No. 4772
$24.90

HOW TO BUILD YOUR OWN UNDERGROUND HOME

How To Build Adobe Houses . . . etc.

TAB BOOKS
BLUE RIDGE SUMMIT, PA. 17214

FIRST EDITION

FIRST PRINTING—OCTOBER 1979
SECOND PRINTING—MAY 1980

Copyright © 1979 by TAB Books Inc.

Reproduction or publication of the content in any manner without express permission of the publisher, is prohibited. No liability is assumed with respect to the use of the information herein.

Printed in the United States of America

Library of Congress Card Number: 79-67187

ISBN 0-8306-0001-9

No. 1172
$11.95

HOW TO BUILD YOUR OWN UNDERGROUND HOME
BY RAY G. SCOTT

BLUE RIDGE SUMMIT, PA. 17214

FIRST EDITION

FIRST PRINTING—OCTOBER 1979
SECOND PRINTING—APRIL 1980
THIRD PRINTING—JUNE 1980

Copyright © 1979 by TAB BOOKS Inc.

Printed in the United States of America

Reproduction or publication of the content in any manner, without express permission of the publisher, is prohibited. No liability is assumed with respect to the use of the information herein.

Library of Congress Cataloging in Publication Data

Scott, Ray G.
   How to build your own underground home.

    "Tab#1172."
    Includes index.
    1. Earth sheltered house—Design and construction.
I. Title.
TH4819.E27S34   690'.8'6   79-16854
ISBN 0-8306-9744-6
ISBN 0-8306-1172-X pbk.

Preface

Prehistoric man became the first underground home dweller by taking refuge from the extreme elements in caves. Even though materials and methods have advanced drastically, I will be the first to admit that subterranian home building has not appealed to the masses of modern times. Its concept is just as logical today as it was back in time, but the catalysts today are financial and ecological because of the continually rising costs and increasing shortages of fuel and electricity. The following is my method of constructing a comfortable, modern geothermic home.

This book is not intended to provide all the technical information included in other publications, such as *Earth Sheltered Housing Design* prepared by the University of Minnesota. It will provide you, the reader, with an insight into the problems which a private home builder might encounter when tackling an unconventional project such as building an underground home.

Ray G. Scott

Acknowledgements

I want to thank my wife, Juanita, and my three children, Michele, Vicki and Chris, whose physical help and encouragement kept me going through another unusual phase of my life, and to my mother for her usual help. Also to Steve McCoy who was always around when I needed him and to the following good friends (In alphabetic order): Larry Bagwell, Curtis Barber, Lester Bull, Nick Crawford, Bill Ertel, Werner Ferrone, Bob Gentry, Don Greenfield, Gurvis Jones, John Neukam, Barry Scott, George Smith and Family, Roger Thompson, Stan Wales, and to these Commercial Businesses: Montgomery Ward: Bel Air, MD; Ralph Currie Carpets: Cockeysville, MD; Classic Kitchens: Bel Air, MD.

Contents

1 Definition and Objectives 11
Mental and Physical Preparation—Benefits—Alternatives

2 Design and Land Must Work Together 21
Well Depths—Excavating—Water Problems—County Regulations—Financing—Lot Size—Into-the-Hill—Level Ground—Below Grade Level—Half-and-Half—Basic Necessities

3 How to Get Work Done 35
Insurance—Best Working Hours

4 When to Hire a Professional and Save Money 41
Property Layout—Lawyer's Fees—Excavating—Building Materials—Concrete—Masonry—Floor Slab—Interior Walls—More Necessary Purchases

5 Codes and Regulations 55
Professional Engineers—Means of Egress—Retaining Walls—Hand Railings—Air Circulation—Electrical Codes and Plumbing—Stairs—Door Openings—Building Codes Appeals Board

6 Site Preparation 67
Driveway—Setback—Septic-Sewer System—Surveying—Moving the Land—Property Lines

7 Preparing and Pouring the Footers 77
The Concrete—Sewer Pipe

8 Walls **87**
Formed and Poured Walls—Block Walls

9 Roof Design and Preparation **97**
Rebar—Wire Mesh—Steel Placement—Alternative Method—Conduit—Chimneys

10 Waterproofing **119**
Moisture Treatments—Smoothness of Roof

11 What About Moisture? **131**
Condensation—Sponge Effect—Humidity—

12 Backfilling and Grading **139**
Tractor-Spread — Trailer-Spread — Crane-Spread —Final Grading—Backhoe Removal—Grass Seed

13 Utilities **147**
Plumbing—Water Pipes—Maintenance—Electric Wiring—Electricians—Wiring—Telephone Wiring—Gas

14 Woodworking **153**
Nails, Nails, Nails—Hanging Doors

15 Adding Trim and Fixtures **157**
Decoration and Layout—Bedrooms—Kitchen—Recycled Materials—Furniture—Carpet and Padding—Paint—Interior Garden—Lighting—Ideas

16 Air Handling **175**
Heating—Cooling

17 Domes and Skylights **179**
Indoor Garden—Cost of Dome—Skylights—Constructing Your Dome

18 Underground Home Ceiling **193**
Roof Slab—Creative Ceilings

19 After Basic Completion **197**
Finishing Touches—Storage Sheds—The Entrance

20 Getting Used to Living Underground **203**
No Windows—Strange Sensations—Radio and Television Reception—Cable Television

21 Alternate Sources of Energy **207**
Heat—Wood Stoves—Coal—Solar Heat—Solar Electric—A Workable Electric Source—Wind Power

22 Underground Home Publicity **213**
Positive Attention—Negative Attention—Public Attention—Private Attention

23 One Year Later 217
Dome Alignment—Dome Foundation—Sun Heat—Crickets—
Snow—Visitors—Utility Bills—Lack of Light—Problem Neighbors

Appendix A 225
Weights and Specific Gravities

Appendix B 231
Underground House Statistics

Appendix C 233
Weight of Basic Materials Used in Underground Construction

Appendix D 235
Slump Test

Appendix E 239
Cement Statistics

Index 253

1

Definition and Objectives

The definition of an underground house at first seems totally self-explanatory, but if you consider the limitless variations of terrain, weather and human nature, you can imagine the extremes that are possible. Therefore, a clarification, along with my definition, is in order here at the beginning of this book. You can imagine the extremes that might occur when somewhere, sometime, someone has set up a permanent residence in a cavern or cave, 100 feet or more below grade surface. On the other hand, there are homes, particularly in California, with approximately 4 inches of soil or sod growing on the roof only to act as an insulator against extreme hot and cold temperatures. These two conditions should definitely be considered the extremes of engineering ease and difficulty.

Therefore, to avoid covering problems and methods of construction that would probably never be encountered by a potential underground home builder reading this book, I have established my parameters of a typical (if there is such a thing) underground home to be 2 to 5 feet under the earth's surface. The biggest reason I have for suggesting 5 feet of earth over the roof of an underground home is that this is the point of best compromise. By compromise, I mean that 4 to 5 feet of earth gives you the most insulation for the least amount of weight. If you consider that earth, with an average amount of small rocks and dampness from rain, weighs around 100 pounds per cubic foot, it is easy to calculate how many cubic feet of dirt you will have over your head. Multiply the number of cubic feet by 90 pounds. This will give you an estimated total weight that your concrete roof slab will have to support. The more weight overhead, the more reinforced concrete you will need and the more it will cost.

According to my personal tests and calculations, 5 feet of earth will give approximately 90 per cent of the insulation value that 10 feet of earth will give you. However, the cost and strength of the roof slab to hold up 10 feet of earth would be unreasonable, probably three or four times more expensive than a slab of concrete capable of holding 5 feet of earth. Figure 1-1 is a bar graph estimating the per cent of insulating value in relation to depth of soil.

Just as the depth into the ground could be varied, the amount of vertical exterior wall surfaces covered by dirt is likewise varied. The previously mentioned sod-roofed homes have no exterior walls covered by dirt. All the walls are conventionally constructed. But the home which I have built and now live in has three and one-half vertical sides covered by a minimum of 4 feet of earth. In all fairness, I've seen a few good designs with only three walls covered by earth. So now having mentioned the extremes for exposed exterior wall surfaces, I'll make this suggestion: If you are really interested in building underground, go all the way. The engineering problems are basically the same regardless of whether you have one side, two sides or all four sides plus the roof covered by earth. However, the benefits are substantially increased in direct proportion to the more exterior vertical wall surfaces covered.

MENTAL AND PHYSICAL PREPARATION

If this definition doesn't scare you, consider one more thing. Before you make the final decision to build under-

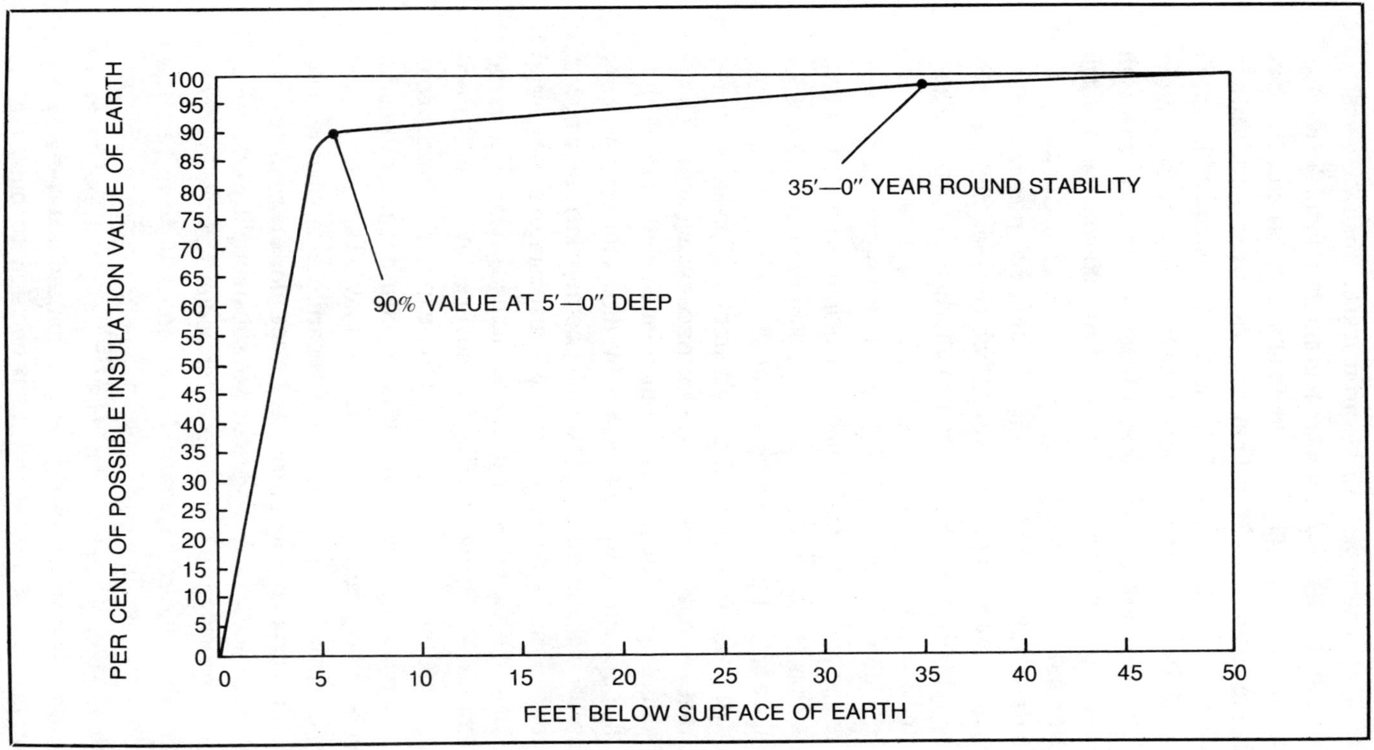

Fig. 1-1. Insulation value of the earth.

ground, you will want to be prepared mentally, as well as physically, to handle a project that is different from the normal. When I say physically and mentally, I mean exactly that. Building a house of any kind will test a person's physical stamina, especially when he tries to do most of the work himself. Remember that a concrete block soaked by rain can weigh nearly 100 pounds, that a shovel of wet dirt can weigh over 25 pounds, that a cubic foot of wet concrete can weigh 100 pounds a cubic foot, a sheet of plywood can weigh 80 pounds and that sheet rock might weigh 120 pounds. These are just a few examples of material weight. See the Appendix at the end of this book if you think building a house of any kind won't be a physical endeavor.

So now you can just imagine the kick-in-the-head when some stranger (or friend) comes along and verbally tears your plans apart with inaccurate and incomplete knowledge or facts, after you have been working all weekend, or a distant relative drops in after a hard day's work and proceeds to tell you that you have a screw loose and probably means it. This is an example of the mental harassment you must be prepared to handle. Sometimes people can unintentionally be downright demoralizing. But then there's always a friend to come by and lift your spirits by telling you that you are doing a good job and how much he likes the idea of building underground. This is the type of friend you need. He is also most likely the same friend you can call on for a helping hand. The person who knocks your project probably won't hang around long enough to get involved or help out.

Contrary to popular belief, most people are not innovators or experimenters, and they don't know how to handle anyone who attempts to be one, except by criticizing. This is probably the truest statement you'll read in this book. In my short life of 38 years, I have so far done quite a few unconventional things; building an underground home is definitely the biggest risk from a financial viewpoint, but it probably won't be my last project. If I've learned one thing by my experiences, it is simply that the overwhelming majority of the population only wants to take a look at the unconventional. Many people will say they would like to do this and that, or someday they'll do such and such, but they really can't come up with a reason for not starting their dream projects immediately. They just procrastinate until it's too late in life to accomplish anything, whether it be an underground house, a sailboat, a trip or a job change. As you read this paragraph, I'm sure you will recognize yourself, friends and family. I hope you, the reader, are daring enough to be innovative whether you decide to build an underground house or not.

I am fortunate that most of my neighbors were and are kind people and seem to be sincere in their friendship and interest. But don't count on this attitude of acceptance of your endeavor. Expect to be called foolish, dumb and worse. If you are lucky and you have nice neighbors, things should go well. Consider yourself fortunate. But I will bet you my last dollar that there will be one joker in your neighborhood, just as there was in mine.

BENEFITS

Now that you know what I consider an underground house to be, and you have been warned of the mental harassments (I'll tell you of more physical problems and legal pitfalls in subsequent chapters), let me now tell you of the benefits you can expect to find.

Fuel Savings

Since temperature, rainfall, winds and storms vary from coast to coast, some of your major objectives may be different from mine. The reason I decided to build my geothermic (sounds more technical than underground) home was definitely the cold winters and the hot summers of Maryland. In the winter the fuel bill in my previous conventional type home was doubling almost every year, and the electricity to run air conditioners in the summer wasn't doing any better.

Nature's Gifts

If you have ever taken a tour of any of the commercially-operated underground caverns, you'll remember seeing a sign somewhere near the beginning stating that the temperature at this point never varies from a specific degree, usually 54° or 55°F, winter or summer. This is one of the great gifts of nature which few of us take advantage of.

As you are probably aware, windmills and wind generators are enjoying a rejuvenated popularity since the fuel shortage of 1973. This is one way of taking advantage of nature's free gifts. Another, of course, is water power to turn a similar generating system. And don't forget that a few of the real back-to-earth folks (who deserve a great deal of credit) are using block ice frozen in the winter to keep cold storage areas cool through summer. As for solar power, I'll only mention it and suggest that you read up on the subject before building this underground house. There are millions of words written on solar energy. It's here now and forever, and it's practical to use.

These gifts of nature, along with many others, are used by only a small segment of the population because it's just not as convenient as they would like it to be. Geothermic heat and earth insulation are just as free, but only tested and used by a minute few. I feel, however, that this will be changing in the near future simply because the cost of all fuels will continue to climb at an unreasonable rate.

Once you are closed in 4 or 5 feet underground with average exterior exposure, you can expect to find year round temperatures stabilizing. Actually the temperature does not stabilize year-round until you are between 30 and 35 feet below the earth's surface, but the interesting fact is that after only 4 feet of dirt and 10 inches of concrete the lowest temperature I have recorded inside my home while under construction during the winter of 1977 was 46°F. This was without man-made heat of any kind. So instead of paying to heat your house in the winter from the mid teens to a comfortable temperature near 72°F, your additional heat requirement will be minimal. Remember, the constant temperature referred to underground is only when there is no life activity. Once you add light bulbs, cooking heat, body heat and appliance heat, the temperature will be much higher and thus leave only a few degrees to be raised by conventional or experimental means. Also note that in the summer these same heat additions are not great enough to require air conditioning. The highest temperature recorded in our home during the summer of 1978 was 79°F. You must realize that every building and every location is as different as the people who build them, so you can expect some of these examples to be more in your favor, or less in your favor depending on your situation. I am only quoting from my own personal experience.

Maintenance

During the time my working design was forming, I nearly overlooked the other major advantages. Consider exterior maintenance. Since an underground home has no trim to paint, windows to wash, or shingles to blow off, and the exposed walls are stone, you do not have to put many hours into constant outside work. The only thing you really need is a good riding lawn mower and a small push power mower.

Permanency

As for a third reason, don't forget that all exterior walls are concrete, as are the ceiling and floor. So if they are designed and constructed correctly, they are impervious to nearly everything. Nothing—insects, fire or water—deteriorates the basic structure. So you can forget the annual termite inspection, rotting beams, etc.

Equally important is the elimination of a major fire potential. If you build your house as I did mine, it is nearly impossible for a fire to get a foothold unless you are a pack rat and cram your storage areas with combustible items. Of course, even an underground home would be vulnerable to this type of carelessness.

Theft Factor

By eliminating all windows, you remove the temptation of vulnerable openings to a petty theft even though we know that the pro is going to find a way to steal regardless of the type of house you have. However, an underground house definitely gives you a feeling of security and stability.

For the Lady of the House

Remember when you don't have windows on every wall, you can arrange furniture in an endless combination because you never block a window. This should be particularly interesting to the woman of the household. Also, she will delight in the fact that she will not have to wash windows, nor will you have to buy as many curtains as in a conventional home.

Property Conservation

Last, but not least, is one of my favorite reasons. I bought approximately 2½ acres of rolling hillside in beautiful Harford County, Maryland. After building a 3600 square foot house, including the garage, I still have 99 per cent of the acreage usable and unobstructed by any man-made objects. Besides, the children can't knock a baseball through my windows.

Now that you know all the good points and are thinking seriously about a subterranean home, as they are sometimes called as opposed to geothermic or underground, I'll tell you a few of the alternatives you can begin to think about.

ALTERNATIVES

The alternatives are unlimited—just let your imagination take over. For example, these houses can be circular, rectangular or square. There are one-story, split-level and probably two-story houses. They are as small as one or two rooms, or as big as my 40 foot x 90 foot, two-level house. Size and shape are only the first of many major decisions you will have to make.

Skylights or domes are usually necessary, sometimes covering indoor gardens, sometimes only providing light to rooms. You could have one dome or six skylights or anything in between. One underground house I know of has the main entrance by a staircase to the center of a circular layout. I consider this an unconventional underground house because of the irregular room shapes. Room locations and exits are your personal choice. The method of construction is what is critical. The most important thing to consider is that room location will have to meet building codes where applicable to your locale. I'll cover codes in a later chapter—read it carefully.

Another factor that enters into alternatives regarding your house design is the land or site you select to build into. Does your design fit the land? Remember, you can build an underground home almost anywhere except a swamp. Once the exact location is established you eliminate many of your alternatives. For example, if the land you decide on is rocky, you will not be excavating as deep as you would if it were a sandy soil with no rocks. And if it faces north instead of south, you certainly would not want to build the open side of glass; just as you shouldn't excavate very deep if standing water is close by. One fact you will notice as your plans begin to progress is that by the time you meet building codes, zoning regulations, neighborhood restrictions and avoid the natural pitfalls, you don't have the limitless possibilities you first pictured. Nevertheless, even after meeting all these regulations, an underground house will still be a challenge to the imagination.

Keep tossing over in your mind all the things you could add to make your home interesting and individualistic.

2

Design and Land Must Work Together

The design of your house and the contour of the land must work together. This is true regardless of what type of home you are building, but never more true than when designing an underground house. It's a fact that any land with a water table low enough to build a conventional home could be used to build an underground home, but a water table varies from site to site. The water table is the depth underground at which you first come in contact with standing water under normal prevailing conditions. It is also a fact that the drier the land, the easier your underground endeavor. Whatever you do, don't buy the first piece of ground you come across. Look around until you have found a couple of acres you really like. If there is such a thing as the ideal location for an underground house, it would be the top of a knoll or hill in the high section of your locale. It is also obvious that you can't always get the best, but since this is one of the most important decisions in your life, make it the best possible. Look very carefully at the drainage adjacent to your potential house location. Pretend that it has been raining for a week and imagine where the run-off would be going. This is the first step to judging the usability of the land.

WELL DEPTHS

Next, check the depth of some of the wells drilled in recent years adjacent to your choice of property. You will be looking for places where well depths are 200 feet or deeper. This tells you that water is not near the surface of the land you will be building on. This is not to say that if the neighbors have a well only 100 feet deep that you can't build an underground home nearby—it's only an indication that moisture is closer to the surface, thus nearer your potential house.

EXCAVATING

The type of problem you could run into is this. If by chance, you started excavating in mid-summer when most sections of the country are entering their driest months, you could be deceived into thinking the land is really ideal, then when the following spring rains begin (as they always do), the land around could turn into a big swamp, holding water like a sponge. If this would happen, of course water would try to come through the concrete wall, floor or roof.

WATER PROBLEMS

The action of water coming through a concrete floor of any house is hydrostatic pressure. Briefly, this is when the soil around the concrete block cannot absorb any more water and the excess water cannot run off because it is surrounded by a less porous-type soil or rock formation. At this point, the water has nowhere to go but through the path of least resistance, usually your concrete floor or block wall. This is a condition you must avoid at all costs when locating your underground house. If possible, wait until you have a rainy period. The greater the rainfall, the better. A positive way to see what the conditions would be around your house if it were already built would be to dig a hole 20 to 25 feet deep. It should be big enough to climb down into, but be careful of caving walls. Examine the soil close—under actual conditions. If you don't have time to do all this investigation, or it is not feasible for some reason or you would prefer to have a professional give you advice, look in the yellow pages of the telephone book under engineers—soil testing or engineering—soil. Every community of a reasonable size will have one or more listed.

Anywhere there is major construction going on, especially road work, there will be soil testing facilities close by. This will cost you, but it is definitely worth the expense if the land you're thinking of buying is questionable. Remember, water leaking in your underground house could make it useless, and you would lose everything that you have invested.

COUNTY REGULATIONS

Last, but not least, your county probably has a department called *Land Use* or some department with a similar title. These local offices are usually a good source to check once you have limited your search for the land to one or two parcels. They have topography maps in great detail concerning the lay of the lands around your proposed home site. Also they have soil testing performed by Farm Bureaus for crop growth. All this information will be helpful to the person trying to make up his mind about a piece of ground. Also, the Health Department in most locales could be helpful, depending on their function within the local government. Be prepared to meet resistance or limited cooperation if these local officials know you are contemplating building underground. My suggestion to you, at this stage, would be to keep your plans to yourself. Remember, this is the voice of experience talking. Use all these sources to their fullest, combine them with good judgment and you shouldn't go wrong.

I strongly suggest that you make the final decision on exact location and get the deed in your name before beginning the design of the building. The reason I say this is that many things can happen on the way to the lawyer's office for final settlement.

FINANCING

You may not get financing at a reasonable rate, or you may not get financing at all. Let me tell you what happened to me because it may very well happen to you and you can plan accordingly. Since I'm building my house in the community that I was born and lived in all my life, as did my parents and relatives before me, you can see that the local banks were definitely on a first name basis with me. Aside from my life-long residence, my credit was flawless. When I decided to build a new house (my underground intentions as of yet unannounced), I stopped by to see my friendly banker. After a short discussion on houses in general, he asked me how much I needed. I gave him my figure and he said no problem. Within a few days a letter came in the mail stating that I could have the amount I requested—just stop in when I was ready to finalize the loan. It was just that easy, even though I was going to be my own contractor. This fact may bother some banks, especially if you don't have the credentials to back up intentions of being your own contractor. But this didn't bother my bank. Remember now, to this point they know nothing of an underground house. So I have the letter of loan approval, but as I am a basically honest individual, I decided to tell the bank of my plans to build underground. As a matter of fact, I even built a scale model of my house (Figs. 2-1 and 2-2) to impress the vice-president. He was impressed all right—so impressed that he said he couldn't possibly approve a loan for a far-out

Fig. 2-1. A scale model of the outside of an underground home.

Fig. 2-2. A scale model of the inside of an underground home.

venture like an underground house. At this point the negotiations began and after a great deal of pleading and promising my life away, they changed their minds and approved my loan. But this was only because of my life-long ties to this particular bank. If a stranger or a younger, less proven individual approached my bank or any other loaning institution for money to build underground, I'm afraid the answer would be short and sweet. No, No, No. This story is not meant to discourage you, but only to emphasize what you are up against mortgage-wise. As for V.H.A. and F.H.A. loans, they are even more difficult to obtain. If you qualify, check into them, but don't waste time begging or waiting for government assistance.

Another problem could be that the restrictions may not allow an underground house, or the soil may be unsuitable. These are just a few of the potential roadblocks to actually getting a deed in your name. If you invest your valuable time and money designing a building for a particular site and the deal falls through, it would be unfortunate and costly. If a professional draws up your blueprints, he will adapt to a particular piece of ground. If you change locations, the prints would have to be revised to suit the new location. This is not necessarily true for a conventional house, but most likely for an underground house.

LOT SIZE

I also suggest that the size of your lot be no smaller than two acres. The reason for this statement is purely cosmetic. Conventional homes can be designed to be attractive side by side on small plots of ground, such as many developments are,

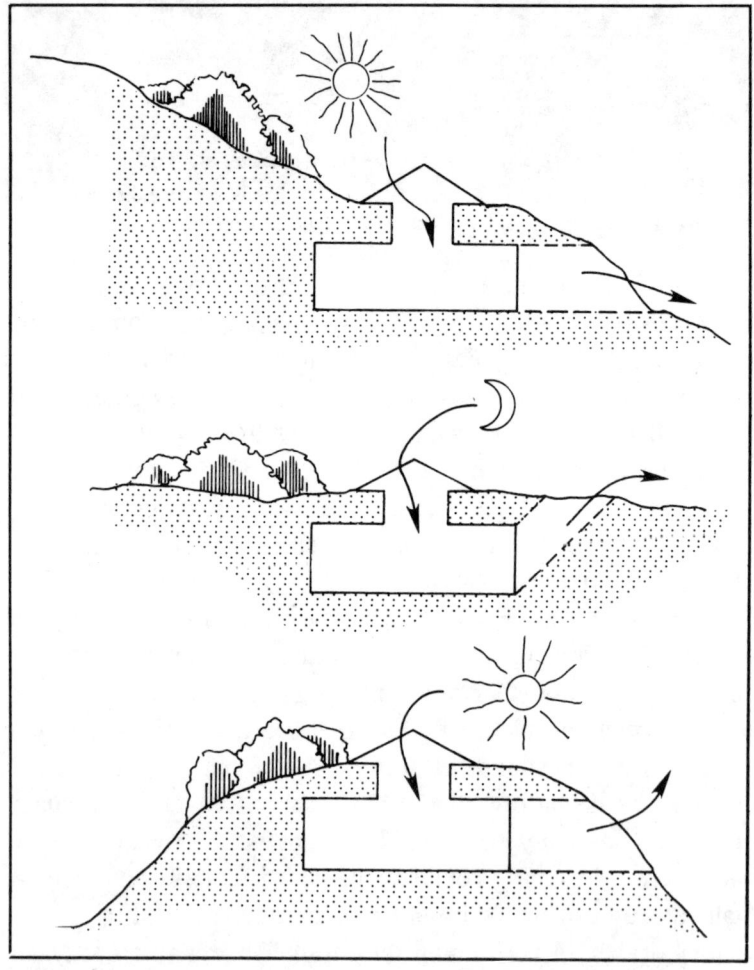

Fig. 2-3. Three basic possibilities for location of an underground home.

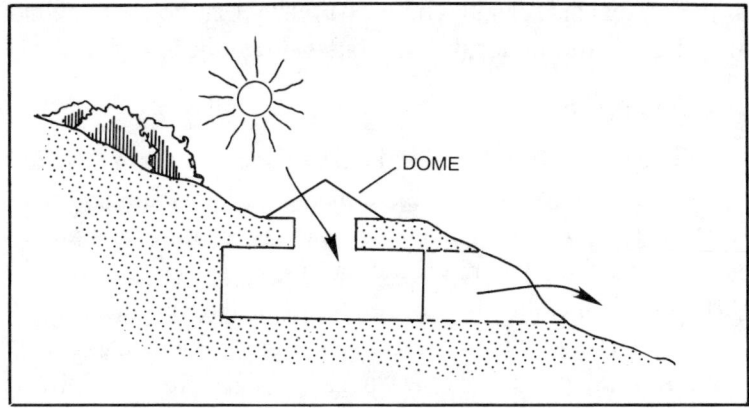
Fig. 2-4. Into-the-hill method of building an underground home.

but in my opinion, an underground home loses much of its appeal when crowded by conventional homes.

Now let's assume that your dream location is a reality. The deed is in your name. If you have picked out a good piece of land, 50 per cent of your potential problems will be eliminated. See Fig. 2-3 and locate the lay of the land that most resembles yours. Note the house location in each situation as I will explain the pros and cons of each as I see it.

INTO-THE-HILL

Into-the-hill is the most popular approach to building underground (Fig. 2-4). This into-the-hill method is by far the easiest to build, especially from a grading viewpoint, because approximately 65 per cent of the cubic footage has to be excavated. The reason this is ideal is that you will need tons and tons of dirt to backfill and complete final grading. This into-the-hill method provides a natural method of moving building materials around by an ordinary truck, because the upper part of the hill allows you to work at roof level. At the same time, the natural slope will give you access to the lower level by normal vehicles. If it were not for the ability to deliver building material to the lower level by truck, you would have to keep a crane of some type on the site to lower the heavier building material, and those cranes are expensive to rent. I suggest, for this reason, above all others, that you try to build the style of the underground house shown in Fig. 2-4.

LEVEL GROUND

The *level-ground method* is to be used as a second choice for quite a few reasons (Fig. 2-5). First, backfilling is much more expensive and difficult because the structure is above ground and since you did not excavate, you have to obtain fill dirt from somewhere to cover it with. This is definitely a course to take as a last resort. I had to buy some extra dirt for my final grading. I called every possible source to check prices of a dumptruck load (approximately 14 tons) and I found the prices (in 1978) ranged from $3 per ton to $10 per ton for the best quality top soil. So you see, buying the good earth isn't a cheap approach. Even if you could get dirt for free, you would have to rent a crane and bucket to put the dirt on top, because it would be unwise to take a bulldozer on your top slab, regardless of its designed strength. This would be expensive and time consuming. The extra equipment combined with the cost of buying and hauling soil will make the style more expensive than you probably want to get involved with. A second point to consider when looking at the ground-level style is that the heat loss and heat absorption is greater when a mass of earth is less in volume and above the natural terrain. There is

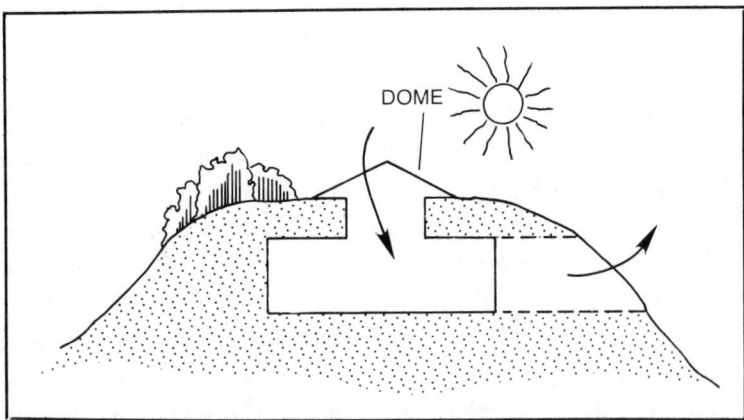

Fig. 2-5. The level-ground approach to an underground home.

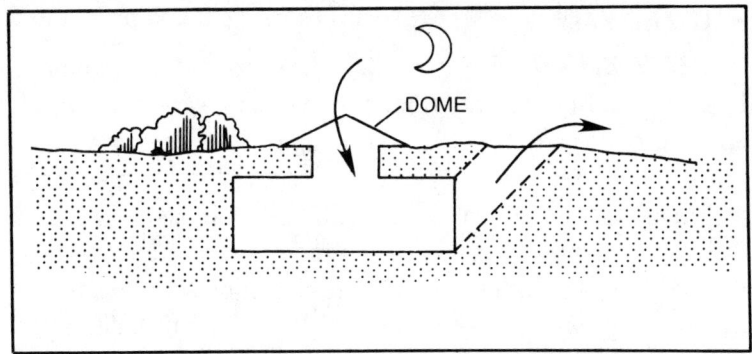

Fig. 2-6. Below-grade level method of construction for an underground home.

one positive aspect of this type. It may be easier to comply with local building codes, simply because you would have the ability to exit from each exterior wall with limited trouble and cost. Also you eliminate the cost of the initial major excavation.

BELOW GRADE LEVEL

The *below-grade-level* is, in my opinion, the least desirable approach (Fig. 2-6). The major reason is that exit and entrance would have to be up and down a set of steps, and a garage entrance would be at the bottom of a hill. This presents a drainage problem, unless a well-designed drain system is installed. In many cases an auxiliary sump pump would be required to pump storm drains up to a natural drain level. In almost any situation where the house is built below a level grade, the drainage system becomes a major endeavor and also very expensive. Consider the possibility of a clogged drain or power blackout. Your house would be flooded. Not a nice thought, but possible. In addition, the pump on this system will require occasional maintenance. If these features don't bother you, then go ahead and use this method.

The construction is basically the same in methods one and two. If there is one benefit to the below-grade-level house, it is that you will not have to haul in additional fill dirt when you are doing the final grading.

HALF-AND-HALF

Half-and-half is a term I've given to the many homes built, as the title indicates, literally half underground and half above ground (Fig. 2-7). At first thought, you could argue that there is no difference between these homes and thousands of conventional homes that have used their club basements as a daily living center. I guess this is technically true, but if you look closely, you will have to agree that there is a real difference. Figure 2-7 shows the major feature that qualifies the *half-and-half* house to be called an underground home. Usually the structure above grade level is used for a garage, storage, an area for solar heat storage tanks or a possibly a work shop. In all fairness, the half-and-half homes researched for this book had less than 20 per cent of the actual floor space above ground, and that 20 per cent was always a nonliving area. One of the advantages of this style is that exits and entrances are more conventional, thus easier to meet building codes on local restrictions. If there are disadvantages, it would be the extra cost of working on two levels and extra precaution that would have to be taken to insure against water seeping along the first level into the lower level.

BASIC NECESSITIES

Now that you're getting down to serious business with this geothermic home idea, don't overlook the forest for the

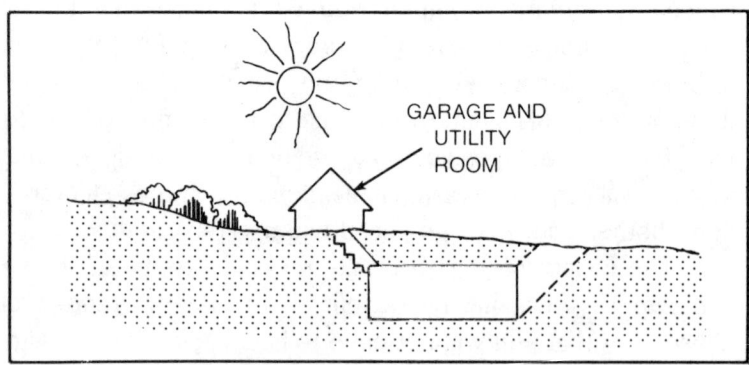

Fig. 2-7. A half-and-half underground home.

trees. You're expecting those unusual problems to show up when you do something as different as this, but don't forget the basic necessities that should be considered regardless of the type of house you are building.

The accessibility to good roads in winter or rainy season should be considered seriously. It's easy to say you like remoteness and getting back to the wilderness, especially when the weather is good and you're excited about a new project and are physically active, but this house will be there a long time and so will the mortgage payments. Stop and think how you will feel about a specific location in 10 years. You've settled down a little, probably have a few more grey hairs and the children are growing like weeds. That beautiful, picturesque, four-acre tract of land you got real—cheap 10 years ago because it was 5 miles to the nearest paved road now presents the problems of daily trips to the store and children walking to meet the bus. This may not be the ideal location you first thought it was.

Also check into the cost of running telephone cables from the road to your house. The cost varies from location to location, as does the method by which the electric company charges you to bring power to your house. The way it works in Harford County, Maryland is like this: the Electric Company will install service lines to the meter, regardless of the distance from the existing power source at no charge to the home owner, providing the meter is installed on the nearest possible corner of the house. If you want the meter on a wall or post farther away than the nearest point, you have to pay the Electric Company so much per additional foot of power line required. Ask precisely what the charges will be. You will find the telephone and electric companies very cooperative organizations when planning the location of lines, meters and the place of line entry into your underground house. I won't go into gas lines because I emphatically suggest you don't even think about liquid gas, propane or natural gas as a fuel. As you know, a leak in a gas line is a serious problem anywhere, but in an underground house, it's more of a concern because of the air tightness of the structure. Don't ask for trouble with these fuels—building underground will present more than enough problems. If you stick strictly to electricity as the utility and a wood or coal burning stove for heating assistance, you'll be safer and happier.

Before signing your life away for a parcel of land, make sure water is available. Most likely you will drill a well, probably deep if you have a good piece of ground. One of the regulations in Harford County, Maryland is that an approved well usually must be drilled before construction can begin. You would be in sad shape to get your money invested in construction and find out there is no water down below. It's a necessity of life.

Well drillers are usually full of valuable information and they can probably predict the depth, quality and quantity of water you will find fairly accurate. Experience has taught them a great deal. So have faith in your well driller. You have the final say as to the location of your well, that is after the health department suggests a particular area. Make sure the well driller agrees with your choice. One important phase of drilling a well is to discuss before hand with the driller the method of payment. Most drillers have a set fee per foot for soft dirt and another for hitting rock, or they will quote you an average of the two prices, regardless of what they strike on their way to water. Also ask them about drilling a second or third hole, if the first or second turn out to be dry. Some drillers do the second drilling for half price. Some have other arrangements. Find out before you start drilling, not after you hit rock.

Once you get water in, you have to get rid of the waste it creates. So sewage disposal is just as important as finding water. Once again the local regulations dictate your septic system's location, size and configuration. Make sure your land is approved for a satisfactory system before you build, even if it is not a standard requirement. Ask for a perc test before buying a piece of ground for a private home, if public sewers aren't close enough to hook into. If the soil is not suitable for a good sewer system, it most likely is not going to give good drainage for your house.

Don't buy property simply because it's cheap. If you do, it will come back to haunt you. Sooner or later you'll pay for buying a marginally acceptable piece of ground. Remember, you don't get something for nothing. Last, but not least, check out all codes, regulations, ordinances and zoning laws that may apply to your choice of property to see if they will cause you a problem.

Some land has restrictions attached to the deed from previous owners. For example, years ago a dedicated farmer could have stipulated in his will that his farm land never be used for anything but farming. This can be done legally, and all of a sudden you could find yourself raising a herd of cattle instead of building an underground home.

Another source of restrictions comes from development preferences. If a housing development has a set of restrictions drawn up, they may include the size of the house, material used and style. I have never heard of one that allowed underground homes, so watch out. Zoning law will be the easiest to comply with. They simply control things like multi-family dwel-

Fig. 2-8. Be sure your land is zoned for a single-family underground house.

ling, commercial ventures or farming. It's very easy to find out if a particular piece of land is zoned for a single-family underground house (Fig. 2-8). Just stop by the county zoning department and look at their zoning map. I think every county in the nation has one.

Now if you are not discouraged, continue reading into chapter three. Remember, I'm trying to save you aggravation and trouble, not discourage you.

3

How To Get Work Done

Since you are building this house yourself, you certainly don't lack energy or interest, so there are only a few things that can slow you down. These include the weather, lack of money or poor planning. The first you have no control over. Money is a personal thing between you and your bank. You know how much you have to work with and how careful you must be with it. This only leaves planning. This you have total control over. Whatever you do, don't confuse planning with designing. Designing is physically locating material items. Planning is the art of allocating your time.

Design will be settled long before you actually begin to build, and you really can't do much changing after you have actually begun pouring concrete and laying block. Once your plans are approved by all necessary authorities and a building permit issued, you can consider the design phase of your project final, except in minor instances.

However, time allocation will continue from day one of construction to the time you use the last paint brush. So you see, this is the important part of building that you have control over. Time is as important as money. Sometimes it is more important because money can't buy time, but in time you can make money.

Once you're committed to building this underground house, figure on one year of continuous work on your part, maybe even more, depending on your desire to get the job done and nature's cooperation.

First of all, don't get behind before you start. Break ground in the early spring. If you wait until mid-summer, you will be in a race with mother nature to beat cold weather. Of course, I'm assuming that you're building the underground house in a region with extreme seasons, such as in Maryland. If you happen to be in the deep South or Southwest, you just have to appreciate our problems of changing seasons. The reason it is imperative to complete all concrete work and get it covered with earth is simple. Concrete expands and contracts like anything else with heat and cold. The expansion and contraction cause cracking which is a condition you need to avoid at any cost. This is why I suggest you plan carefully to be able to pour your roof slab during a time period where the temperature doesn't get below freezing or vary to extremes of hot and cold. You must realize that if your building were being built in a locale where the temperature might reach 100°F during a day in September, but fall to 40°F at night causing a 60°F differential, cracking could develop. This condition would probably do more damage than actually pouring concrete at 50°F and having the temperature drop to 32°F at night. The extreme differential is what causes the cracking problem and should be avoided at any cost. How's that for a planning problem?

I can't begin to tell you how to plan well personally. I don't think any book can. You are born with that ability. It's almost a talent—like singing. Fortunately, I was born with a planning ability a little above average. However, I know that if I had been even better at planning, my job would have been much easier. Just think a little bit ahead. Don't overlook little things, like small tools, nails or a water cooler.

A good example is something that happened to me. I had a gas generator on the site to use while building the scaffolding for the roof. I rushed to the site early in the morning with my power saw, started the generator and, lo and behold, I'd forgotten my extension cord. For the want of an extension cord hours of work were lost until I left the site and picked one up. Now I was ready to cut boards, and I did, for about 15 minutes. Then the generator ran out of gas. As if this wasn't bad enough, I didn't have a container to get gas in. So by the time I got a can out to the gas station, back to the site, started the generator and was ready to work, I was starved and ready for lunch. Of course, I didn't brown bag a lunch at first because I didn't realize how much time it takes to drive three miles, get a sandwich and soda and get back to work. I soon learned to brown bag a sandwich on those days in which I planned to put in a full day's work. If there is food and drink on the site, I found I could get an average of two more hours a day of working time. This really adds up in a year.

I have to admit that this day I described was unusual for me, but it is an example of what good planning and a little thought can prevent.

As for how to get additional working time, this is the eternal problem of a do-it-yourselfer. I presume the reader of this book to be working a regular 40-hour week to pay for the other 128 hours and the house. Let's also assume that you use 10 hours a week travelling to and from work and to and from the building site; you probably need seven hours of sleep a night; and time to eat. Let's say that is 10 hours a week. This gives you a total of 109 hours just to eat, sleep and work at your regular occupation. That leaves 59 hours to take care of personal business, see your family, socialize and build a house. So you see, there's really no time to waste in idle talk. You cannot waste effort of any kind.

One of the fine lines you will have to walk when building an underground house is tactfully dealing with and handling friendly, inquisitive people. This sounds like an unfriendly gesture, but it is not. Here's what I mean. Naturally an underground house is interesting. Maybe some day there will be enough underground homes around so that the majority of the public will have seen one or possibly have been inside of one. Once this happens, of course, the novelty will be missing and the curiosity seekers will not visit you, but this is definitely in the future era. Be prepared for the present day, because as the word of your innovative project spreads, your friends and neighbors will stop by to talk with you about your house. This is the problem. How do you politely keep on working while they are asking you basic questions? Remember, after a while, you have answered every question many times and explained the details to many people. But each time the questions are asked, it is the first time for your friend. Soon you will find yourself talking more than working. However, it is good to know that people are interested, so you just do your best to work and talk, talk and work. Most people will volunteer a helping hand and that is something you can always use.

INSURANCE

This brings me to another subject that should be mentioned in conjunction with an underground house. Insurance. With all the visitors you will have on your property from beginning to end, I suggest you obtain a good insurance policy covering personal liability. As I'm sure you are aware, it's awfully easy to have an injury on a construction site, especially in the early stages when the terrain is full of ditches, rubble, nails, loose timber and so on. Ask your lawyer about posting the property as a means of liability protection, but don't count on a *no trespassing sign* to protect you against a lawsuit if someone would get hurt, because it would be voided by your personal invitation to visitors or workers. You are still liable for these people. Anyway you slice it, you need a good insurance policy.

BEST WORKING HOURS

As for working time, I found the best time to work uninterrupted was to start at sunrise. I don't mean just early—I mean exactly at sun-up. Somewhere around 5 a.m. Once you get used to these early hours you'll find work progresses must faster than evening work. It's also invigorating and the sunrises seem to be good for the mind. To be honest with you, I found the weekends, holidays and vacation days to be the time to get the big jobs done. You'll find that the larger phases of construction need to be completed by continued hours of working. You can literally never get a big job done (for example, plumbing) if you do it 15 minutes at a time, one day at a time. It will take 15 minutes to get the necessary tools and supplies together and ready for work, whether that work period is to be for 10 minutes or 10 hours. This is another way to save valuable time by planning. So if you have only a few minutes to work, do something that can be completed in that time frame, if at all possible. One such job would be hanging a door. Or use the time to prepare a particular area for a bigger job. Keep this train of thought in mind and you will find you have saved days by the time you're finished building.

The early mornings and evenings I used to take care of small things. If you can arrange to take a vacation at times when a big job needs to be completed, then you are fortunate. There's nothing worse than having a complete week off from your normal job, have it pass and accomplish nothing significant. It can really demoralize and frustrate you if it happens.

Still another phase of getting work done is affected by availability of material. This is where planning far ahead on your part can prevent a problem. When ordering material, be sure to give the supplier long enough advance notice to deliver supplies by the time you need them. Don't wait until the last minute and then waste time because you are missing one 2 x 4 or one concrete block. Don't forget, you're not the only one ordering supplies. Don't expect the vender to jump at your request for immediate delivery.

If there is one way above all others to save time, it is to complete one craft throughout the house. For example, if you are putting furring strips on the block walls, start in one room and continue throughout the house. The same goes for plumbing, electric, sheet rock, painting or whatever. If you try to complete one room at a time, from scratch to final trim, and then move on to the next room, you will spend most of your time putting tools away and getting new ones out. Also by completing one job throughout the house, you become skilled at the particular job. The only thing to be said against this method is that it gets boring. For example, hammering nails for three days and then painting for three days becomes very monotonous. Jumping around can break this monotony, but it wastes valuable time.

Probably the most effective time saving idea that I will mention is following: When you have help available, whether it's a friend, relative, paid worker, young or old, male or female, don't overlook the fact that everyone can do some type of work. But, if you ask the wrong person to do the wrong job, you either have to hold their hand or do the job over. Don't ask a child to do a man's work and vice versa. This way neither person will become frustrated by being asked to do a job they can't handle. Use your labor, whoever or whenever, effectively.

About the only other thing which is really important as far as saving time and making work easier is to have work that needs to be completed inside and outside even after you are under roof. In Harford County, Maryland, just as in most other locales, the weather varies considerably. Even in mid-winter, we have occasional time periods of warmer than usual temperature. When this happens, get something done outside that can't be completed in bad weather, because in the warm weather there are surely going to be days that rain prevents outside work. I know of people who would just cancel that day's work. But if you're really anxious to complete your house, you can always find something constructive to do whether it's winter or summer, night or day.

4

When to Hire a Professional and Save Money

It is easy for me to tell you to plan ahead and save money when this was something I found most difficult to do successfully. Since you are reading this book, I have to assume that if you build, you are planning to do some of the work yourself. Should you decide not to build underground, this chapter will be a help regardless of the style of house you decide on, as long as you do 50 per cent of the buying and building yourself.

As we all know, there is always more than one way to do anything. This is never more true than when building a house. The crafts which I have found easy, you may not and vice versa. So as you read on, keep this in mind and pick the subjects you feel comfortable with.

PROPERTY LAYOUT

One of the easiest ways to begin your project and save a few dollars right from the start is to locate and lay out your house corners on your property, once you own it. All you need is approximately 30 wooden stakes about 1″ × 3″ × 48″, roughly 400′ of surveyor's string, a surveyor's transit, a plumb, a bob and a 100 foot steel tape measure. Most likely, a local rental company will rent a transit to you and can show you how to use it. There is no need to buy a transit. They are expensive, and you will only need this instrument in the beginning phase of building lay out. It is one of the few items that I suggest you rent as a method of saving money. In addition, transits around construction sites have been known to grow legs and walk away from their owners, never to be seen again.

After a short lesson with your transit and a few practice readings, you can lay out the corners of your house as well as anyone. Just go slow and double check yourself. Be sure to check local regulations regarding side clearances to your property line. Your house usually has to be at least 10 feet from your side boundary, but check the code to be sure.

By telling you to locate your house corners I am not suggesting that you try to locate permanent boundary survey markers. These are two different jobs, and this is a job for a professional surveyor. Also, most localities require a certified surveyor to check these boundaries and a practicing lawyer to record the deed.

LAWYER'S FEES

Lawyer's fees connected with buying property or recording mortgages are occasionally a rip-off. Ask friends who have recently purchased land or a house what their charges were.

One of the biggest surprises connected with home building or buying that everyone encounters is that—the actual cost of the property that is asked by the seller is only the top of the iceburg as far as cost goes. If anyone you know has recently purchased real estate, they will attest to this. I'm relaying this warning especially to the younger person buying his first property. Here is a totally mythical example only to show the progression of dollars required to buy a parcel of land to build on. Remember the figures and items are estimated because they vary drastically from locale to locale.

Sample Purchase

Here is an example ad in a newspaper: Two-acre lot; ½ wooded; nice view, $20,00. The sum advertised may seem reasonable to you, but don't relax and write a check yet. At the very beginning a perc test is required to insure the health department that a septic system will work well on this level. If this is required, add $100 to $200 depending on how easily accessible the land is. If you actually agree to buy the land, it must be surveyed. Add $200 to $500 depending on how complex the shape is. Next you need a lawyer for the title search. This covers hidden ownerships or liens placed against this property by previous owners. Add about $500 for a normal search. Of course, there is a tax just as in buying a car. In Maryland, there is a 5 per cent sales tax. So a piece of land costing $20,000 would be taxed for $1,000. Yours may be higher or lower. Now you have a registering fee. This is for recording your ownership on the courthouse records and everywhere else the law requires. This could run over $200 depending on where you are. Then there is a stamp tax. This is exactly what it implies. A little seal is attached to the documents as they go through the legal channels. This is a local tax as opposed to the state sales tax. Add $50.

Real Estate Tax

Of course, we must not be prejudiced against real estate tax. You pay real estate tax proportional to the fraction of the tax year that you will own this new property. For example, if the tax bill is $500 for a year, but you buy this property exactly halfway through the year, you owe one-half of that year's tax bill. Add $250.

Already this $20,000 piece of ground could be as high as $22,700, and you could continue to add little hidden costs that you might encounter. When I say hidden costs, I'm not indicating that the system is trying to deceive you. I only mean that these costs are not spelled out in big black letters to a first-time property buyer, and since most people don't buy homes and property on a frequent basis, I'm sure many people tend to forget what was involved in buying their property. Also the cost changes from year to year.

Also, these costs do not include the hook-up of utility, surcharges, highway access costs, permits or anything other than getting the deed in your name. These additional subjects will be covered in later chapters. Fortunately, I have a reliable friend who is a lawyer and another who is a banker, so I felt comfortable. However, I can't caution you enough to check for undisclosed costs. As for tax stamps, local taxes, fees, etc., you're stuck. They're everywhere and inescapable. So for now, accept them.

EXCAVATING

Now that you have your land, are happy with it and are ready to break ground, let a local excavator with a good bulldozer do the heavy digging and grading. Even if you could afford a dozer, you'd probably waste days learning how to use one well enough to dig a foundation. A professional can usually do a foundation in one or two days. Once the foundation excavation is complete, you can begin to do work yourself.

If you're dexterious enough to operate a backhoe, you can invest some of your money for a good return. For clarification, a backhoe is a rubber-tired tractor with a scooping bucket on the rear and a bigger scooping bucket on the front. Both are hydraulically operated and easy to operate with a little help from an experienced operator. These mechanical work horses are invaluable around a construction site. For example, after the dozer digs the hole and cuts a driveway, you can dig your own footers, spread your own gravel base in the driveway and move or drag anything that needs moving. These used backhoes are available (as of 1978) through dealers or private sales at a cost of between $3,000 and $8,000. It really makes no difference what the price is, as long as it's a good value. The point is that if you service it regularly and don't misuse it, you can get your full price back when you sell it after your home is complete. Remember, this same tractor will most likely do all of your fine grading, leaving only hand manicuring to complete your lawn.

The most important thing is that these vehicles can work close to your underground home and in many cases can work and grade even on the roof. However, do this only if your advising engineer says it is safe to do so. The uses you will find for this tractor are unlimited. Remember, shop carefully to find a good buy. Then don't panic to sell this vehicle immediately when you are finished because they always retain their resale value. You may even pick up a few extra dollars doing small digging jobs in the neighborhood.

BUILDING MATERIALS

Now that you've rented a transit and bought a backhoe, you're ready to buy building material. By building an underground home using my method, poured concrete and concrete block are the two biggest single purchases you'll make, so check supplier prices carefully. For example, my house required nearly 8,000 concrete blocks. When checking prices with the four major suppliers in my area, I found delivered price of a standard 12" concrete block to vary as much as 15 cents a block. It doesn't take a genius to figure the savings here. If you have a method of hauling and unloading these blocks, you can save a bundle more, but most people don't have access to the equipment to move pallets of block (you need a heavy-duty forklift), so leave the job of delivery to the block compnay. Don't make plans to lay these blocks until you actually see them on your site. Block companies are famous for missing their delivery date by days, especially to a first-time or private home builder. The reason is simple. They have good intentions when the dispatcher says he will deliver on a particular day and time, but he knows you are an individual. Then a big contractor who is a regular customer calls an hour after you do and wants 5,000 blocks delivered the next day. You can easily figure out who is going to get their blocks on schedule. It's not you. By the way, most block companies have seconds. These are blocks with cracks or chips. They are just as good as the first grade once mortar is applied. Ask about them. They could be used for interior walls at an additional savings. However, don't use them on the exterior walls.

CONCRETE

Now for the concrete—remember you have to pour footers before you can lay block. (Refer to chapter 8 for details on how to prepare footers.) Once your footers are ready for concrete, don't even consider mixing you own. Buy from a local concrete delivery company. There are two standard methods that concrete companies use to deliver concrete to your site.

Cement Mixer

Once way is the conventional barrel-on-the-back type that you commonly know as a cement mixer. This type mixes cement, gravel, sand and water as they drive down the road or on your site. The only problem is that they are batch mixed. This means that if you order 6 yards of concrete, they load the cylinder with the appropriate amount of cement, sand and gravel. The only thing left out is the water. This is added when it reaches your site. However, the catch is that you now own and pay for all six cubic yards of concrete even if you over estimated and can only use four cubic yards.

Rectangular Tank

The second method of delivering concrete is the newer, rectangular-tank type. This type of concrete truck carries all of the ingredients—cement, sand, gravel and water—in separate containers. Once ready to pour, they begin to blend these components together forming a slurry mix of concrete only seconds before it comes out of the truck. With this method you only pay for what you use. Since everything is unmixed until immediately prior to pouring, the truck can stop pouring at anytime you designate and return to its home plant without wasting anything.

They do, however, charge a fee if you order a small amount, usually an additional 10 per cent. You will have to pay this fee if the total yards used from one truck is less than about 5 cubic yards. This second method also avoids any panic rush to pour if a problem arises, whereas the first method requires dumping to begin immediately after the water is added and continued pouring until the truck is completely empty, even if the excess is dumped in your driveway.

Since most companies in a given area will charge the same per cubic yard, the only other advantage you gain is service. If you are pouring your footers yourself, try to be ready for the first load of the morning from the concrete company. The reasoning is that this is the only load that will be on a known time schedule. After delivery of the first load, the driver returns to the company and loads up to begin his next assigned delivery. So the later in the day, the more delays he has encountered on previous assignments. Therefore, you could wait for hours for a load to be delivered. In all fairness to the concrete companies, it is difficult to stay on a schedule. Once I had a crew of friends over to help and the truck was three hours late, so we just stood around wasting time.

Again, if you have a choice, definitely buy from a company that mixes concrete on the site because you'll only pay for what you use. This is better than a pre-mix company because you order in advance and have to pay for the full load whether you use it or not. Contrary to what you estimated your concrete usage would be, you'll probably miss by at least a half yard due to inexperience and possibly an uneven pouring surface.

MASONRY

Now that your footers are poured and blocks delivered, let an experienced block mason lay your block. However, here's your chance to save again. Get a price to lay the block from at least three different small block laying companies with good reputations. Check their work and reliability in advance and don't pay for anything until the job is done to your satisfaction. It should take about three successive days of good working weather to finish the exterior walls of a standard underground house, if there is such a thing. Anytime you're working with a small contractor, ask his price. Once the work is done and you're ready to pay the bill, ask if he gives a discount for paying in cash. Sometimes they will give you a good discount for paying in cash, because they avoid the risk of a bad check. Also when dealing with a small contractor, get a clear understanding as to who is ordering and paying for sand, mortar and water. The total price is usually the same whether you take care of these items or the block layer does. It's just a serious delay to have block and workers, but no sand. If you can work with your block layer and have him agree to lay one day's worth of block around the total perimeter of you're house, maybe three, four or five block high (Figs. 4-1 and 4-2), and then leave the site and come back at a later date at no extra charge, it will be much easier to pour the concrete floor. If your mason has to continue laying block until the walls are at their maxiumum height, it only makes it harder to move men and equipment around to pour the concrete floor.

FLOOR SLAB

Back to saving money. Hire a concrete finisher to pour the smooth floor slab. This is one of the most important jobs in building your underground house. If the floor sets up uneven

Fig. 4-1. If possible, lay three courses of block, then pour the floor.

Fig. 4-2. Pouring a concrete floor.

or rough or cracked, it's a major problem because you will most likely be putting carpet and tile directly over the concrete and a smooth level surface is absolutely necessary. Find out who the contractors prefer. Right here I should mention that a good way to find the best people in the trades of plumbing, block laying, concrete finishing, etc., is to look for the one that can't give you immediate service. He's naturally in demand. The guy who is sitting by his phone and can start tomorrow is not busy for a reason. Find out why. I found it was better to wait for the busy man than hire an idle contractor. I'm not telling you not to give a new man a chance, but be careful. The concrete finishers will give you a price in cents per square foot. Once again, find out what this covers. How smooth should the pouring bed be? What about level pegs?

For clarification, level pegs are only wooden or steel pegs driven in the ground so that the top of each peg is level with the others and to the grade level that you want your finished concrete to be. As your concrete flows and you work it smooth, it should end up level with the tops of these pegs. This way you don't have to use any type of leveling device to insure a level floor or footer. If the pegs were put in accurately, then the floor should be level.

Pouring a slab of concrete is another way to save a few dollars. If your area is unlevel, fill low spots with gravel. Gravel is much cheaper than filling these holes with concrete. For example, a cubic yard of concrete, as of 1978, was approximately $35 delivered. A cubic yard of small stone would be approximately $3 delivered. This is quite a difference in cost if you're only filling a hole.

Fig. 4-3. Inside section of marked block knocked out to tie the interior wall.

INTERIOR WALLS

A second reason for pouring the floor after a couple of courses of exterior wall block are laid and before the interior walls are started is because of the difficulty of leveling and smoothing concrete one room at a time. There is absolutely nothing to be gained by pouring concrete after interior walls are up. Don't even consider this method.

A third reason to put interior walls up after floor slab is complete is that it is very easy to lay out the walls in their actual position. This is how I located my interior walls (Fig. 4-3).

Once your floor is finished, take the width of your interior wall block and cut a board that width. Usually in an underground home you can use 6" concrete block for interior walls, unless your engineer says otherwise. This board should be approximately 8' long for ease of handling. Now with a 100 foot tape measure and a can of bright spray paint (why not red) and a chalk line begin to lay the entire floor plan on the concrete floor. Spray along both edges of the board leaving a wall location mark (Figs. 4-4 and 4-5). This system is good because it gives you a chance to check actual sizes of rooms rather than looking at a blueprint. Plus, by this time you need a psychological lift and you will feel a sense of accomplishment seeing your rooms in full scale. Also, now is the time to make a change in wall location, not later. So walk through the make-believe rooms. Check out door locations, openings, closets, room sizes and anything else you can think of.

MORE NECESSARY PURCHASES

Now that you have things started, there's no turning back. There are a few more things to buy, preferably used. Watch for a bargain on an acetylene cutting torch outfit. They are easy to use and you'll need it to cut the metal rebar that you'll be putting in the concrete roof and retaining walls. They are hard to find, but you will need one and renting it is expensive. Plus, if you rent by the day, you are rushed to get

Fig. 4-4. Lay out interior walls with paint.

your cutting done and return the torch outfit. This is a good way to have an accident or make a stupid mistake.

Also buy a good radial-arm saw new or used. It will be one of the most valuable tools you acquire, and you'll probably keep it forever. Check prices closely and watch motor and blade sizes. Ask your friends and experts about sizes and

Fig. 4-5. Look at the actual room sizes as outlined by the paint. Make any changes in wall locations now.

brand names. Remember you're not a professional carpenter so don't buy the super contractor's model. Just buy the size you need.

Another thing I bought that has proved to be a life saver is an old station wagon. I found a 1963 Ford. The body was shot but the motor and transmission were in good shape. I have come to call it my "poor man's pick-up." If you price pick-up trucks you'll know why. An old station wagon can haul (one way or another) 90 per cent of the supplies a pick-up truck can. My theory was that the old station wagon couldn't be hurt any worse than it was so I loaded block sand, wood, steel concrete and anything and everything in it. If it has to go to the junk yard it was money well spent to have an "almost pick-up truck" for building this house without paying for and destroying a good truck. Give it thought.

Needless to say you'll need the basic tools. They all should be in good condition. In following chapters I will point out additional ways to save money as I discuss more specific stages of construction. Congratulations! You're doing a good job. By the way, how are the building inspectors treating you?

5

Codes and Regulations

Probably the largest single stumbling block you are going to face is how to comply with the local building codes. Once you face the facts that most building inspectors are long-term government employees and must constantly justify their existence you can easily understand why the mention of an underground house can start a panic. If they inspect and approve any phase of your building project and heaven forbid something drastic happened like a fire or a collapsing wall, they are a possible link in the responsibility chain. So therefore, they will take no chances of looking bad in their job performance. Consequently, they usually just overdo everything. They will stick strictly to the book. If it's mentioned in their code book, they aren't interested, because they are not liable. To prove my point, one regulation in our local codes covers hand railings. I have a set of four steps leading from the interior area down to the garage level. A hand rail is a must by codes for safety reasons. Any time you have three or more steps there must be a railing. Of course, I can't really say anything against the hand rail regulation except that it seems to be more of a nitpicking, harassing technique than of any real physical value. This code is now enforced diligently in our county.

In chapter 9 I describe how I built the support structure for pouring the concrete roof slab. You will have noted that in my roof alone, there are more than 140 tons of concrete, 10 tons of steel, 800 tons of dirt plus a two-ton dome. But to this day, no official or inspector has questioned the strength or method of construction, because it's not mentioned in their code books to do so. Pouring this roof alone could have killed as many as 15 people if it had collapsed in mid-construction, but officially no one cares. I say officially because it is just that.

PROFESSIONAL ENGINEERS

The official stance that my local inspection department took was that I must get a professional engineer to put his stamp or seal on my drawing. This seal I mention is a legal signature that indicates that the signing engineer has checked strength and material and agrees that the architectural drawing is satisfactory. This type of engineer is tested by the state for proof of his ability. Then he is given permission to charge a fee for checking these drawings, thus taking a share of the responsibility. So you see, as long as the engineer had his name on the drawing, the county inspection department could say that he was responsible if something wasn't designed correctly. To verify this fact, I can tell you that on the day I poured 3 yards of concrete in a footer, I had two separate visits from official sources, just to see if I was doing it right. Quite a paradox, but I'm sure you'll see it as you build. They are geared to conventional home building and not underground homes. I should also like to add that this is truer the more rural your location. If you were to build a strange structure in a district where high-rise office buildings, large industrial complexes and big apartment complexes are constantly under construction, the inspectors there have seen and are familiar with practically any type of construction problem.

On the other extreme, at the present time, there are still some areas of the United States that have no building codes at all. God bless their nonmeddling souls. It's a pleasure to realize that some communities still believe that the best government is the least governing.

If you intend to build in a community that has a complete set of building codes and zoning regulations, I'll remind you of a few things that will give you and them concern.

MEANS OF EGRESS

Probably the most difficult to comply with is a term called *means of egress*. This meaning exits. This covers doors, windows, holes or anything else that could be used as fire escapes. Usually the codes require two exits from each room except the bathroom. Obviously when you build underground the windows are the first to go, thus a problem.

Sprinkler System

The solution that was proposed to me was to use a commercial sprinkler system in place of the missing windows. If you price their systems, you'll soon find it unreasonable from a cost viewpoint. In my house an acceptable sprinkler system would have cost approximately $10,000. Needless to say, I couldn't accept that.

Smoke Detectors

Therefore, after much negotiations, conflict and letter writing, we (the county and I) agreed that a smoke detector in each room would be adequate. However, even on our compromises we ran into a snag. My idea of a good smoke detector was a battery-operated model made by any of the major smoke detector manufacturers. When I say battery-operated, I mean the type that doesn't require hook-up to the 120-volt house electricity. They only require small voltage batteries, usually one 9-volt battery that lasts for over a year. My logic for this type is understandable, I think. If the house electricity is out of order by storm or if a fire starts in the electrical circuit, it usually blows the fuse or breaker, thus shutting down the power to the detector that is supposed to be on guard. But a battery-operated model is on guard at all times. These battery models usually have a warning system that would sound when the battery is wearing down and ready for replacement. The county inspectors, as usual, had a different view of the same subject. They say that human nature, more often then not, will forget to replace the run-down battery so that the detector system will most likely be inoperative after the first battery wears down. I felt I was right, but I admit that it's all in how you analyze the problem.

Series of Corridors

There is another alternative to meeting egress (fire escape routes) regulations. That is by a series of corridors leading from each room (Fig. 5-1). The reason a corridor or hallway is required is because most local codes say you must be able to escape to the exterior by means of a window or door, without going through another room. For example, you cannot escape out of your bedroom into the living room to get to the nearest door or window. Your bedroom must have a window that leads to the outside and a doorway that leads to a corridor, since corridors are not considered rooms by definition. Now you can easily see why underground homes get into conflict when you eliminate all of the exterior windows. To meet all codes by the corridor system, you would have to waste a lot of square feet of expensive floor space, plus isolate some living areas. Corridors are not my personal idea of a solution, though you may work out an acceptable arrangement.

In summary of this fire escape problem, you have basically four choices to consider before you finalize your plans:

- Provide a corridor to each room
- Provide an appproved sprinkler system
- Provide approved smoke detectors in each room
- Provide escape from each room through the roof

It is my opinion that the third solution is a very economical and logical approach, since that is the way I solved the problem.

The fourth solution is listed more in gest than for serious consideration. I hope it's obvious that the more holes you have

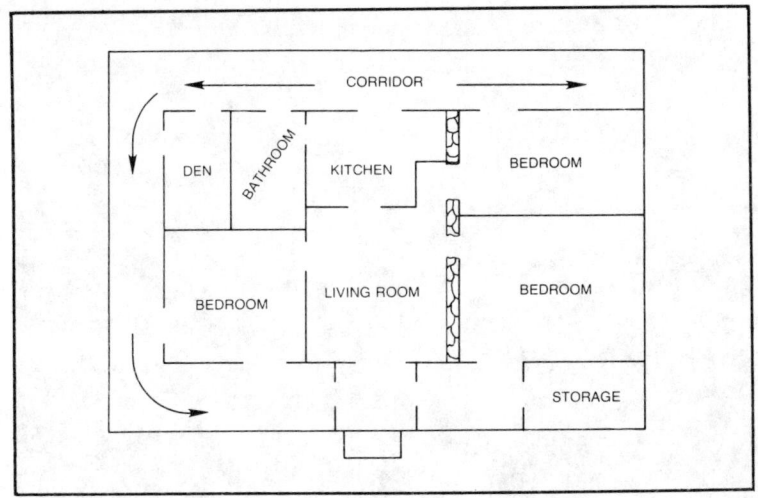

Fig. 5-1. Typical example of using corridors as means of egress.

in your roof, the more problems you will undoubtedly have. Also the cost could be prohibitive.

RETAINING WALLS

Another area that could cause you some trouble when trying to meet codes is retaining walls. Most underground homes have more than their share of retaining walls, depending on the design, of course. Most localities have regulations as to maximum height and method of construction. Try to arrange your design to eliminate exterior retaining walls, if at all possible. If you can't, figure the cost closely. They are extremely expensive to build if they meet the code.

If you expect a retaining wall to stand on its own when the force of mother nature, by means of freezing and thawing the soil, combined with the weight of the soil, is trying to push it over, then you are naive (Fig. 5-2). You can reinforce the wall with enough steel and enough concrete to insure that it will stand and not crack against any of the elements, but it is difficult. One of my solutions to retaining walls is to always brace one against another with steel-reinforced concrete (Fig. 5-3). If you have only one retaining wall, you can always tie it to an anchor post of some type (Fig. 5-4).

Fig. 5-2. A large retaining wall is unsupported in final stage of construction.

Additional suggestions on how to tie a retaining wall back could be lengthy and it is a subject that has been written about in detail. Ask a good contractor or engineer, or search the library for books on this subject. It will be worth your time to particularly look into the use of railroad ties. Most railroad ties which you can buy now have never been used on a railroad and they aren't really the same thing. The old-time railroad ties were pressure cooked in creosote (a preservative) to prevent rotting. The new so-called ties have only been dipped in a preservative and will not last as long as a real tie. Building retaining walls of ties is a difficult, back-breaking job. So use something that will stay in place as long as possible.

HAND RAILINGS

Another subject that will require close attention to complete your house is hand railings. There is usually a difference between safe conditions and meeting the codes. I ran into a problem with my interior garden (Figs. 5-5 and 5-6). When a garden is covered by a dome, it is a personal judgment as to whether it is considered exterior or interior. If indeed the inspector feels it is exterior, then hand rail, doors and electrical boxes must meet one segment of the code. If he decides it is interior, then he will turn to another page in his book. As I mentioned, hand railing requirements are different depending on the use of your garden or atrium. If you plan to use an

Fig. 5-3. Two retaining walls held apart by the roof structure.

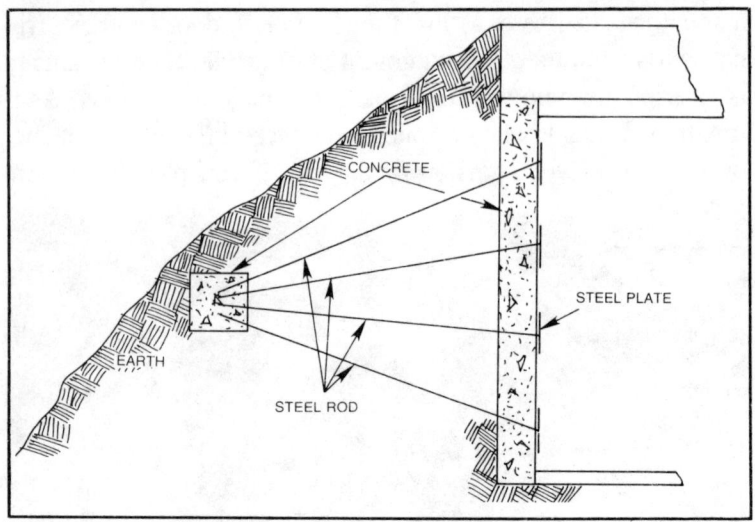

Fig. 5-4. Alternate method of holding a retaining wall.

above-floor level to grow year-round plants, then you are required to have a railing, even if you only use it once a year. If it is just for decoration, then no railing is required. Still another problem area could be glass doors. The codes sometimes say sliding glass doors are not allowed as a principal means of eggress. This becomes particularly complicated when these doors enter into your garden. Is it exterior space or interior space?

Most local building codes were patterned after a basic set of national regulations and sometime in the past these codes have been adopted as the gospel truth. In addition, many subdivisions have drawn up a few amendments to the national codes. Most of these amendments are pets of some local developer and in no way are intended to serve your benefit, only your expense. For this reason, everywhere in this country will probably take a different approach to the building of an underground house.

AIR CIRCULATION

Air circulation is one area that is touchy and important. If your house is like mine when complete, you will have only a wood stove for heat. I'm not suggesting that you don't put conventional heating in if you feel comfortable doing it, but the majority of underground home owners find wood heating is the most satisfying, even over solar heat. If you use conventional heat with a duct system, then all air circulation problems will

Fig. 5-5. Partial view of a garden in the final stage of construction.

63

Fig. 5-6. An exterior garden and walkway.

be easily met. But if a wood stove is in your future, then concentrate on the area of circulation. Just because you heat one room easily and quickly doesn't mean the hot air will move from room to room. You need a circulation system, but as you know a wood stove needs the same oxygen that you need to breathe. As the fire burns and you breathe, this oxygen must be replenished. So you do need a duct to the outside world. Here is where the codes will conflict with your good judgment about the size and location of the fresh air intake supply. The inspector's logic here is that in a conventional home fresh air is drawn in around windows, under doors, etc., regardless of the new caulking and installed insulation strips. I know from experience that all you need to do is circulate the air inside the house. The exterior doors would have to be opened approximately once a day to provide all the fresh air necessary to live comfortably. This is particularly true if you have a large dome or breathing skylight. Remember, if you keep bringing in outside air in the winter when it's not required, you defeat the purpose of underground living. Of course, the same is true in the summer. In summary of fresh air, I like and need fresh air as much as anyone, but enough is enough. Don't change air more frequently than necessary.

ELECTRICAL CODES AND PLUMBING

Plumbing and electrical codes will be mentioned only in passing. There doesn't seem to be much of a problem with building underground and meeting plumbing and electrical codes. Electric wires and water pipes don't know the difference so at least these two phases of utility installation should be simple (Fig. 5-7).

I will tell you to watch out for the sewer drain vent pipes. Don't put them through the roof. Run them with the water pipes along the block wall and vent them to the exterior vertical walls. These drain air vents are required to be 2" in diameter to allow proper air intake into the septic system. The reason these drains are required is that if you release a large amount of water into a drain line at a certain point, it creates a vacuum as it drains to a drain field. This vacuum draws the standing water out of the traps in the sinks at another point. Once the water has reached the septic tank, the trap at the second point will be empty and allow sewer odor to seep back up the pipe into the living area.

STAIRS

Still another area that you might watch out for and design around is the steps. The reason to avoid steps in an under-

Fig. 5-7. Typical water pipe attached to 1 × 3 firring strip on block wall.

ground house is, once again, written in the sacred scrolls of building codes because a principal means of egress cannot contain steps upward, only downward. Therefore, since you are already down, you can't continue in that direction. You must eventually come up. This is a code that varies from locale to locale, so check your particular situation out carefully.

DOOR OPENINGS

This chapter will be closed with one last code for you to check on. Most likely all doors opening to all living areas from utility rooms, storage rooms, garages, laundry rooms or furnace rooms must be made of solid wood approximately 1½" thick with no windows. They also must have an approved burn rate. The reasoning is that it will contain a fire in these work areas long enough for you to escape past (not through) the door.

As you go through these trials and tribulations, you'll find you cannot meet certain codes, or it is really impractical to do so. If that is the case, there is a means of appeal if the building inspector will not suggest an alternative to your problem.

BUILDING CODES APPEALS BOARD

This course is usually referred to the building codes appeals board. They are usually politically appointed members for a specific term. They have absolutely no power to change a regulation. For example, they cannot give you approval to eliminate a door if a door is called for by code. Most codes make use of the overworked and all-encompassing word *approved*. If you put a hand railing along a stairway and use a piece of wood 2" × 2" thick, the inspector may disapprove the railing. You can ask for an appeal to the appeals board saying that 2" × 2" is strong enough and should be accepted. Then they will rule either for you or against you. They will never say a 2" is not okay but 2" × 3" is okay. This means that they will not suggest what is acceptable, only give you a yes or no answer.

6
Site Preparation

Site preparation for an underground house is definitely more critical than that of a conventional home since most underground homes are on the side of a hill. This terrain will be covered first and in most detail.

Chapter 2 covered what to look for and what to avoid when finding your ideal location. There is an interrelation between these two chapters. As you read on, you will notice that I am explaining location to you as if your land were in the two- to three-acre range. I think of this as the minimum size for an underground house. It is obvious that if you have 10 or 15 acres you should have little trouble locating the ideal spot for everything. Therefore, I will only point out the things to watch for if your land is in the two- to three-acre range (Figs. 6-1 through 6-3).

Once your boundaries are clearly and accurately marked by surveyors' stakes, find an observation point where you can see most of your property and study the contour.

DRIVEWAY

You also have to give a lot of thought to where you are going to cut your dirveway. This is the first excavation that

Fig. 6-1. A two- to three-acre lot.

usually takes place. I suggest you put your driveway on one side or the other as opposed to down the middle of your property (Figs. 6-4 and 6-5). If your driveway is in the center of your yard, you split the lawn into two parcels, both of which may not be big enough to use for recreation areas.

SETBACK

You must also know what the restrictions are on *setback*. Setback is a term that your locality has established to name a suitable distance from the public highway where you can build your house. This distance is different for each piece of land. The reason for this regulation is to prevent someone from setting a new house right up against the roadside. There is also a regulation controlling how closely you can build to your neighbors' property line. This dimension is usually 10 to 20 feet. If you have a three-acre tract to build on and you follow all of the possible regulations, you will soon notice that you don't have as much choice as you first thought concerning the location of your house.

Fig. 6-2. The minimum size lot for an underground home is at least two acres.

SEPTIC-SEWER SYSTEM

Before you start driving markers in the ground locating the corners of your house, have you cleared the location of your septic-sewer system with the health department? If not,

Fig. 6-3. Preparing your site.

Fig. 6-4. Cutting your driveway out of your land.

be sure to check with them. And don't forget the well is also covered by regulations. Usually the local health department handles this. Of course, I'm assuming that your land is covered by codes because most land near major population centers is heavily regulated, especially if it's a small parcel and not of farm size.

Fig. 6-5. Your driveway should be on one side of your property.

SURVEYING

Now, back to site preparation (Fig. 6-6). It's time to begin putting stakes in the ground. You can locate the corners of your house yourself with a transit, or you can hire a professional surveyor. If you do it yourself, follow this method. You

Fig. 6-6. The lot before excavation.

Fig. 6-7. The lot one day after excavation.

must have a set of drawings of your house by now. Add 10 feet to the width and length. The reason for this is that the stakes you drive in to the ground when laying a house do not indicate the actual exterior wall corners but the corners of excavation (Fig. 6-7). The bulldozer operator will use these stakes as a guide to dig the home. The purpose of the extra 10 feet on the length and width is that the block layer or form builders need room to walk and work around the actual wall once they are started (Fig. 6-8). Also the drain field is laid in this same space once the walls are started.

As soon as this same dozer cuts your driveway and you agree that it's the right location, bring in gravel for a driveway bed. Look in the yellow pages under *gravel* or *quarries*. Common terminology around Maryland is *crusher run*. This is a gravel and dust mixture that is as cheap as any gravel and packs to make a good road bed. You want this driveway passable for your delivery trucks right from the start because they will not deliver material if there is a chance of getting stuck on the job site. You can't blame them for that because their trucks are expensive and serve as their basic means of livelihood. Besides, you could be liable for towing bills or damage to the trucks.

Whatever you do, don't let anyone talk you into paving your driveway with blacktop or macadam the first year. Let the gravel pack and settle for at least one year. Of course, if you are going to concrete your driveway, that's a different story. Concrete could be poured as soon as the house is

Fig. 6-8. Four foot walking space and drain pipe.

complete as long as it's not over unpacked fill dirt. Don't concrete or macadam your driveway and let heavy delivery trucks drive over it the first month it has been poured. Give it a chance to cure. A couple of months should be sufficient. If it cracks after two months, it wasn't put down or reinforced properly in the first place. Then your problems are just beginning as far as driveways go.

Give some more thought to putting anything down on your driveway other than gravel. The tax assessors love people who improve their property by a hard driveway. It's not fair, but it's the system of tax assessment.

MOWING THE LAND

If your land is grown over with weeds or undergrowth, find a way to mow it to grass length while the excavation is going on. Every neighborhood has someone with a big field mower behind a farm tractor who will do this for a reasonable price. You'll want to actually see the surface of the land that will become your future lawn. If it is grown over with brush, I don't care how many times you walk over a piece of land, you never see everything. For example, big rocks that require a dozer to move may be just below the surface. Move them before the dozer leaves the site. It's impossible to move a rock as big as a refrigerator, even with the backhoe I hope you bought earlier.

The next reason for mowing the land is to eliminate rodents, insects and allergenic weeds. It will also allow the land to dry out.

If you have a wooded area on your property, try to cut down underbrush, dead trees and unhealthy trees to allow the stronger ones to develop into good shade trees. Talk to a professional regarding the selection of the trees you save as opposed to the ones that get the axe. Some may be rare or otherwise valuable. Some may be dying and unnoticeable. Some may be thorny or have poison berries or leaves. Don't go in and methodically cut down all the living trees and bushes, on the premise that you will have to buy from a nursery anyway when the house is complete. It's usually a waste of natural beauty and nursery plants are expensive and very difficult to start. Keep your underground house surrounded by a natural setting as much as possible. You'll be happier in the long run and so will your neighbors.

PROPERTY LINES

Another thing to do regarding site preparation, which I strongly suggest, is that once the official survey is made by a professional and the property markers officially set, remove any wooden posts and drive steel pipes in their place. Do this at least every 50 feet along your neighbor's property line on all sides. Drive them to grade level, but make sure you can find them if you need to.

Some wise man once said, "Fences make the best neighbors." This at first may sound like a cold or unfriendly attitude, but it is not. Personalities change, situations change and neighbors change, and there's nothing that will cause hard feelings faster than two people who think they both own the same rose bush on a common boundary. I don't necessarily agree with the fence theory, but at least make sure it's obvious where the property lines are, right from the start.

The reason I point this out is that with both homes I have built the question has come up as to whom is using whose property to plan proverbial rose bushes.

Due to the fact that you are building a "strange" home in the eyes of most people, the world you live in may not be ready to jump on your bandwagon or beat a path to your door. In fact, they could be downright nasty, once your intentions to live underground are made public. So cover all possible sources of contention, especially those boundaries. There's no use in asking for any extra unfavorable reaction.

As site preparation continues, have your dozer operator grade off approximately 6" of top soil to form a mound. This method will prevent wasting top soil that you will need for final grading. If you don't pile your top soil aside, it will be covered by the lesser-grade under soil dug from footers, foundation or the driveway. If you think the extra grading effort to save top soil isn't worth the extra money you might have to pay a dozer operator, you'd better check the price of a truckload of good top soil. You'll agree that it's easier and more economical to save even an ounce of good soil rather than pay to haul it in at final-grading time.

7

Preparing and Pouring the Footers

Preparing footers for an underground house is much more critical than those of a conventional home, because of the excessive weight bearing on them. The consequences, also, are more critical. Cracking walls will lead to leaks.

Dig your footers correctly and accurately and it will be time well spent. To begin with, a conventional house footer is usually required by code to be 16" wide by 8" deep. I recommend that for an underground house over 2000 square feet that you increase the width to 24" wide and 12" deep. Also add reinforcing steel rods as an added safety factor against settling cracks. The amount of steel rod added to the footer is immaterial. The more the better, but it is expensive. So use good judgment and ask for advice. In my opinion, four pieces of steel rebar 3/4" in diameter would be idea (Fig. 7-1).

The important thing about preparing and digging footers is that they are level and square. Also, the corners are at right angles. The reason to keep the corners square is basic. All that weight pushing down on the footer is trying to push it into the ground further (Figs. 7-2 and 7-3). To exaggerate this point, suppose the footers were only 1" wide and pointed on the bottom. They would act as a knife edge and would keep

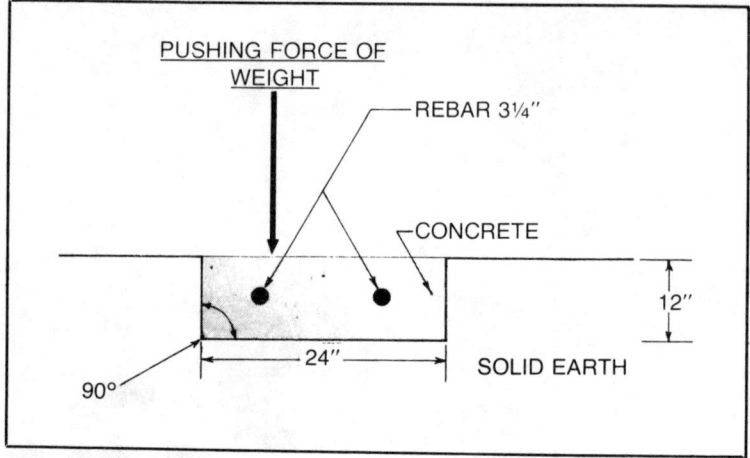

Fig. 7-1. Typical section of footer with rebar.

settling deeper and deeper. It's the wide, flat surface that stops settling in the same way that snow shoes stop you from settling in the snow.

This footer will be dug by a backhoe, either driven by a professional or by you. Either way the footers will be dug by a backhoe and cleaned up by hand labor and a square-tipped shovel. In preparation for the backhoe to begin digging, you have to place guide lines on the dirt for the operator to follow. Use a common field line that can be bought at any hardware store. Lay out the location of each footer edge (not center line) in the same way that football stripes are applied. The backhoe operator will then dig beside this white line you put down. Notice I said mark the edges of the footer. If your addition and subtraction is not accurate, you will be digging footers where there are no walls and vice versa.

Now that these white lines of lime are in place and the machine is digging, you need two additional helpers and a good transit.

Set the transit up totally outside the perimeter of the house foundation by at least 25 feet. This will prevent having to relocate the transit as the backhoe maneuvers closer.

As the backhoe is digging, you and a helper will continually measure the depth of his diggings to maintain a uniform ditch. Approximately every 4 feet drive a wooden or steel stake in the center of the footer. These stakes are driven in the ground until the tops of all the stakes are level with each other, as established by the transit reading. The stakes are spaced equally as the machine digs, and your helper takes readings on the transit. This continues until all the footers are complete.

Fig. 7-2. Typical 20" wide footers.

Up to this point, the footer preparation is the same as in a conventional building. The big difference is the fact that every wall is a bearing wall. Therefore, every wall requires a footer underneath. This may not sound like a major point, but consider the fact that by putting footers under every interior wall, the amount of digging, hand shoveling, concrete, steel and so forth is approximately two and a half times as much as a conventional house. For example, my house, above the ground, would have required 260 feet of footer. By being underground it actually required over 570 feet of footer. So you see how the cost and labor can add up fast. This, coupled with the extra width and depth I suggested earlier, could cause your underground house footers to actually cost over four times that of a conventional house.

Do not take these footers lightly. If you do, you will not only waste time and money, but you could endanger the complete integrity of the structure.

THE CONCRETE

Pouring the fresh concrete is a job you can handle with a little help from your friends, whether it's footers, sidewalks or your roof. First of all, all concrete companies sell concrete by the cubic yard delivered. You are responsible for telling them how much to deliver, and you are responsible for the distribution of this concrete. To figure how much you will need for a specific pour, you simply figure the cubic yards of the area to be filled—length times width times height. These dimensions are usually discussed in feet and inches so be careful when converting to cubic yards. There are 27 cubic feet in a cubic yard. I have heard stories from the concrete truck drivers about do-it-yourselfers who forgot that they were buying a cubic yard instead of a square yard and found themselves either far too short of concrete, or with enough to concrete the entire neighborhood. Remember, when you are talking to the concrete company on the telephone, he has no idea what you're doing. So he takes your request to be the gospel truth, whether you ask for one yard or 100 yards. Be careful with the simple arithmetic. It could be costly if you make a mistake. Also remember that once the truck arrives with your order, it's your concrete. Concrete does not make round trips. If you have a footer to be filled that actually requires 5 yards, but through your mistake in ordering the truck arrives with 8

Fig. 7-3. Drive the stakes approximately every 4 feet into the center of the footer until the tops of the stakes are level.

Fig. 7-4. Accidents are caused by carelessness.

yards, you pay for your order and the excess gets dumped on your property for you to clean up later.

Once the truck arrives, the driver will know how close to get to your diggings. Let this decision be his. Most of them are experienced and are responsible for their trucks. However, I happened to get a driver who was a little more of a cowboy than a truck driver. Figures 7-4 through 7-6 illustrate the results of carelessness and poor judgment. This time the driver was only severly shaken. It's a miracle that this accident was not fatal, but the truck was totally destroyed. So let him make the decision as to how and where he will dump the concrete. When pouring concrete down a hole, the risks can be very great at times, especially when building an underground house.

Once the concrete truck starts pouring wet concrete in your footer, all you need is a good rake and shovel. The driver will ask you whether you want it wet or dry. He only means with more or less water added. If the concrete flows along the footer easily by raking, then keep that consistency. Put the stakes in the footer to insure the proper level for the concrete. Don't forget to watch them closely as the concrete flows. They are now the only guide you have to keep the concrete level enough to lay the block on. I'll remind you right here that the interior footers of an undergrund house need not be as

Fig. 7-5. Poor judgement caused this truck to be totally destroyed.

level as you may think, because a 4" to 6" slab of concrete gets poured over these interior footers. Don't try to pour footers and slab at the same time. It's a big job and there's no advantage to be gained except very little time. The best reason for not pouring footers and slab at one time is that if you have good drainage soil, it will be a sandy, mica soil and very loosely packed as opposed to a clay-type soil. It is often very difficult

Fig. 7-6. Fortunately, the driver of this mishap was only severely shaken.

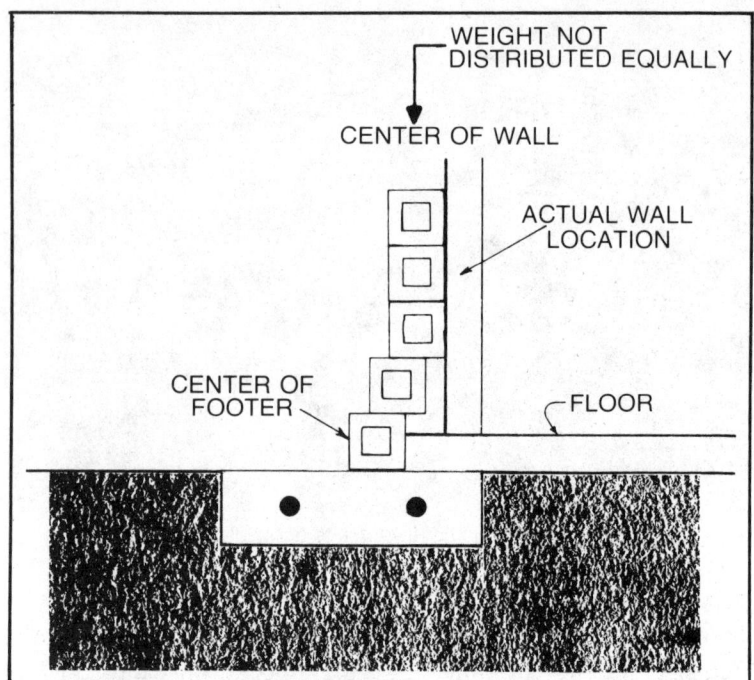

Fig. 7-7. An exaggerated method of misalignment.

to keep footer ditches from caving in along the edges. If the side of your footer ditch does cave in, you either lose strength or waste concrete. If you pour the footer and continue pouring more concrete to make the floor slab, the edges will most likely collapse. This is my opinion, and I'm sure some people reading this will disagree, but remember I'm living in my house and everything is working well.

Now back to the footers you're pouring. In most cases the concrete will flow freely 10 or 15 feet with little raking and shoveling. Once the raking becomes difficult, ask the driver to move to another spot if he thinks he can do so safely, and continue to dump until all the footers are filled to the top of the leveling pegs. There is no need to use a trowel on the footers. The surface, as it settles and hardens, is smooth enough as long as it is level to plus or minus a ½". If you misjudge and the footers set up out of level, the block layer can correct the mistake, but it is a slow procedure and most block layers hate to begin laying block on footers that are unlevel or out of square.

The principle of right (90°) angle corners is the foundation of basic building construction. The entire weight of your house plus the earth covering it rest on these footers. If by chance you poured them out of square, then the block layer will have to shift his first course of block to the edge of the footer to compensate for your error (Fig. 7-7). Once he does this, the weight is not distributed evenly and a crack in the footer, wall or even roof is likely to happen in the future. If you are not confident in your ability to keep the footers accurate and square, hire someone to help you. You can't end up with a successful underground house if the foundation is a weak link.

SEWER PIPE

Once the footers are poured and set up, check all the cast iron sewer pipe you placed (Figs. 7-8 and 7-9). This is the only time you will get a chance to do anything about mistakes or damaged pipes. The plumbing inspector has approved your system most likely, but that doesn't stop accidental breaking

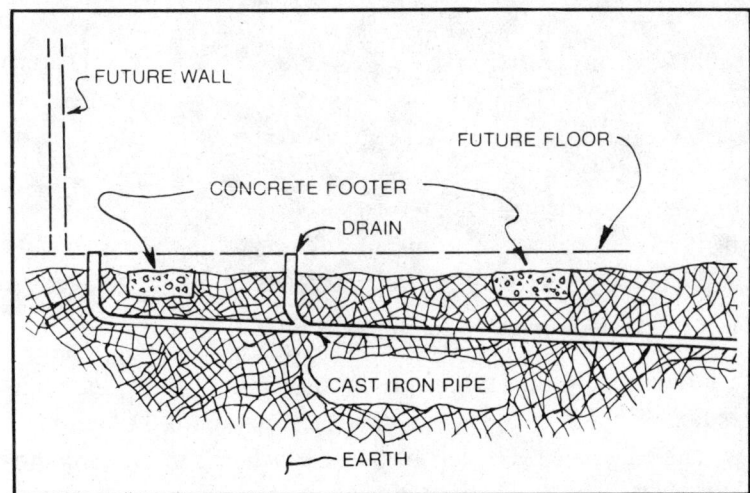

Fig. 7-8. Cast iron drain pipes are tunneled under footers. They are not placed prior to pouring.

Fig. 7-9. All pipes must be thoroughly checked.

or movement as final footer preparation takes place. The next chance you will get to correct a drain pipe will be at great expense, because you will be using a jack hammer to break the floor apart. Check the pipe; it will be a load off your mind later on.

8
Walls

There are only two basic methods for constructing the walls of an underground house, as opposed to the endless methods and materials available to conventional, above-ground home constructions. Above-ground construction lends itself to plastic, wood, glass, stone, brick, metal, concrete and any combination of the above, but in underground construction the material is limited to one type—concrete. There are two possible ways of erecting this concrete:

- Pouring concrete in forms
- Laying concrete block.

FORMED AND POURED WALLS

This method is the strongest, most difficult and most expensive. Needless to say, any advantage you gain you pay for. As I'm sure you are aware by now, there is always more than one way to do any job. The same goes for pouring concrete walls. Insert a section of steel into the poured footers immediately after they are all leveled out. These pieces of steel should stick out of the center of the concrete about 12". So if you poured your footers 12" deep, the steel rebar would have to be cut into approximately 24" lengths. Put these steel pieces on 2 foot centers everywhere a wall will be. Remember to skip putting a post in the section of footer where a doorway will be. If you forget or misjudge, you can simply cut it off later. It's not that big of a deal. The reason for these steel posts is to tie the walls solidly to the footer to prevent any possible movement. This method also increases strength. This is the type of construction you would use if cost were not a major factor.

The alternative to tying the walls to the footers is simply to set the wall on top of the footer and rely on the actual bonding of concrete to concrete, rather than a steel connection.

Once you decide on the method of setting the poured concrete wall on the footer, the actual wall-forming preparation is the same. You can locate form builders or renters in the yellow pages of most major cities. Renting forms will be the easiest and the most economical if you can find them. Erecting these forms is a laborious job, and you should have someone experienced in form erecting to assist you. If you rent these forms, remember, you are responsible for any pieces that you damage or intentionally modify. Also there is always the chance of collapsing forms and the extra labor and expense used to clean up the mess. It just isn't worth the extra trouble and cost to pour exterior walls.

BLOCK WALLS

I'll state right here that it is my preference to use concrete block for all walls, exterior and interior, instead of poured concrete. Think about the pouring method, analyze it, then forget it.

Check around and get a respectable block layer and contract price for the complete job. This is where your good judgment comes in. No one can help you make a choice. Only you have the facts and you have to live with it.

A good block laying crew will take about 10 working days to put up an average underground house. It will then be ready to begin preparations for the roof. Figures 8-2 through 8-5 illustrate the different stages of block work. Construct all walls, even closets, out of block. Exterior walls should never be less than 12" thick. They are just right at that width to put rebar in and fill with concrete for strength. A post of rebar and filled concrete should be created any place that an interior wall does not intersect with an exterior wall. For a distance exceeding 10 feet, these posts should be approximately 4 feet long or three block (Fig. 8-6). Use rebar about ¾" in diameter and insert a length down each hole in the block all the way to the footer if possible. The interior wall can be 6" concrete block and doesn't need to be filled with concrete except in rare conditions. The are several reasons why you don't fill interior block with concrete. First, cost is prohibitive. Second—your electrician will use the hollow block to feed some of his wire through to meet certain codes. The wires can only be fed to the recepticle box by way of the hollow concrete block. (Fig. 8-7). Third, and most importantly, you'll probably have to knock at least one hole in the interior wall due to oversight of some trivial dimension. Have you ever tried to knock a hole in solid concrete? Forget it unless you have a power air hammer. I'll tell you a few of the reasons I had to knock out block after

Fig. 8-1. Concrete forms in place for a conventional house.

Fig. 8-2. Early stages of block laying.

they were set in place. I forgot to leave openings to the back of the bathtubs to allow access to the plumbing (Fig. 8-8). Also, there had to be a hole for a vent pipe out of each bathroom. However, this I didn't forget. I planned to locate this as the construction progressed. Also, don't forget that the water pipes have to go through the walls to the kitchen and bath. In

Fig. 8-3. The mid-stage of block laying.

Fig. 8-4. Block laying continues.

Fig. 8-5. Final stages of block laying.

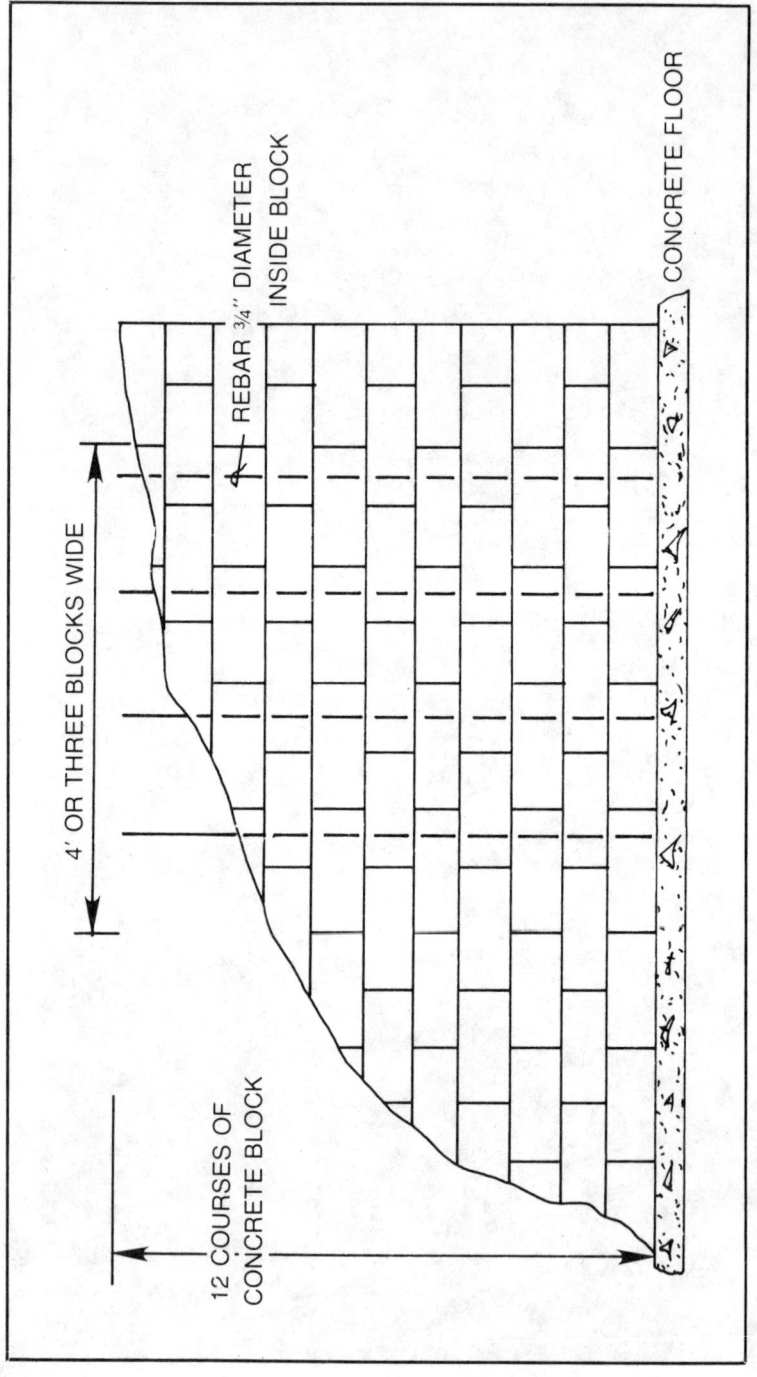

Fig. 8-6. Four lengths of rebar make a post.

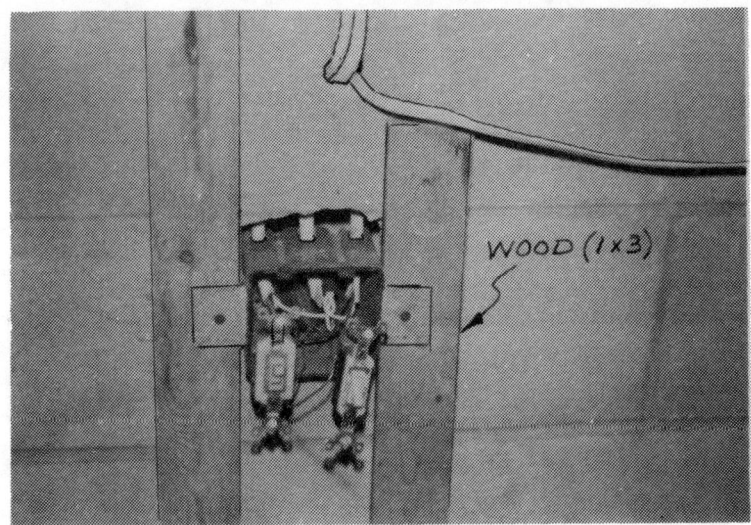

Fig. 8-7. Electric receptacle and wire in concrete block.

my house the copper pipes pass through the walls at approximately eight different places. This would be a major job if the walls were solid concrete.

Another place that I had to chip away the block was where I tried to install my one-piece fiberglass tub and shower unit. I found the unit to be ½" wider than my door opening. This was

Fig. 8-8. Rough access hole to plumbing behind the bathtub.

an oversight that didn't cause a real problem because we just broke away the block as needed.

Instead of knocking block out for everything you should plan better than I did and install vents and heat ducts as the block is laid. This sounds easier than it is. Vent and air ducts sometimes have to be relocated because natural air currents are drastically affected by being underground. I found that where I thought air would circulate naturally, it didn't, and vice-versa. Thus, I had to relocate numerous openings in the concrete block. I suggest you try to locate the vent openings as the block goes up, but don't be surprised if you miss a few.

As your block work progresses day by day you will, for the first time, see a house developing before your eyes and realize you're really undertaking an enormous project. There's no turning back at this point, so you had better like what you see so far.

9

Roof Design and Preparation

Now that you have all the walls up and level at ceiling height, you come to another really critical part—preparing the shoring (Figs. 9-1 and 9-2), the substructure and braces for pouring concrete. What you are actually doing is building a platform capable of holding as much as 250 pounds per square foot. This includes steel, approximately 10″ of wet concrete and a worker smoothing this concrete. Holding wet concrete until it sets is like holding onto the proverbial burlap bag full of bobcats. Wet concrete wants to go everywhere except where you want it. If it finds a small hole, it will make the hole bigger and bigger until it breaks through. This method completes the roof in one pouring with no joints. Then there are no seams and no leaks. This is also the method that you can do yourself with a little luck and some help from your friends. Be realistic when evaluating your abilities to build your own shoring and substructure and pouring the slab. You may want to have a contractor do it. Doing it yourself is a back-breaking job. But you can save approximately $10,000!

Here's how I did my shoring (Fig. 9-3): laid rough cut lumber down on the concrete floor, wall to wall, every 18″. You can get this type of lumber at saw mills, usually very cheap. It's the strips that are cut from a log before they get to the center where the good boards are cut from.

I did not glue this rough lumber to the concrete floor (Figs. 9-4 through 9-6). It is not necessary to go to that extra time and cost. Check around for this wood. You'll find it. Later, when you're finished your house, cut this wood up and use it in your fireplace. I paid two cents a foot for random length over 8 feet long, and I picked this wood up to save money, rather than pay a delivery cost.

For your next step you will definitely need three or four people willing to work. Don't try to erect scaffolding by my method without sufficient labor, free or otherwise.

Once you have laid rough lumber on the floor and nailed a section of 2 × 4s along the ceiling height, stand a 2 × 4 upright under the first piece of rough lumber. Try to start in a corner.

With a few more 2 × 4s nailed between the top and bottom rough lumber, you can lay a sheet of ½" sheeting grade exterior plywood on the top. As your helpers hold this arrangement together, you climb up to the top of the block wall and nail through the plywood and the rough lumber into one of the upright 2 × 4s. You now have the beginning of your support. Your supports will be the same throughout the rest of the house.

If, at this point, you are considering leaving out the rough cut lumber, don't, because the results will be catastrophic. The rough lumber prevents the extreme weight of the future concrete from punching a hole through the concrete floor or through the ½" plywood. It is a must.

Now back to the actual erecting. Continue to set 2 × 4s upright, watching closely to keep them at 16" centers, maximum. If your centers are a little less than 16", that will do.

Continue this method until one room is complete. Be sure to have a good piece of rough lumber at each joint of the plywood, because this is the weakest point of the plywood.

The sad thing about this method is that you are constantly cutting plywood sheets. Therefore, they can't be sold later. But don't waste the plywood—save all the small pieces. They

Fig. 9-1. All interior walls are complete and the shoring is started.

Fig. 9-2. The process of shoring is underway.

will fit somewhere as things progress. One good thing in your favor now is that you can climb up and walk around on this plywood platform that you're building.

Before you buy these 2 × 4 × 8s, I suggest you try to keep the ceiling very close to 8 feet, because sheet rock and

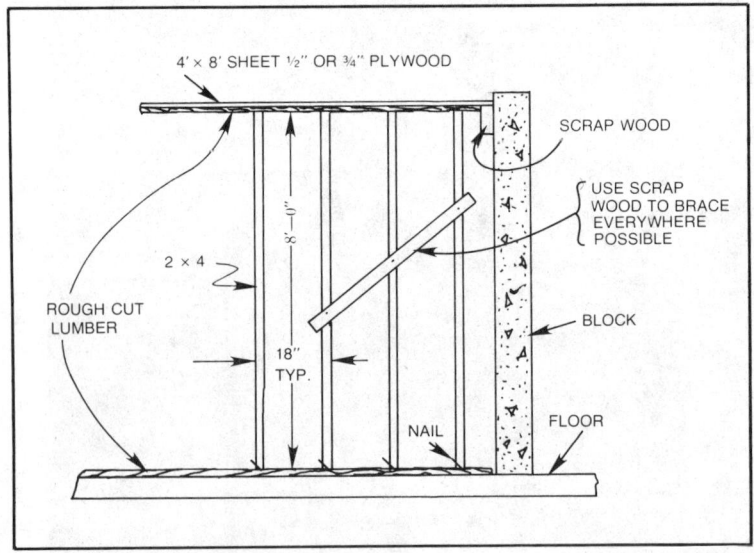

Fig. 9-3. A typical shoring arrangement.

Fig. 9-4. If you look closely, you'll see that the wood strips are not fastened to the floor.

Fig. 9-5. Wood strips are not fastened to the floor.

paneling come in 4 × 8 foot sheets. If your ceiling ends up 7' 11" high, you will have to cut each piece of sheet rock or paneling. That's quite a job. The way you control your ceiling height is by the length of the 2 × 4s. If you buy standard 2 × 4 × 8s and set them on rough lumber, add another rough board on top, both of which are approximately 1" thick and then set a sheet of ½" plywood on that, it's easy to figure that your

Fig. 9-6. Another view of rough wood and 2 x 4 supports.

ceiling will then be 8' 2½" tall when these are removed. That's too tall. Cut 2" off each 2 × 4 × 8 before you use it. If you do, you will end up with a ceiling approximately 8 feet in height. Whatever you do, don't try to use precut 2 × 4s. Precut 2 × 4s are approximately 2' 8¼" long. This would make the ceiling too low.

Each room is shored up and braced individually. Do not let the wood go over the top of the black wall (Fig. 9-7). This method locks all the walls in place with concrete. In addition, it

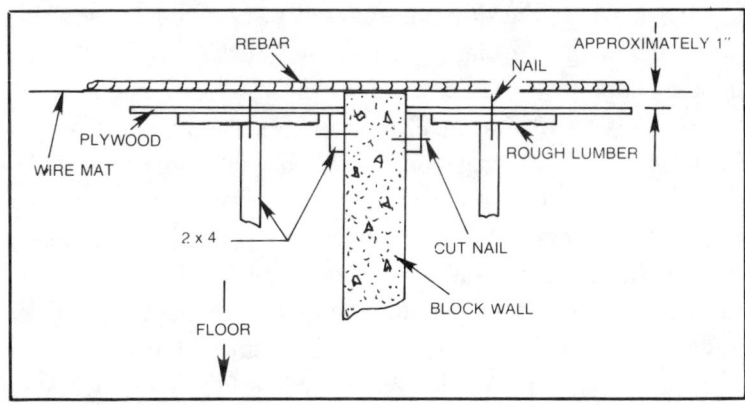

Fig. 9-7. The wood should not go over the top of the block wall.

103

holds all of your shoring secure from moving left, right, forward or backward. Most importantly, the rebar lays on the top of the block, thus avoiding an extreme load on the shoring. Once the shoring is up in all rooms, go back and check each 2 × 4 to make sure it is plumb and toenailed with at least two 10-penny nails, top and bottom. Remember one slip of a 2 × 4 and down comes the wet concrete. I can't warn you enough about this. A slip could bankrupt you. If you add the cost of the concrete, the cost of the lumber, your labor and the cost of cleaning up wet concrete once it has fallen, you can easily see why this could be the only mistake you'll make because it will also be the last.

Now that all the supports are moving toward completion and you can walk around on this platform, you're ready for the next step.

Stuff each open concrete block with paper. Save the concrete mortar bags from the block layer. Tear them in half in each hole of the concrete block to prevent concrete from flowing down the block. Filled block are too expensive and unnecessary for strength. Make sure your engineer agrees that all walls do not need to be filled with concrete. Some probably will, but don't fill any walls that aren't necessary.

Now your shoring is up completely, all the holes are stuffed with paper and you are ready to spread plastic. This plastic is to prevent the concrete from sticking to the plywood so that it will come down easily and will be resaleable. Use construction grade plastic that comes in big rolls from any building supply store. Cover all the plywood with one sheet of plastic. If you tear a small hole in the plastic, don't worry because a little concrete on the wood won't hurt anything.

There is no doubt that the most critical part of your underground house will be the roof. Put your time and money into the design of the slab. It will be money well spent. A good professional engineer should look your plans over, make suggestions and lay out a steel reinforcement bar pattern for you for a small fee. About $200 would be fair. When working up the original floor plan, be sure to keep the rooms near

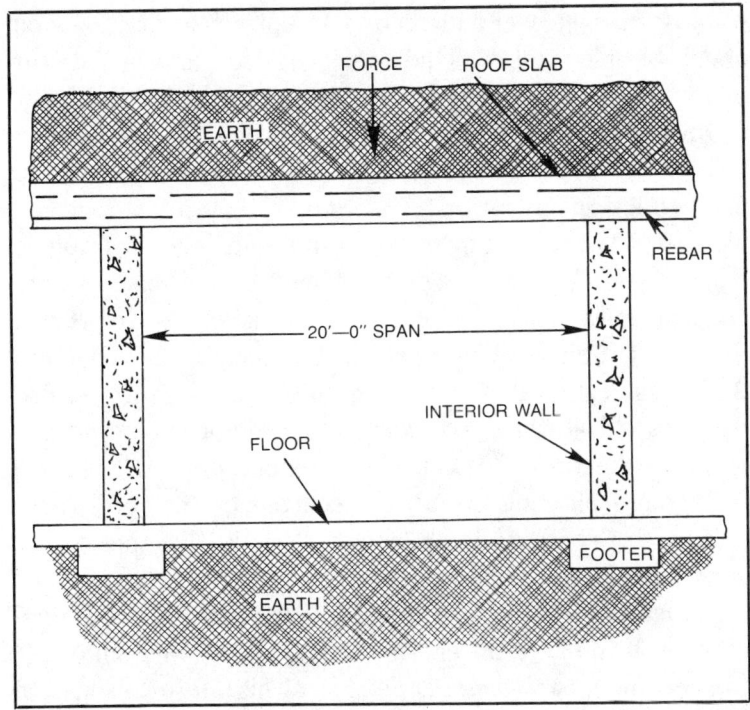

Fig. 9-8. Maximum span should be 20 feet.

conventional size. Since your interior walls are bearing walls and physically holding up the roof and dirt, you want to avoid spanning a long distance. The method of construction, cost and the reinforcement involved then becomes more critical and a bigger job than the average person can handle or afford. The widest span I recommend is 20 feet (Fig. 9-8).

A rule of common sense I would suggest for you to follow is that when laying out a floor plan, add the length and the width. The total should not exceed 38 feet. For example, a room which is 16 feet by 20 feet would equal 36 feet, or a utility room could be 25 feet by 8 feet to equal 33 feet. Remember this is only my rule of thumb. Trust your engineer as a final authority.

If your living requirements are average, 20 feet is as wide as any room usually needs to be. The engineer designing the strength of your roof will need an exact layout of your floor plan. If you have ever had a course in high school drafting, you should be able to make all the drawings necessary to build your house. If you don't feel comfortable doing this drawing, your engineer will have someone make a reliable set for you.

To locate an engineer, look in the yellow pages of the phone book under *construction engineer*. Any city of reasonable size will have a listing of one or more engineers capable of helping you. When you contact him, tell him exactly what you're planning and ask him what he would charge to provide you with a drawing showing rebar size, location and concrete thickness. Talk with this engineer at great length concerning the facts and details of your house. All the information you give him must be very accurate. For example, you can't tell him that you're planning on 5 feet of dirt over the roof when, indeed, this depth might be 10 feet. You must be specific and accurate with information.

Figure 9-9 is a sample drawing. Once again, check around for rates if you have the choice. This price will vary quite a bit from engineer to engineer depending on his interest in unusual dwellings, ecology or your plans in general. These are professionals and if they can possibly give you a break on price, they will, especially if they know you plan on building this structure yourself. They make up any financial break they give you on the next multi-million dollar project they design.

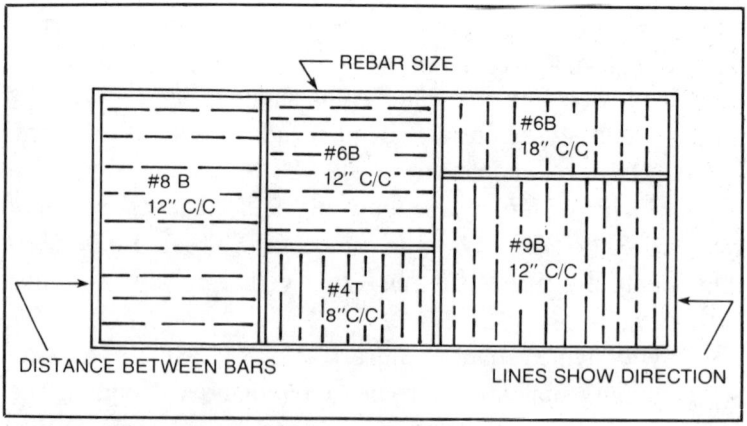

Fig. 9-9. Typical rebar drawing.

Another place to check for a good engineer is your local college. Some of those professors are sure to be engineers or have an engineering background. Before making a commitment to any engineer, check with the building code department to see if a professional engineer's stamp is required. I am not familiar with any locale in which a stamp or seal is mandatory for a private dwelling, but check to be sure. It will definitely cost more for an engineer to put his official seal on your drawings because this means he is legally responsible for the design. Just make sure the person figuring the strength of materials in your roof is qualified and interested in underground homes.

REBAR

Rebar is steel rod approximately 40 feet long and comes in diameters from ⅜" to over 1". These bars or rods are for strengthening concrete and nothing more. Your roof will probably use all diameters and lengths, depending on room widths. This is where your cutting torch comes in handy.

This cutting torch is by far the easiest and most universal method for placing, bending and cutting rebar because by heating the steel, you can make the bends that will be required in some places. There are other methods of cutting this rebar. You could use a circular saw with a metal cutting blade. This method is slower but still gets the job done. However, the bending will now have to be done by brute strength—yours. When large companies lay rebar, they have long-handled shears or cutters like a pair of bit-cutting pliers that will actually shear through some thicknesses. You, as a small contractor, may have a hard time locating this tool at a reasonable price.

This rebar will be delivered to your site in long lengths, which you will have to cut and bend to form the pattern designed by the engineer. Rebar can be bought from a used steel dealer listed in the yellow pages. The term "used" is misleading, because it's not used, it was simply previously owned and left over from a big construction project. Buy it if possible. Used rebar is about half the price of new rebar.

WIRE MESH

Another type of steel used for added strength in concrete is called *concrete mat* or *wire mesh*. It's a roll of heavy steel screen resembling a roll of fencing. It is manufactured in many sizes. This wire mesh adds additional strength to prevent cracking. I covered my entire roof with steel mat (Figs. 9-10 through 9-13), then the rebar was put in place. Discuss wire mesh and rebar with a couple of experts, especially the technique of tying rebar and steel together. When rebar is laid in a criss-cross pattern, it must be tied together with a piece of wire to prevent the steel from rolling and shifting as you walk on it (Figs. 9-14 and 9-15). Common stove pipe wire is often used. You must consider that wet concrete will be dropped on this steel from approximately 4 feet above. That's a great deal of weight trying to move your rebar around. It is critical that rebar does not move. Take your time and do it right. As the rebar is being laid in place, it cannot be touching the wood scaffolding. It must be raised off of the wood by at least an inch. See your engineered roof design for the exact height. This is so that the concrete flows easily under and completely surrounds the steel. There are wire pegs sold for this purpose, or you can use pieces of concrete block. Either way works fine.

Again, placing this rebar is most critical. It is physically impossible for one person to drag a 40 foot length, ⅝" in diameter piece of rebar around on top of the scaffolding. You will need an extra person to control the steel. Once you have maneuvered just one piece of this rebar around, you will know what I mean by it being difficult to handle. Only experience will make it easier. Last, but not least, be careful as you cut through a length of steel. If it happens to be laying on an uneven surface, such as the ground, and you cut through the steel, one piece or the other could spring up and hit you in the face. The reason I tell you this is that that is exactly what

Fig. 9-10. The entire roof is covered with wire mesh.

happened on my job. The steel looked very relaxed, but when the cut was made, one end sprang up and caught me in the face. It could have been serious, but I was lucky. You might not be.

STEEL PLACEMENT

Now you have worked your way to the steel placement phase. Anyone can do this just by using common sense and following the instructions of your engineer or concrete expert. I fenced in the perimeter of my roof with block to form a totally closed area for pouring concrete. Once you get this far, you're at the critical point of your project. Don't let your wood frame work become exposed to rain, wind, etc., for a long period of time. Constant wetting of the plywood will cause it to separate and buckle, thus losing some of its strength. The sooner you pour concrete on the erected shoring, the better.

At this point you'll have all shoring in place, all holes filled and plastic in place as well as steel in place and raised off the plywood by at least 1". It will also be laying on the blockwork. Finally, you must have a solid level that is an easily accessible spot immediately adjacent to the building for the concrete trucks.

As an alternative for shoring, instead of buying a truck load of plywood and 2 × 4s and building your own shoring, you could rent all scaffolding from a forming company listed in the yellow pages under *concrete forming*. They do not use the 2 × 4 method. They are very professional and use wood beams like railroad ties and a series of jacks. The catch to renting is that it's expensive. To rent all forming for the roof of my house for one week would have cost over $2,000. Plus I would have to pay for all of the plywood to be cut, and that adds up fast. Since most of the room sizes are not in intervals of 4' × 8', this requires you to cut numerous pieces of plywood. For this reason I shopped around for a volume price on plywood and 2 × 4s, bought them new, used them and sold them used through the newspaper at two-thirds the original cost.

Fig. 9-11. Wire mesh adds additional strength.

Fig. 9-12. Wire mesh prevents cracking.

Either method will work. You're the judge of your own ability and your accessibility to free physical labor. Okay, now back to pouring your roof. Just as everything else, there is more than one way to get concrete from truck to roof. The first way is a concrete pump. You can rent this equipment for about $300 a day. A concrete pump is just that. It pumps liquid concrete over distances up to 60 feet away. The problem with a pump is that it's slow and you need someone to hold a hose constantly at approximately every 10 feet of length because the throbbing effect of the pump tends to make the line uncontrollable. The second method, which is the recommended one, is a crane. They rent for about $300 a day, with one operator. The choice is yours. Discuss it with the local experts, especially the concrete finishers in your area. If you use a crane, it will take approximately six hours from start to finish for an average house. The crane will have two buckets. The concrete truck backs up to one bucket and fills it. Then the crane lifts that bucket to the farthest corner and dumps it. While this happening, the truck is loading the second bucket. By the time it is full, the crane will be returning with the first bucket, which is now empty. Keep repeating this sequence

Fig. 9-13. Wire mesh is another type of steel used for added strength.

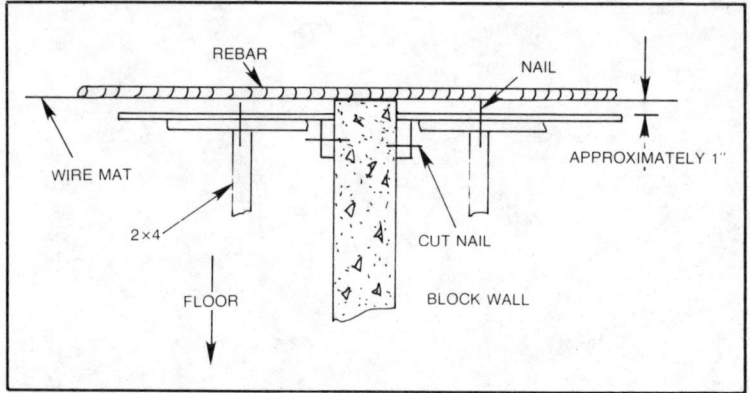

Fig. 9-14. Tying rebar to the mesh.

until the roof is covered to the depth you have pre-established (Figs. 9-16 and 9-17). As the concrete is dumped, you need labor (and lots of it) to level it and a finisher to smooth it. The smoother the surface, the less moisture the concrete will absorb when covered with dirt. However, don't use the buffing machine such as you will use on your floor. There is no advantage in getting the roof as smooth as your floor. One other thing to remember is to have someone shake the steel lightly by any method possible. You could use a pick as the concrete flows across your steel network. This insures that the concrete reaches all cracks and crevices and completely surrounds the steel. Concrete must totally surround all steel. The minimum thickness under the steel should be 1".

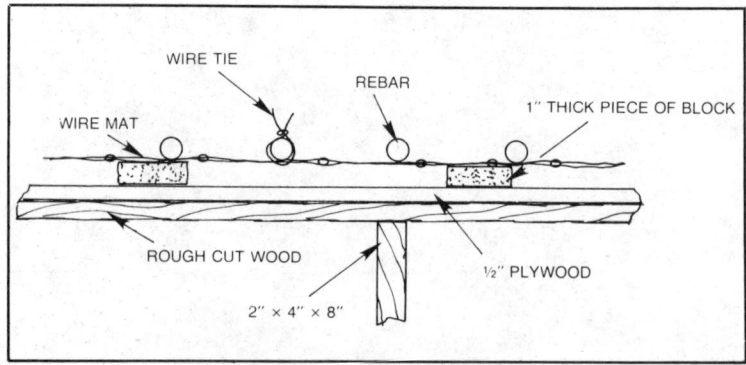

Fig. 9-15. Typical section showing rebar tied to the mat.

Fig. 9-16. A bucket of concrete is moved about by a large crane.

DO NOT use an electric or hydraulic vibrator to settle the concrete. It's not necessary and causes tremendous stress on the shoring. If your experts suggest a vibrator, watch out.

One hour after the last bucket is dumped and raked, you can relax. If it hasn't collasped by then, it will be there until

Fig. 9-17. A bucket of concrete is poured on your roof.

dooms day. You are now halfway to completion of your geothermic house!

ALTERNATIVE METHOD

There are other ways to accomplish the same goal. Here's an alternative.

If once again you check the phone book under concrete products, you'll find precast or prestressed concrete. There are companies that make slabs of concrete predesigned to carry any weight you require. These slabs usually have a maximum length and width somewhere around 20 feet long by 4 feet wide. As you can figure, this gives you quite a few joints that are sealed in a variety of ways, but are almost always covered with a second layer of poured concrete or sprayed insulation, such as foam. These companies will set these precast pieces in place of your walls for a price. The big advantage of this system is that there is no scaffolding to erect. It is rigid and it can be placed in one day. Of course, the disadvantage to this method is cost and the possibility of leaks.

Discuss all aspects of your roof with professionals. Talk to more than one person in each trade. They can all give you valuable information, but in the end you have to make the final decisions as to how and who. See Table 9-1 for some estimated costs of a roof.

Table 9-1. Cost of Roof.

METHOD	*ESTIMATED COST	ADVANTAGE	DISADVANTAGE
BUCKET AND CRANE	$8,000	FAST	NONE
PUMP	$8,000	IF CRANE UNAVAILABLE	EXTRA LABOR; SLOW
PRE-CAST	$14,000	ONE-DAY INSTALLATION; LESS LABOR	EXPENSIVE; SEAMS TO PATCH, POSSIBLE LEAKS
DIRECT DUMP	$7,800	NO RENT OF CRANE OR PUMP	LOTS OF LABOR AND WHEELBARROW; SLOW
CONTRACTOR EVERYTHING	$20,000	NO RESPONSIBILITY TO YOU	COST

*ESTIMATED COST FOR 3,600 SQUARE FEET INCLUDING ALL FORMING, PREPARATIONS, ETC.

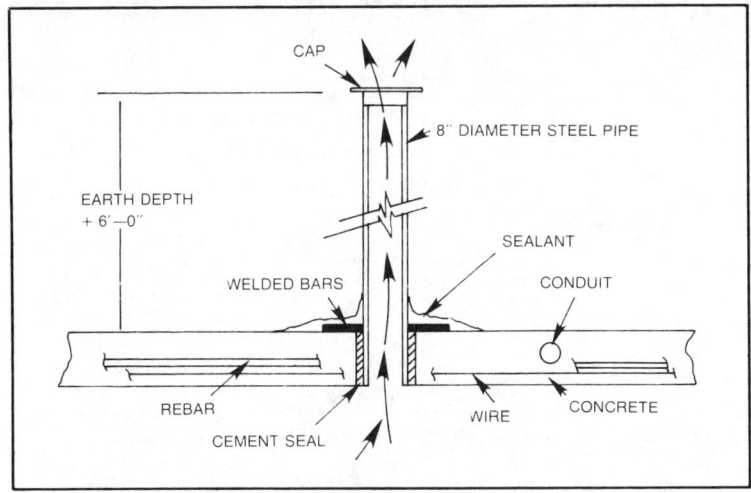

Fig. 9-18. Application of electrical conduit.

CONDUIT

It is a very good idea to lay down P.V.C. conduit (approximately 2" diameter) on the steel before the concrete is poured (Fig. 9-18). This is for the main runs of your electrical wires. Be sure to let the electrician that is working with you locate and install this conduit. The codes are once again very tricky. The reason this is an alternative is that if your house is small, say 40 feet by 25 feet, the cost of putting pipe in the ceiling concrete would probably be more expensive than running wire around the walls. But if you want hanging ceiling lights, you should definitely give the conduit consideration. I put conduit in the concrete because my house is 90 feet long and 40 feet wide and I wanted ceiling lights in some rooms. This installation is not hard to do.

CHIMNEYS

After all rebars and shoring are in place, locate exactly where you want the chimney hole to be. Secure to the plywood anything you find that is 8" to 9" in diameter, maybe an old bucket or can. This will leave a hole in the roof for your future chimney. It is ridiculous to jack-hammer a hole in the roof after the concrete is poured and set up.

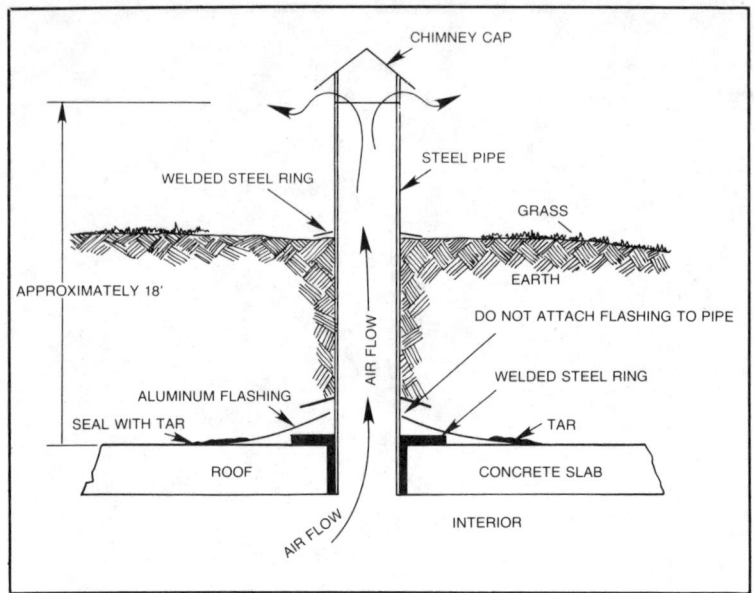

Fig. 9-19. Typical chimney installation.

As for building a chimney, in my opinion there is only one method that is solid and practical. Buy a length of approximately 8" diameter steel pipe however high you want your chimney to be and weld bars to the sides (Fig. 9-19). These bars rest on the concrete and hold the pipe upright until you fill around the pipe with concrete and tar it over this new seam. It's that simple and works well. Standard chimneys will crack immediately after the first freeze because the block above ground level freezes solid and is forced to shift. However, the block 4 feet underground does not freeze and is mortared stationary to the roof which doesn't move, thus causing cracking. Watch this chimney phase closely. You can't live underground without one or even two.

Do not put any holes in the roof except for the chimney. Holes are just too hard to keep waterproof. Any venting can be put through the exterior walls just as easily as through the roof.

10

Waterproofing

When you mention underground homes or subterranian structures of any kind, people immediately and always think of a damp and dark hole. I'm sure their experience with older buildings used for storage or warehousing, and unfinished house basements with inefficient drainage and lighting are the culprit for this bad reputation. This is rightly so since many times the drainage is inadequate due to poor grading or planning.

Just as almost everything in the world has changed in the past 25 years, so have building materials, methods and equipment. For one example, urethane foam used for insulation was unavailable to the general public as recently as five years ago, and polyethylene and styrofoam have become commonplace for home construction.

Before going any further, I'll give my definition of waterproofing. It's simply preventing excessive damaging moisture from reaching the interior of your home. This can be done in a variety of ways with a variety of building materials. First, I'll give some examples of extreme methods to insure a moisture-free house. However, remember that no matter what you do or how well you do it, there's always the possibility of a moisture problem requiring mechanical assistance, such as pumps or at least dehumidifiers. I just want you to be aware of the potential problems. It's a risk you will have to take when building underground.

MOISTURE TREATMENTS

Now for the methods. Once you have excavated the land to your desired level, poured your footers and are ready for the walls, you may realize that you could have poured solid cement reinforced walls instead of concrete block walls. Solid concrete is a superior barrier against running water only. Whatever your exterior walls are, they should now be treated to prevent moisture vapor from penetrating to the interior.

Tar Baby

I used two heavy coats of hot tar, sprayed on by a commercial *tar baby*. Tar babies can be found in the yellow pages of the phone book under waterproofing—tar. Two coats of tar are sprayed on. The second coat is sprayed on after the first has dried. This method is far superior to one heavy coat. Another reason in favor of the second method is that any high spot or edge will only absorb a thin layer of tar. Additional tar will only settle to the low spots leaving the high spots only lightly covered. By spraying one average coat everywhere, letting it dry and spraying a second equivalent coat a day or so later, the build-up is uniform. This is the most common method.

Polyethylene Layers

If you want to go to additional expense, you can wrap the entire structure with two or three layers of polyethylene (Fig. 10-1). You can buy polyethylene in 100-foot rolls by 20 feet wide and four milligrams thick (about the thickness of a sheet of paper) from most building supply stores. Once the tar is on the block and dry to the touch you can begin to wrap the building, ending with two or three layers over the entire structure. Try to keep the polyethylene smooth and wrinkle-

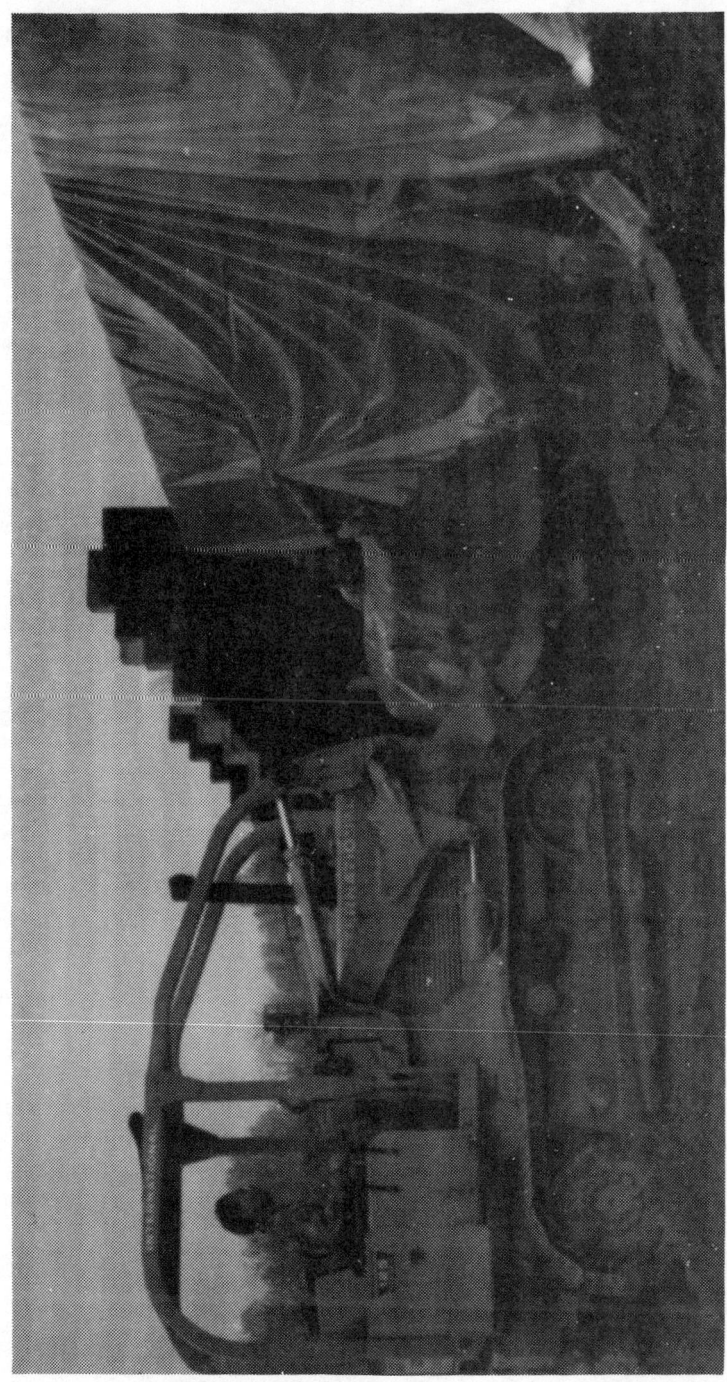

Fig. 10-1. Polyethylene used as wrapping.

free. I used polyethylene sheeting but found that the wrinkles were a real problem because a mild breeze always seemed to be blowing. This proved to be more trouble than it was worth. Just for information's sake, polyethylene sheeting will not deteriorate underground but sunlight will deteriorate this material. Tests indicate that polyethylene that has been underground is still intact after 20 years. The only reason I am reluctant to urge you to use polyethylene is if you tear one hole in it as you back fill the dirt, you will lose most of the potential waterproofing value.

Pressed Insulation Board

Following the wrapping of the structure, you can begin to backfill gently (Figs. 10-2 through 10-6). Take care not to tear the plastic if you do use it. If you want to take another precaution, buy *pressed insulation board*. They are usually about ½" thick. It is as cheap as any building material you can buy in 4 × 8 sheets. Line the exterior walls with this material The only purpose it will serve is to cushion the rock and dirt as it falls against the polyethylene wrapping. If your soil and drainage is good this should be all you need. If you want to go to real extremes and you have an indication that your soil isn't as good as it should be, this next method should work for you. But it is expensive.

The most common method to keep water away from concrete floors is a series of pipes covered with gravel, leading to a drain line away from the house (Fig. 10-7). The less drastic method is to lay a couple of layers of the polyethylene down before pouring the concrete. These polyethylene sheets were the only prevention I took to stop moisture from penetrating through the floor and it seems to be doing the job. In reality I don't think anything would usually be required if the soil is of a good drainage quality.

Clay as a Water Barrier

One more thing you can do to help insure the proper runoff of excessive water is to have clay soil trucked to your

Fig. 10-2. First stages of backfilling.

Fig. 10-3. After the plastic is laid, you can begin the process of backfilling.

Fig. 10-4. Looking over the backfilling job.

Fig. 10-5. Backfilling continues.

Fig. 10-6. Both backfilling and excavation require heavy machinery.

Fig. 10-7. The land is dug out for a drain line.

site from wherever you can find it and grade from 6″ to 1 foot of clay over the roof (Fig. 10-8). Good quality clay will have a consistency similar to modeling clay. It should be graded to a peak and another 3 or 4 feet of good top soil added on top of the clay. Then if water happens to seep that far down, the clay barrier will cause the water to divert off the roof.

The condition you can create with clay by forming a pitch to the top of the concrete roof slab to divert water away from any opening can be formed into the concrete slab as it is poured. It is possible to pour the concrete with a pitch suitable enough to insure that water cannot flow toward an opening such as your garden or chimney opening. At the same time you could lay standard perforated drainage pipes in a bed of gravel directly on top of the concrete.

Use whichever system you feel safe with and top it all off with a crop of excellent quality grass. Once a good sod base has developed, keep it manicured smoothly and cut as short as reasonable. Follow your local landscaping expert's advice as to the length you can cut the grass depending on the temperature, rainfall and other conditions affecting the ability of your grass to survive. I mixed two grass seeds together in a 50:50 ration. One seed sprouted in three days when watered, but was an annual. This was only to prevent erosion until the permanent seed caught hold.

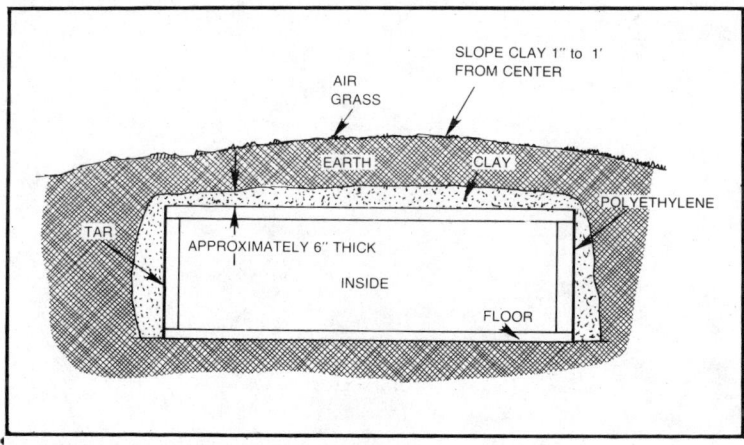

Fig. 10-8. Clay could be used as a natural water barrier.

SMOOTHNESS OF ROOF

One additional fact about waterproofing deals with the smoothness of the roof's concrete. The rougher the surface, the more moisture the concrete will absorb. If the slab is polished smooth, water will not penetrate the surface. Obviously, there is a happy medium to work for.

11

What About Moisture?

Whenever the subject of an underground home comes up in conversation, the same questions consistently pop up. What about moisture? Doesn't the house smell musty? Aren't there drops of water on the ceiling? Why isn't an underground home just like a basement? These questions are definitely logical, so I'll try to explain why an underground house has no real moisture problems.

Everyone has been in an old house with a clammy-feeling basement at one time or another. They have a problem because the waterproofing applied to many conventional home basements is only one step better than nothing at all. Then the grading is quite often done with mainly cosmetic results in mind rather than keeping water away from the foundation. Also, the top of a basement is exposed to a fluctuating temperature. In addition, the absence of activity in a basement causes a lack of the required air circulation. These are all reasons why a basement smells musty. The reason my house doesn't have these problems is basic. My grading was given top consideration for maximum water runoff. Then my waterproofing was applied cautiously.

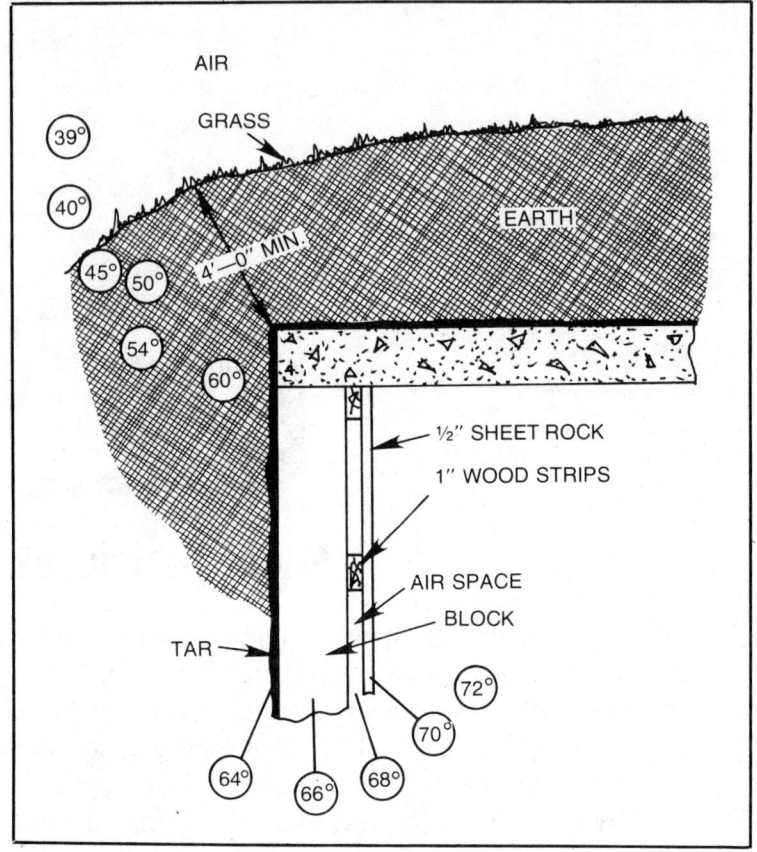

Fig. 11-1. Very slight temperature differential.

CONDENSATION

Once these physical moisture barriers are complete, the remaining moisture problem is the result of the law of physics. Condensation is the direct result of temperature differential and the percentage of humidity of the outside air. The temperature differential I'm talking about is best exemplified by what happens when the windshield of your car fogs up when you first start to drive when it's cold outside. The reason fog appears on the interior of the glass is that your body heat and breath are warm. Approximately ¼" on the other side of the glass is a temperature of probably 50° or colder. The ¼" thick glass is the point to consider. Remember hot and cold separated by a thin membrane will cause moisture to form on the warmer side.

The reason my walls do not sweat can easily be illustrated. The temperatures shown on Figs. 11-1 through 11-3 are estimated to help explain the point.

In Fig. 11-1 you will note that the temperature differential isn't present. However, Fig. 11-2 shows how great the temperature differential could be in a conventional basement. As you see, it is a similar condition to the cold car example.

In short, if the temperature is similar on each side of the walls, the remaining moisture problem can be handled with a standard room dehumidifier. The reason I don't have a problem around my doors is that the living area is separated from the outside temperature by a foyer arrangement (Fig. 11-3).

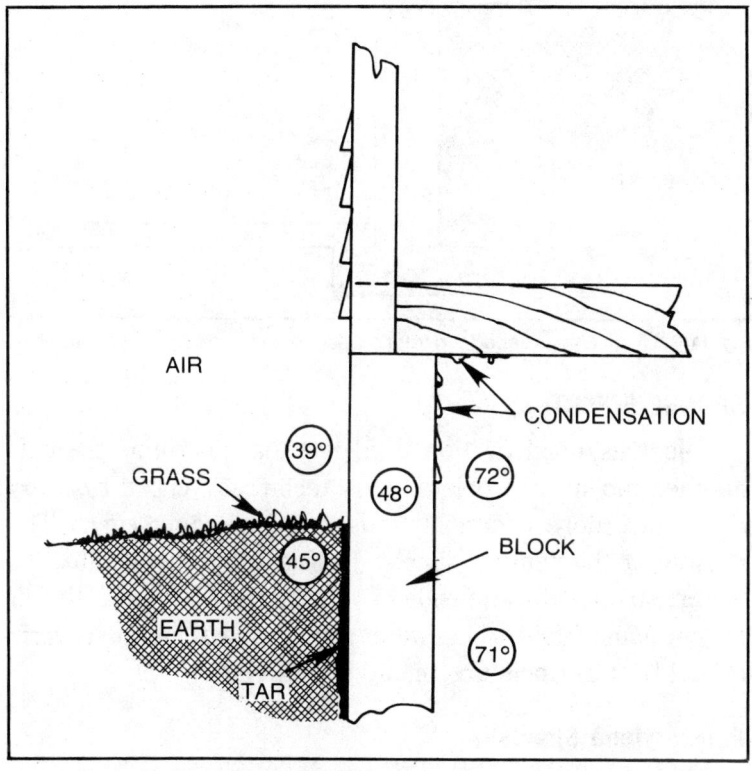

Fig. 11-2. Conventional house showing extreme temperature differential in degrees Fahrenheit from inside to outside.

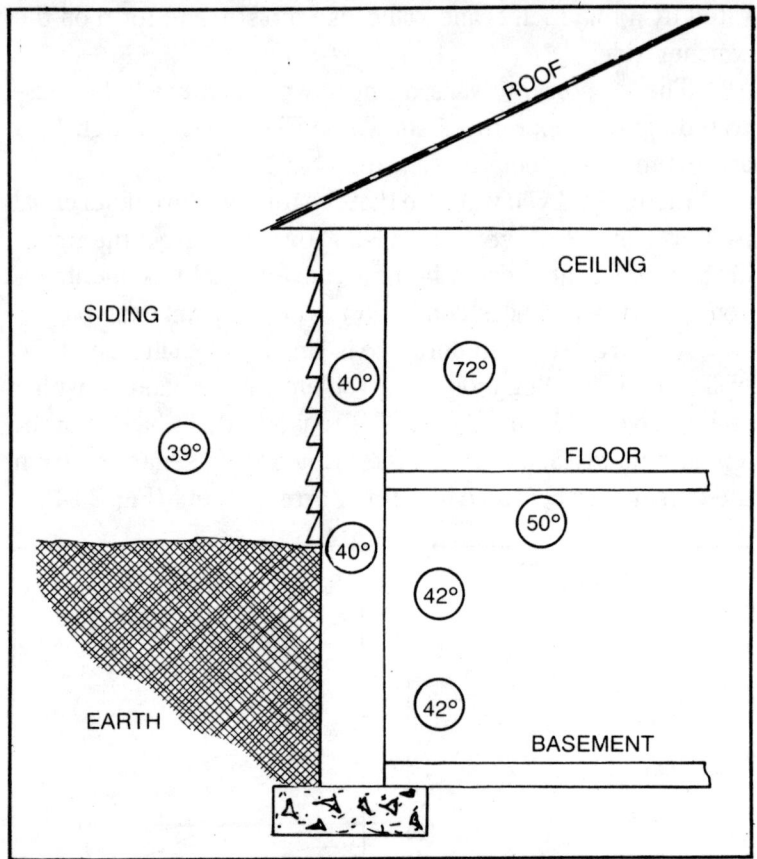

Fig. 11-3. Living area is separated from outside temperature by a foyer arrangement.

SPONGE EFFECT

Just as condensation is a potential problem, there is another moisture problem. It is technically called *capillary draw*, but more commonly it is called a *sponge effect*. The reason for the name is simple. Just as a dry sponge absorbs water, so does the air inside of your house. However, the air in your house is absorbing water from the earth because warm air holds more moisture than does cold air.

Polyethylene Sheets

There is, however, a couple of methods to prevent the sponging of humid air, or at least to help slow it down. The first

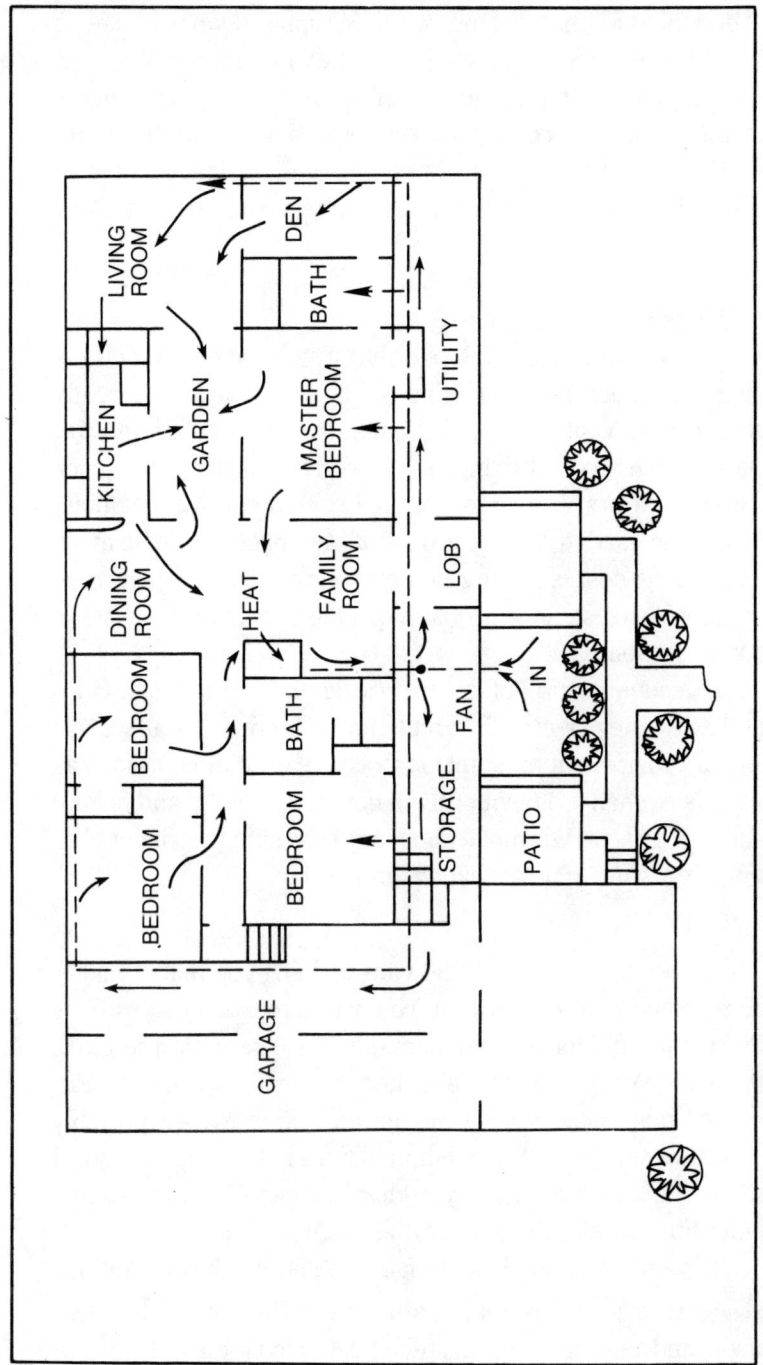

Fig. 11-4. Dotted line shows air movement by duct system.

method is one that I employed. Wrapping your house in polyethylene sheets is valued for helping to prevent this sponging effect of moisture coming from the earth to the interior. However, remember that once a hole is in this material, the water will definitely find it and be trapped inside against the block rather than be absorbed back into the drier earth.

Air Pockets

The second method is one that if you have followed my building suggestions up to this point, you will have already included it in your house. This system is the 1" air pocket created by the wood furring strips used to hold the sheet rock up. Air pockets are the best way to prevent sponging of moist air from the earth to the interior. A 2" air space would be more ideal, but the cost of furring all the walls with a 2" strip of wood instead of a 1" strip is probably prohibitive from a cost and labor standpoint.

The construction of my exterior and interior walls, combined with the special air circulation system I installed, are adequate to prevent most major moisture problems, as long as the air is exchanged frequently in corners, closets and behind furniture. This air will move about with the simplest of ventilating systems using a mechanical in-line fan.

HUMIDITY

However, remember that I am warning you that humidity will be a slight problem that you will have to deal with. A standard large room size dehumidifier will remove the extra humidity. Now, don't be shcoked by that statement. Remember that anywhere in the United States except possibly the southwest, people use dehumidifiers in their conventional houses. I'm just reminding you that you can expect the same simple humidity problems as in any other house.

It is a fact that each section of the country has conditions and weather patterns that are uniquely their own. For this reason and due to the long technical calculations, I am not going to go into great detail about how to figure heat loads, humidifier sizes, etc. However, there is one term that should be mentioned. That term is *dew-point*. This is the temperature at which moisture droplets will form. This is not a constant point. It fluctuates with the percent of humidity in the outside atmosphere. You learn a great deal about dew-point as you discuss the construction of an underground house. After lengthy discussions with numerous experts in the field of air handling, I proceeded to install an air handling system. Dew-point is another law of physics that applies to warm air holding more moisture in vapor form than colder air. This explains the lessening of a humidity problem in the winter.

Another thing you can do to lessen the possibility of a moisture problem is to insulate hot and cold water pipes. Also, insulate the hot water heater.

Moisture is a problem, but it can be conquered, probably as easy as any other problem connected with an underground house.

12

Backfilling and Grading

By the time you get this far you will have approximately 75 per cent of your money invested, listened to plenty of ridicule and put in hundreds of hours of hard work. Don't make a major mistake now. Whatever you do, don't do any grading near the building for at least three weeks after the concrete roof slab is poured. Even then I suggest you tread softly until the concrete is cured for five weeks. At this point I'll tell you of a change I will make on the next underground home I build. I will not try to waterproof the entire structure at one time. Note in Fig. 12-1 that I did not backfill against the exterior walls until the roof slab was complete. My reasoning for this was to keep the complete surface, four walls and roof exposed so that they could be sprayed with a hot tar-like sealer and then wrapped in the sheets of polyethylene as previously discussed. This cavity was approximately 3 feet wide and 15 feet deep. It was constantly breaking away and then needed to be hand shoveled out. Try throwing a ton of wet dirt shovel by shovel 15 feet in the air over your shoulder and you will soon see that wrapping the structure in one piece isn't worth the effort. If I had it to do over again, I would complete the exterior walls and spray them with two coats of tar to within 1 foot of the roof slab line.

After the wrapping of the plastic and about one day of drying, I would begin pushing dirt against the wall, first checking to see that the drain pipe at the base isn't disturbed by the first load of dirt falling from as high as 15 feet. By backfilling as I suggest, not as I did, you will eliminate four of the major problems I had all during early construction. The first problem, as I said before, was the constant collapsing of the dirt before I had the tar sprayed. Secondly, it was a constant safety hazard and more than once I dropped tools into the hole and had to systematically climb down to retrieve them.

This is another good place for me to explain the inconsistency that abides in the bureaucracy of any department of permits and regulations. Follow this logic, if you will. As I was grading, an official stopped by to tell me that I needed a barrier of some type to stop soil from washing into a small stream nearby 300 feet away. Now this was and is a hillside of natural vegetation of underbrush, trees, bushes, etc., but he wanted me to provide a barrier of bales of hay or straw staked to the ground to prevent erosion into the small stream. The part that irritated me was that this excavation was never mentioned as a safety hazard to human beings. It bothered me, so I eventually put up a make shift warning fence. But the inspection officials never mentioned it. Another paradox of bureaucracy.

By doing the grading at two different times the dirt against the wall has time to settle, especially after a heavy rain. Do not do any of the grading until all interior block walls are tied in place to the exterior walls or these exterior walls will crack or collapse. If you now fill the dirt against the exterior wall, it will be easier to move around while preparing scaffolding for the roof pouring.

TRACTOR-SPREAD

Now begin to spread the dirt over the roof for curing unless your engineer says otherwise. Leave the underside shoring up until you have at least 3 feet of dirt spread smoothly over the complete structure. Do this with a small tractor, initially, similar to the one in Fig. 12-2. One like this can usually

Fig. 12-1. View of roof prior to start of grading.

be rented by the day or week. The reason I say a small tractor and 3 feet of dirt is that the dirt transfers the weight of the tractor uniformly downward onto the roof slab as opposed to the weight of the tractor being distributed to only the four wheels of the tractor. Putting the dirt over the slab roof safely is one of the most hazardous phases of building this house. As I mentioned, the small tractor with a front bucket is one method of moving dirt. It is also the preferred method.

TRAILER-SPREAD

If you have a light, compact car like a Volkswagen, and a small utility trailer like the smallest open-bed ones you can rent from rental outfits, you are also ready to move dirt. Pull the empty trailer to the source of dirt. Load the trailer, but use common sense as to how full to fill the trailer. Then drive the car and trailer onto the roof only after you have spread at least 6" to a foot of dirt.

Whichever method you use, don't drive tractor, car or anything else directly over the tar or plastic. The tar, as thick as you have on your roof, will literally never dry hard and any vehicle will slip and slide as if on frozen water. You can get around doing this by hand by backing the trailer to the edge, dumping the first load and spreading it roughly. Then back over that load and dump the next. Keep leap-frogging backward until you have enough dirt spread to drive forward and make a circle, thus cutting down on the time it takes you to make a single trip. Naturally if you are using a small tractor, you dump frontward and continue the same procedure. Just don't drive on plastic or tar.

CRANE-SPREAD

Still another method that is to be considered, depending on availability and cost to you, is the crane. It could be the same one that you probably used to dump concrete. Use the largest bucket available and fill it with dirt using your backhoe. The crane will then very accurately place the dirt. The only disadvantage is cost.

Fig. 12-2. This small tractor was used until 3 feet of dirt was in place.

Whatever method you choose to use, be careful when working close to the edge. This dirt is loose and will roll and pack. This can easily upset tractors.

FINAL GRADING

After five weeks, if the 3 feet of dirt and the supports are still in place, it will most likely be safe enough to take your backhoe on top of the structure. Remove the bucket from the back. This is easily done, so don't take a chance carrying all the extra weight of the bucket onto the roof. Only the scoop on the front will be required. Once you are finished running around up on the roof with your backhoe, then put the aft bucket on and finish up the rest of your grading. The reason you can't continue to use a small tractor or trailer is because that will only move or carry approximately a quarter yard of dirt, while a backhoe tractor will carry one-half to three-quarters of a yard at one trip. You'll be thankful for the extra hauling capacity when you start dumping dirt over the edge to build up a sloped wall, if that is your design. Don't drive on the roof unless you have complete control of the tractor! Next to driving a grading vehicle on the roof, the most dangerous thing you can do is operate a bulldozer or large tractor close to an unsupported wall while pushing soft dirt. The weight of the vehicle pressing down on soft dirt displaces it. This dirt must go somewhere and it will try to push the nearest block or concrete wall away.

As final grading progresses, don't be surprised if you have to haul dirt to your site before you're done. I thought I had enough dirt to literally cover half the neighborhood, only to find out I needed another 125 tons of dirt. The need for additional fill dirt all depends on the lay of your land, the amount of dirt you have excavated and the design. If it is necessary to bring in additional dirt, check every price in town. I found good, clean fill dirt, not top soil, ranged from $1 a ton to $5 a ton. So you can easily add up the potential savings. If good top soil is required, the price is much higher. Therefore, don't use top soil for fill, and don't use fill for top soil. Only a few inches are required to grow good grass.

BACKHOE REMOVAL

As the grading and filling phase of your subterranian home draws to a close, you will find that this backhoe I suggested you buy is no longer required. Once the rough driveway is in and all the major grading is complete, begin to look for a buyer for this heavy equipment. If you made a good buy and didn't misuse your tractor, you will probably make enough profit to buy a large riding lawn mower with a snow blade and a small trailer in addition to grass cutting equipment.

GRASS SEED

As final grading takes place by hand raking and shoveling, be sure to plant the best grass seed and fertilize it as recommended by the experts in your area. Even grass seed varies from locale to locale. In final grading check into the use of sod—pre-grown grass. I tried to use it on a steep grade, and after the first heavy rain, it came tumbling down under its own weight. I had better luck planting fast-growing grass seed with good grass seed than I did with sod. With every condition being different, use your own good judgment and ask people in your area for advice.

13

Utilities

By now you ought to be pleased with your construction ability. You have a solid concrete shell floor, roof and block walls. From here on to final completion it will get easier physically, but at times the mental pressure will begin to get to you. If the building inspectors haven't hassled you or some neighbors are not up in arms, you're very lucky. But I'm sure you have all those minor problems under control.

PLUMBING

So now to the subject of plumbing. This is one of the easiest trades to do yourself. Most local codes will allow the home owner to do his own plumbing with a special homeowner permit. The best thing about plumbing, both water and drain, is that it's safe for an amateur to work with. Common sense will tell that drains always run downhill. The codes say that a good drain drops ¼" for every foot of length. Of course, this rate of drop is not always true, especially in drains which are 2" in diameter or smaller. If you followed the codes, you should have 4" cast iron drains under the concrete slab. This is a nationally accepted code. However, once above ground the codes are as different as day and night. Some local codes allow the use of polyvinyl-chloride pipes, commonly called PVC pipes. Some places require copper or steel. Other places allow common plastic to be used in certain drains. All I can tell you is to check your plumbing codes. They are usually fair and easy to meet, especially the drain phase of plumbing.

WATER PIPES

As you read the regulations covering portable water pipes, you will notice that if copper is required, it will be either ½" or ¾" in diameter depending on how many branch lines are involved. Regardless of the size required, this pipe is really called hard copper tubing and it is bought in lengths approximately 20 feet long. There is a special copper pipe cutter that is inexpensive and invaluable when doing your own plumbing. Buy one. Do not use a hacksaw. After the pipes are cut and ready to be soldered into a fitting, they must be cleaned with a wire brush or steel wool. Each part to be soldered must have a bright, shiny finish. Once these parts are shiny, they are treated with a soldering flux paste. This is an acid base paste, similar to toothpaste, that cuts any trace of oil or grease off of the copper. Solder will not stick to copper if it is coated with grease. This procedure must be followed to insure a water tight connection.

Plastic (PVC) pipe can be used in place of copper pipe in some instances. I suggest you use PVC for cold water pipes where possible. It is so much easier to work with than copper. PVC won't rust, and it's easy to cut and put together. You will most likely have to use quite a bit of copper pipe to meet the codes. Don't waste it because it is expensive.

Another important thing to remember is to always buy the best quality valves, pipe, fittings, faucets, etc., to install in places that are difficult to get at for repairs. It's one thing to have a leak in an open area that is easily accessible for repairs, but it is a nightmare to get to a leak in some obscure cubbyhole without wall demolition. Quality is equally important when getting the spigots for bath and kitchen. Cheap units will rust away before you know it, and they are difficult, if not impossible, to repair.

MAINTENANCE

I realize this isn't unique to underground houses. But one of my reasons for going underground was to eliminate as much year-round maintenance as possible. It doesn't make much sense to do away with exterior maintenance problems and build in interior problems. The same theory is even more true when buying your deep well pump and installing it. Buy a reputable brand submersible deep well pump. They are easy to hook up although it is a somewhat physically back-breaking job when lowering that heavy pump and plastic pipe 300 feet down a 6" or 7" diameter steel casing. The point is that once it's down, it should be good for 10 years or more. Follow instructions closely, double checking the plastic for leaks. Check out all phases of wiring before lowering the unit down into the well casing. Be extremely careful because pipe and electric lines slide down the steel casing.

Pull up all of this pipe with the pump hanging on the end. This time the line is full of water and the water weighs approximately 62 pounds per cubic foot. It won't take you long to realize how heavy this is going to be. It could easily exceed 400 pounds.

ELECTRIC WIRING

If you are careful, you won't waste your valuable time on something as unnecessary as frayed electric wires. Question your wholesale suppliers. They are usually very cooperative. If you have a little extra money, I would suggest letting a professional do this pump installation ritual. It's a gamble doing it yourself.

If you followed my earlier suggestion and installed plastic conduit in the roof slab, your electric wiring runs will be much easier than if you plan to run all wiring around walls. If you are doing your own wiring I assume you must have some knowledge of the subject or know someone who does. Most electric codes will allow the home owner to work on his own house but won't allow anyone to help. Some locales even have a test you must pass.

ELECTRICIANS

If you have the money and are low in electrical experience, I'd suggest you let a registered electrician do the wiring. Electricity is one of the most difficult and most dangerous of all the trades.

If you do decide to hire an electrician, check around and get one for a good price. If you do it yourself, go to the wholesale outlets for parts. They will sell to an individual in large quantities. You save a bundle over a small retail outlet.

WIRING

If you're doing the electrical work yourself and you now have all the materials, the runs are made just as if it were the basement of a conventional home. The underground idea does not present any problems with wiring. Wires are clamped to the block wall in straight runs and all turns are made in 90° if possible. When roughing-in receptacle and switch boxes, they are mounted to the block wall by nailing and gluing a firring strip (usually 1" by 3"), alongside of a hole knocked carefully in the concrete block. Locate the web of the block before you start. Mount ears of the receptacle box to the wood. Feed wires per code and continue until all the wires are in place. Then go around and cement in all excess areas around the box. If codes allow and non-metalic receptacle boxes are available, try to use them. Even if a wire should short out against the sides of the box, it would not ground out. I used them and they worked great. Once all wire is in place, use a felt tip marker (black or blue) and identify each wall. You should identify them by name, indicating direction and spelling out any other information you feel might be valuable in the future. Print this information in letters approximately 2" high. Then take a clear black and white photograph. This way you can go back years later and locate wiring if necessary for additions or any other reasons. Be sure to wait until you get all the firring strips in place before you photograph, because it's good to know where the strips are also. As a rule of thumb, take the photo just before the sheet rock goes up.

TELEPHONE WIRING

I consider the telephone an important utility and since it is a necessity of life, why not prewire your house for the telephone just as you did for the electric? Here is another area where you can save money. The receptacle boxes used for telephone outlets are the same as the receptacle boxes used for a standard electric outlet. The boxes are installed into the concrete block exactly as if they were to be used for electricity. You can make arrangements with the phone company to install these boxes yourself, saving approximately $10 an outlet. Once you install the boxes in the locations of your choice, the telephone company will come in and complete the wiring installation. As I said earlier, the telephone company will work with you in most cases. Even though I installed a phone outlet in every room, I only installed two phones with jack cords. You can unplug either phone and carry it to any room in the house without paying for extra telephones. Ask the phone company how you can install the boxes and save money.

GAS

Natural gas or LP gas is a utility, but I'm only mentioning the word to remind you, as I did earlier—DON'T USE ANY OF THE LIQUID FUELS OR VAPOR GASES. Stick to electricity for everything. Remember, you don't have windows to open in emergencies.

All utilities—plumbing, sewers, electric, telephone—are basically the same when building either an underground house or building any standard structure. The point to remember is that when all walls are block, it is obvious that you will have a problem moving or changing any utility once the final walls are in place.

By now you should be seeing the light at the end of that overworked tunnel. The nicest thing about reaching this stage is the convenience factor. For the first time you can plug saws into any receptacle for temporary use instead of hunting for those elusive extension cords. For the first time a light bulb is in a temporary receptacle, instead of a drop light. Also, water is now available for washing or mixing cement or whatever else is required. The bathrooms may even be hooked up by now. This is your first taste of convenience. Up until this point you were really roughing it. Believe me, I remember what it was like to reach this plateau.

14

Woodworking

It's a fact that approximately 80 per cent of an underground house is concrete. You might think that your woodworking ability won't be tested. How wrong you are! Your woodworking skills will be put to the test in the way of hanging doors, trim and baseboard molding. This is where a radial-arm saw will be very valuable. The fine trim of an underground house is very similar to that of a conventional house.

NAILS, NAILS, NAILS

However, before the trim phase comes to pass, you will have to pound over 3,000 nails into concrete. If you have never driven a nail into a concrete block, you don't know what you're missing. It takes approximately 50 times the force to drive a nail into concrete than into wood. These 3,000 nails will be used to attach 1″ × 3″ wood strips to the block wall. The 3″ strips should be evenly spaced. Whatever you do, don't leave spaces wider than 18″. If you do the sheet rock will flex or possibly break.

Before these wood strips are attached to the block wall, you should apply some type of adhesive designed for gripping wood to concrete. Readily available at any building supply store is adhesive in tubes like caulk. It is applied with a standard caulking gun. This adhesive is commonly called *panel cement*. Apply a bead of panel cement to each board in a similar way to applying toothpaste to your toothbrush. Once these boards are nailed up and the cement hardens, these strips will never fall.

Let me explain about the type of nail you should use. There are two basic types available. One is called a *masonry nail*. It is common to use this type when attaching wood to solid concrete, like a floor slab. The other type of nail available is called a *cut nail*. They are rectangular in section and from my personal experience, I found that these cut nails were easier to drive into the concrete block. Drive a nail approximately every 2 feet. A rule-of-thumb to go by is this: The nail should be ½" longer than the board you are attaching. As you are hammering these boards up, you will notice a technique is required to get this arm-breaking job done. You will soon see that the nails go into the block very tightly. Then if you give the nail one last hit just to make sure it is tight, then all of a sudden it will pop loose. This is because of the vibration caused by the hammer hitting the surface of the board and not the nail.

As the first nail in a particular board is driven in tight, move along about 2 feet and drive another. Once the next nail is started into the wood, hold your free hand on the wood to dampen the vibration. Continue this procedure until you have all the firring strips in place.

These firring strips are, of course, necessary to hold the sheet rock or paneling on the wall. However, the 1" air pocket created as the covering goes up serves as a great insulator against temperature change or humidity.

HANGING DOORS

This is a bad feature of finishing off an underground home. When building a conventional home, it is standard procedure to use 2" × 4" interior wall studding. Therefore, interior walls always turn out to be approximately 4½" thick. Because of this dimensional consistency, some companies manufacture a prehung door assembly. This is exactly what the name infers. The door is already attached to the frame with hinges and all final trim. The builder just inserts this assembly in place and "presto," the entire doorway is complete. Simple, isn't it?

But if you built an underground house to the specifications I indicated, you now have all of your interior walls at least 8" thick. Add it up. The walls are 6" concrete block—actually 5½" wide. The firring strips on both sides of the wall are ¾" thick each. And don't forget the two pieces of ½" sheet rock. This adds up to a thickness of 8".

Since underground homes have not really taken over the building world, no manufacturer makes prehung doors to fit 8" thick walls. By now you have guessed it. An underground home builder has to completely build his door assembly from blank lumber, even to the point of drilling holes for and attaching door knobs.

This may not sound like a big deal, but it is. Hanging a prehung door assembly takes about half an hour. Building a doorway assembly from scratch takes even an expert carpenter 10 times as long to finish. Also, the quality is never as good as the factory-assembled units. Another fact you have to face is that you can't possibly build a door assembly as cheap as you could buy one if it were available.

There is a special tool available to insure that the door knob hole is in the correct position every time. This drill assembly is expensive and hard to find, but you must use it to insure accuracy. See if you can rent or borrow this tool. Buy one only as a last resort, because you will probably never use it again.

15

Adding Trim and Fixtures

While reading this book, you've noticed I'm giving my personal advice and opinions. Remember, I've already lived in my underground house for a year so I know the reaction your friends, the general public, neighbors and the inspectors will have. As for technical advice, any engineer can figure the strength of material, electric requirements and other specific sciences. It's the non-exact areas that can make or break the success of your home.

DECORATION AND LAYOUT

As you begin to plan interior decoration, do it with an open mind. I suggest you use unusual materials and designs and layouts (Figs. 15-1 through 15-3). Don't forget an underground home is unusual and it takes a special personality to own, build or design one. Once you are committed to going underground, you have to face the criticism anyway so you might as well add a few strange colors and designs. Why not have mirrors on the ceiling? Use whatever ideas you have hidden away in the back of your mind that you thought you could never use.

Fig. 15-1. Be original with your room layout.

BEDROOMS

We gave an open, warm feeling to each of our bedrooms by the use of special wall murals (Figs. 15-4 through 15-6). These murals are available from major wallpaper suppliers and range in cost from $40 to $150. Surely you'll find a design to fit

Fig. 15-2. Use unusual materials and designs in your room layout.

Fig. 15-3. These authentic, bleached barn boards are over 100 years old.

your personality and taste. The mural, such as the woods scene in Fig. 15-7, gives a warm sensation to any room, especially one without windows.

KITCHEN

Due to the fact that you don't have windows on any wall, you can really use the unobstructed walls to your advantage. In addition to murals, consider full wall bookcases or room-length shelves. You'll be surprised at the uses you will find for all of the additional wall space. Figures 15-8 through 15-10 are pictures of our kitchen. We used earth colors. Otherwise, it's very conventional even if it is 6 feet underground.

RECYCLED MATERIALS

Since most underground homes are built with energy savings in mind, why not carry that theme a little farther? Recycle—especially building materials. Authentic old barn wood is a good place to start. It will take some searching of the old farms and countryside to find wood that the owner will let you buy at a reasonable cost, or maybe even give to you. The end result of disinfected, trimmed barn boards in a hallway or family room is a very attractive appearance, complimentary to

Fig. 15-4. Cartoon-type mural on two walls in bright colors.

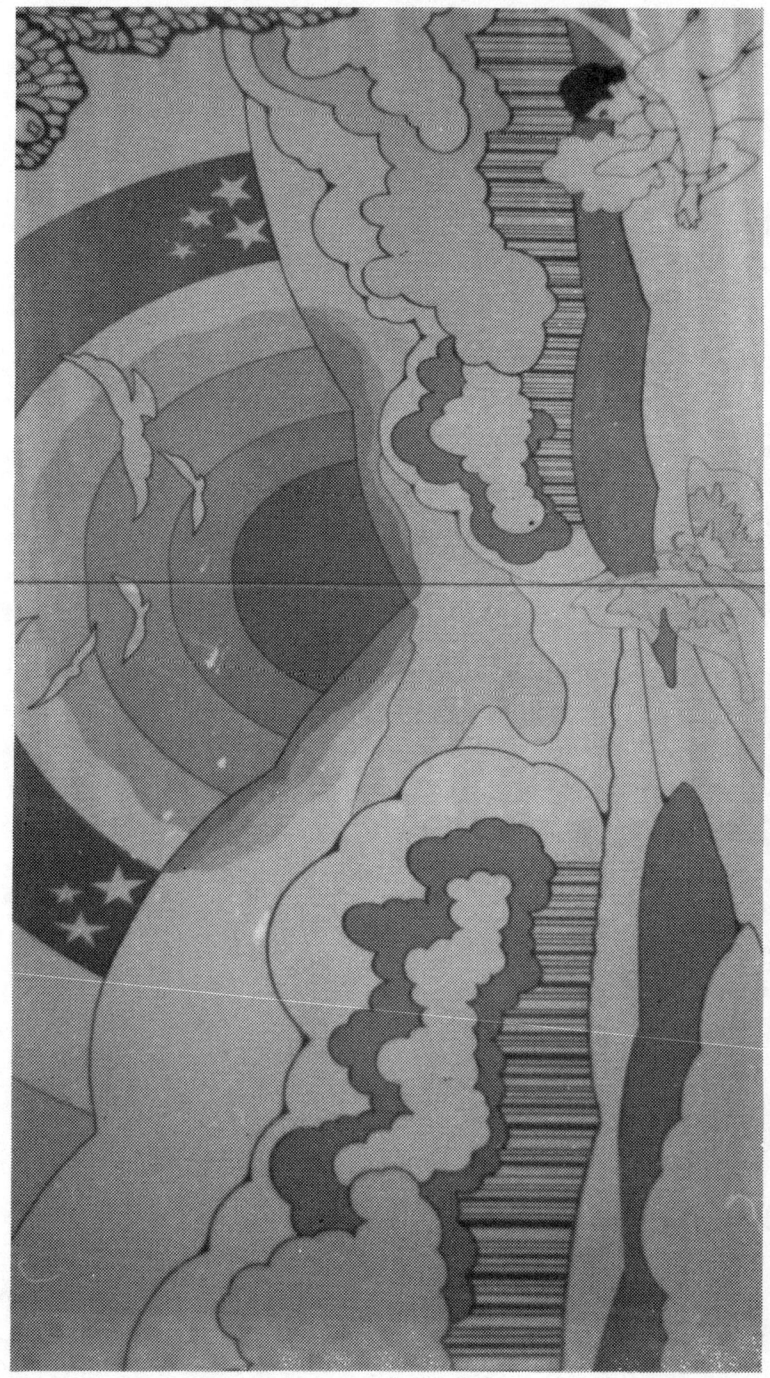

Fig. 15-5. A close-up of a wall mural covering two walls in a bedroom.

Fig. 15-6. This space-age wall mural gives a wide open feeling to this bedroom.

Fig. 15-7. Wall murals offer a room an open and warm atmosphere.

any underground house (Fig. 15-11). Also, you can find brick from an old building for steps, walls, shelves, floors, etc. Old brick or stone is relatively easy to find (Fig. 15-12).

FURNITURE

Then there's the furniture. Why not refinish old or previously owned furniture to suit your taste? You'll be mentally

Fig. 15-8. The kitchen of an underground house.

Fig. 15-9. This kitchen resembles many conventional homes' kitchens.

and financially rewarded if you take the time to salvage some of the past to go with your home of the future.

CARPET AND PADDING

Once you are ready for carpet and padding, shop around. Prices and quality are as different as day and night. As you probably realize, the carpet will be the single most eye-catching item in your house. Carpet just jumps out at you as you enter a home, especially if the quality is good. Also remember that the bright, light colors will reflect light and give a warm, dry feeling to your house. There is no use adding to the stigma of a cave by using drab colors. They will only add to the cave feeling some of your visitors may visualize.

PAINT

The same goes for paint. Always use light, bright colors. I suggest earthy colors: greens, yellows, browns, etc. Once again, the choice is yours.

Another suggestion I think you will find helpful when painting is the use of "sandpaint". This is a commercial product that is nothing more than a sand product added to laytex paint.

Fig. 15-10. This kitchen is totally electric.

Fig. 15-11. Old barn wood adorns the wall of this hallway.

It is thick, like paste, and is applied with a sponge. It really gives a different effect to sheet rock walls. In addition, you do not have to sand the sheet rock as smooth when sand paint is going to be used. Check it out. You'll like it. One disadvantage of this paint is that it can't be washed. So please don't use this rough surface where dirt will easily accumulate.

INTERIOR GARDEN

One of the spots in your house that will receive the most attention, simply because no one else has one, is your interior

Fig. 15-12. Brick used on this wall is over 125 years old. The stove also serves as this underground home's only means of heat.

Fig. 15-13. Hanging plants form the ceiling overhead in the garden.

garden. If you didn't include one, you'll soon wish you had (Fig. 15-13). In our garden area we used 2″ × 6″ wood blocks about 12″ long marking a walkway with an unusual pattern. We also hang many live plants over our head from the dome (Fig. 15-14). At times they even form a ceiling of live plants overhead as we walk through. Clinging ivy is another way to cover the block walls in your atrium.

Fig. 15-14. Plants hang from the skylight dome.

LIGHTING

Another subject that is only as limited as your imagination is lighting, especially in the garden. Give thought to dimmer switches, ground-level lights, hanging or side-mounted fixtures. Regardless of where, how or the quantity of light

Fig. 15-15. Your eating area will provide a place to explore endless decorating ideas.

Fig. 15-16. Light fixtures and carpet accent the bathroom.

fixtures, why not experiment with colored bulbs, especially blues and greens. Any good electrical supply store will have an ample supply to choose from. Once you start installing lighting outside, why not consider lighting the edges of the driveway with small D.C. exterior lights? Remember, the driveway is one of the few things that is visible from the road.

One fixture or device that we made use of was the commercial electric timers that are available everywhere. For

Fig. 15-17. Your bathroom is even open for a unique design.

example, we are experimenting with turning lights on and off in the garden as night falls and morning comes in. Another use for these timers is to turn your hot water heater on and off at times when hot water is not required. I realize lighting and timers are not restricted to underground homes, but they do give you another dimension to work with, especially for electrical conservation.

IDEAS

My wife collected pictures of interesting ideas of conventional homes from home and garden magazines. All we did was ignore the windows and then we found that many of the ideas could be used underground as well as above ground. If you don't have a collection of pictures, remember the local library has back issues of most magazines. For a few more ideas, see Figs. 15-15 through 15-17.

16

Air Handling

This is a phase that can cost you a fortune if you don't approach it with a great deal of logical thought. Due to the fact that the total air tightness will be underground, many of the conventional rules of thumb will have to be ignored.

HEATING

Any heating-ventilation contractor can install conventional sheet metal duct systems, such as the ones you will find in any conventional house. If you note any house with forced hot air, it has at least two vents per room. One is a return and the others are for incoming hot air. These vents are connected to a sheet metal duct system that comes from and returns to a central heating plant. Other possible ways of heating include electric and hot water baseboard heat. Many people use only woodstoves to heat their underground home. The metal duct system is by far the most expensive, most difficult and most inefficient system to use in an underground house. The reason is that the contractor would have to break through concrete walls at least three times per room. In my case, with ten heated rooms, that would be at least 30 holes broken by hand in concrete block or solid concrete. This costs time and money, not to mention weakening the structure.

A second negative reason not to use a metal duct system is that the sheet rock walls would have to be built around the duct to cover it when finishing a room's interior. This in itself is a time consuming job.

My system is simple, but efficient. It cost approximately one-tenth of the cost of a conventional hot air system and in many ways it is twice as efficient and flexible. The general idea that I used follows.

Start with the room where your woodstove is located. This should be in a centrally located room. As this room heats up by the radiant heat of the stove, it is nothing more than a big hot air plenum, serving the same purpose as a plenum chamber or a furnace. By installing a miniature motor approximately one-hundredth of a horsepower with approximately an 8" diameter fan blade into the wall, the fan will draw hot air out of the main room into the next room. By using a variable speed control such as a light dimmer switch, you can vary the speed of this fan motor. Thus you control the volume of air that flows through the wall. By repeating this procedure in any adjacent room, you can circulate the air as necessary.

Do not forget that by drawing air into a room, there must be a vent to allow the same volume of air to escape. In some cases, I used a small grill for this escaping air, but in most rooms the doors were cut to clear the carpet by approximately ½". This ½" clearance allows the pressure to escape very satisfactorily. Of course, if the door is open, there is no problem at all. The air flow will continue to circulate by using only this small in-the-wall motor and no duct system. The only additional venting necessary is to have a clear unobstructed path for fresh, exterior air to be drawn in as the hot air goes up the chimney. In my house, as in many others, all that is required is to vent air into the atrium or garden area. If your garden dome is not air tight, as most are not, further venting in the dome is unnecessary. This is the main reason for not making this foundation a solid unit.

COOLING

In the warmer months when the wood stove is not used, the fans serve the same purpose of keeping the air moving, thus avoiding a stale or musty odor. By using a standard, good quality room dehumidifier in one or more rooms depending on the severity of the humidity problem, and letting these fans circulate the room air past these dehumidifiers, it is relatively simple to control the humidity in the entire house without a complex system of duct work or expensive central heating-humidifying unit. The disadvantage of putting a hole in the wall is that now sound can travel very wasily from room to room. This condition can be nearly eliminated by side-stepping this air flow with a simple duct system you construct yourself as the wall board goes up.

This allows the air to go through the wall, then travel behind the sheet rock until the grill vent is installed on the opposite wall approximately 4 feet away from the concrete opening. This method is only a minor adaptation to the direct air flow, but it is a major barrier to sound waves.

In my house these fans run nearly 75 per cent of the time, year round. This may sound like we're using a great deal of power, but don't forget that each one is only one-hundredth of a horsepower or a collective total of one-fifth of a horsepower for my entire house. Most conventional furnaces have motors that draw more than twice the power that these require. This is just another advantage of building underground.

17

Domes and Skylights

From the data I have collected on underground homes, I figure that 85 per cent of them have either a skylight or a dome. Approximately 75 per cent have some type of interior garden or atrium, or courtyard. I highly recommend that you consider including a garden in your plans due to the absence of windows. You need a method of natural light access to eliminate any trace of a cave-like atmosphere. Because your house is below grade level, a dome is much easier to build and install than if you tried to put one on a conventional house roof that is 20 feet off the ground.

INDOOR GARDEN

My garden is approximately 8 feet wide by 16 feet long. This seems to be the average size, especially when you consider the cost of building or buying a dome. The dome or skylight is another place where a person handy with tools will save money. I built my dome in the shape of a pyramid and covered it with acrylic plastic ¼" thick. It measures 16 feet wide by 24 feet long by 8 feet high. To see my dome under construction, refer to Fig. 17-1. Figure 17-2 shows the method of construction.

As for building the super structure of a dome, all you need is a hand circular saw with a special aluminum cutting blade, a square, a tape measure, a good aluminum welder and a place to work. Don't use any material for structural support but aluminum, because it's light weight, easy to cut and it won't rust or need painting. You can buy aluminum from any steel supplier listed in the yellow pages. Check at least three or four suppliers because the price of aluminum varies quite a bit. Aluminum is sold by the pound, so the more you buy, the cheaper the pound rate. Therefore, buy all you need at one time and pick it up if possible. Shipping of irregular shapes is always costly. If you decide to build your own, try to stick to a shape similar to my pyramid style shown near completion in Figure 17-3. Avoid curves because the bending of plastic covering is very difficult without the proper specialized plastic heating equipment.

COST OF DOME

If you are still undecided about whether to build your own dome or buy one already complete, consider these facts: I completed my dome (technically not a dome) at a cost less than $3,000. The equivalent structure commercially built would have cost more than $9,000, not delivered and not totally assembled. I was afraid to ask about a delivery charge. There is another drawback—you'll find only a few dome manufacturers interested in talking to a private home owner since most of their work is with commercial building contractors specializing in shopping malls and office buildings. However, if by now you are considering doing without a dome or a skylight, I'll try again to convince you to include one at any cost.

Besides the element of natural light, consider the pleasures of a year-round growing area, for exotic plants or a small vegetable garden.

In addition, an atrium will give you the ideal place for natural ventilation or air-draw because of its height above grade level.

Fig. 17-1. Dome under construction.

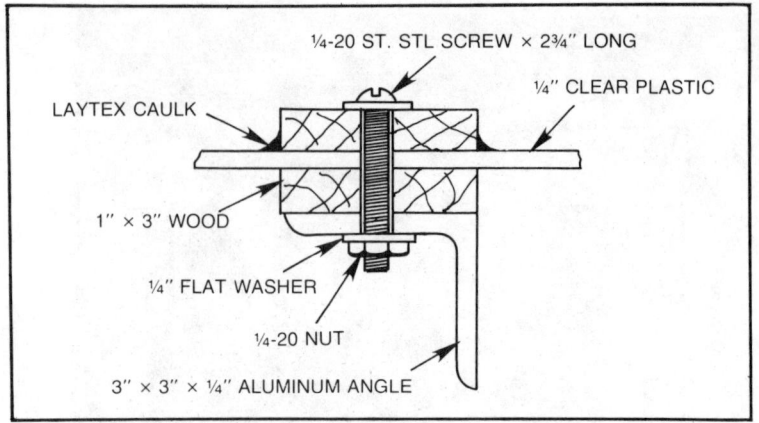

Fig. 17-2. Typical section of dome structure.

Now for the major reason. A garden or atrium covered by a dome of some type will give you a place to provide emergency exits in order to comply with some local building codes. Check codes carefully as you design your garden and dome. As I've said in almost every chapter, consider all possibilities before locking in on a design. See Figs. 17-4 and 17-5 photos of my garden in mid-construction, and Figs. 17-6 and 17-7 for photos of it near completion.

SKYLIGHTS

Skylights, as opposed to domes, are usually considered only to let light in. They are mostly transluscent, and probably will be much easier to buy than build because the shipping costs aren't prohibitive. Check the large building supply stores as a source. These are a few of the possibilities. It's your choice once again.

CONSTRUCTING YOUR DOME

If you decide you want a dome, find a good aluminum welder who will work with you. If he can't work on your site, then at least be near enough to make moving the welded frame possible (Fig. 17-8). Never install the plastic panes until the dome is in place and set on a stable foundation. The flexing will break the plastic panes every time. Check prices and explain

Fig. 17-3. Dome near structural completion.

Fig. 17-4. View of the garden during mid-construction.

Fig. 17-5. Progress is being made on this dome.

Fig. 17-6. Dome is near completion.

Fig. 17-7. Dome in place over garden.

your project to the welder. Keep looking until you find one who is interested in your underground house, not just your cash. Try to arrange to do the sawing, fitting, holding and grinding yourself. Let the welder weld. You'll both be satisfied and the finished product will show it. If in doubt about strength, return to the engineer who helped with the roof. If he was accurate with the roof strength, the dome will be a breeze.

Once you find this person capable of welding aluminum and he agrees to help you, you have to have all aluminum angle and flat bar delivered. Aluminum angle of 3″ × 3″ × ¼″ and aluminum flat bar of ¼″ × 3″ should be sufficient to build a normal dome. To avoid cutting aluminum at the wrong angle or too short, use cardboard to make a template at the joints. Use a good tape measure and triple check the dimensions after tack welding and before permanent welding. Continue this procedure until the dome's super structure is complete. Once welding is finished, use a grinder to smooth welded joints so that the plastic and wood will lay flat.

Once your framework is complete and ready for installation, you need to construct a foundation to set this structure on. I stacked 8″ concrete blocks from roof slab to ground level (Fig. 17-9). Then I set 8″ by 9″ railroad ties around the perimeter. Finally the structure rested on the ties and was bolted down. The reason I stacked block with no mortar was to let the dome breathe and to allow some moisture to seep through to the earth inside the dome.

In all fairness to you, beware of this method. I understand that it may be against some building codes in some locales. Let me mention something very interesting about the indoor gardens of underground homes. One inspector will say that a garden area like mine is an outdoor area and that exterior building codes apply to electrical outlets, water lines, etc. The next inspector will say that the same area is definitely an interior room and that interior codes apply. Let them fight it out. I consider it an indoor area.

Fig. 17-8. Method of moving dome after construction.

Back to the completion of this dome. There are only a couple of choices of material for panes. There are many acrylics on the market suitable for panes in a dome. One such example is plexiglass. Check all suppliers for prices of 4' × 8' sheets of ¼" clear acrylics. Do not use anything more than ¼" thick. The expansion and contraction is a factor to consider when using as much plastic as you will use. One-quarter inch will be strong enough, yet the weight will not be too great.

You also have the option of using tinted colors in acrylic plastic, but they are more expensive. But do give some thought to the idea of installing tinted panes. You have to live with it for a long time. However, I personally suggest you stick to clear because the sky and clouds will begin to look strange through pink or yellow or whatever tinted panes you might choose.

Another thing I would suggest while designing your dome is that you do not make any of the sections bigger than can be covered by a 4' × 8' sheets of acrylic. Buy these by the gross from a wholesaler. Don't buy them from the local hardware store, or you'll go broke. Space the bolting pattern so that a bolt ends up within 3" of each end of the pane and at 12" intervals. There is an easy way to make sure that each sheet of plastic is cut to exact shape and you don't make a mistake and ruin a costly 4' × 8' sheet. With the help of two extra people to help hold a sheet in place over the frame, move it around until it fits an open space with a minimum amount of waste (Fig. 17-10). Now use a straightedge and a crayon to draw a straight line where you want to cut. Continue this process until all panes are cut. As you cut a pane, put it in place to avoid scratching or breaking. Whatever you do, leave the paper on and keep the sheets out of the sunlight until cut, then remove paper at installation. If the sheets are exposed to sunlight for more than a few days, the paper becomes brittle and is difficult, if not impossible, to remove. Ask you supplier. He may be an expert on plastic or just a part-time salesman, but it won't hurt to ask. After all these procedures are followed and the dome is built, installed and all the panes are in place, the

Fig. 17-9. Stacking 8" block forms a mortarless foundation.

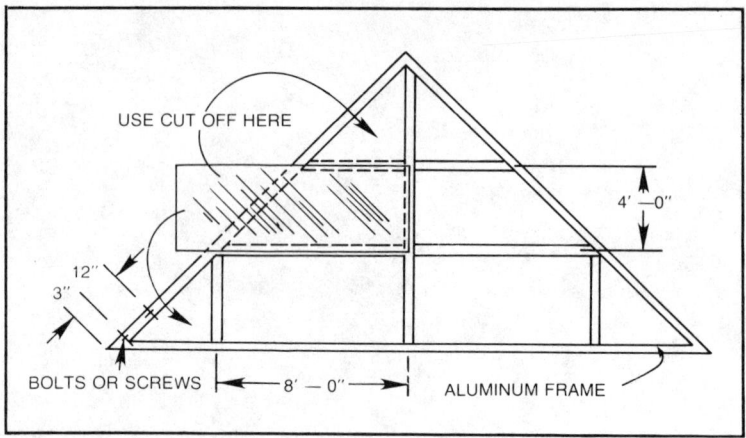

Fig. 17-10. Method of cutting plastic to correct shape.

final step is to caulk each seam using an acrylic caulk. Any good quality will work fine. Finally, the dome must be bolted to the railroad ties by using lag bolts, approximately 6" long.

As a safety reminder, do not watch the welder as he is welding. The light flash will burn your eyes. Even a reflection off of a wall will cause a severe burn or possible blindness. Be very careful if welding is a subject you are not familiar with.

Another possibility for building a dome is using prefabricated panels in triangular shapes. Look in the classified section of the how-to-do; plus magazines, such as *Mother Earth News, Mechanics Illustrated, Popular Science,* etc., for geodesic panels.

18

Underground Home Ceiling

Have you ever stopped to think recently about what your ceiling is going to look like when your house is complete? I realize that with all the other problems of building an underground home, you haven't really had time to worry about the cosmetic effects of the concrete slab—your roof. However, if you stop and think about it, you'll discover this 10" concrete slab has two sides, one of which is on the inside of your house. This could possibly be your finished interior ceiling.

ROOF SLAB

If you poured your roof slab in one piece over a sheet of plastic and you have removed all the scaffolding, you will notice the unique pattern formed in the concrete by the plastic. Most likely, this will be suitable for a finished ceiling texture. All that was required was to paint the concrete roof with flat latex paint.

I've mentioned this natural way of completing your ceiling, because although there are other ways of finishing your ceiling interior, they are definitely a job to install.

A fact you must accept is that, with all of your shoring, reinforcing and other construction involved in pouring the roof, it is not logical to expect the underside of your roof to turn out smooth and level. It will definitely have high and low spots, thus preventing you from attaching sheet rock directly to the underside of the concrete.

The uneven surface is not the only determining factor. Probably the largest barrier you will discover is that you cannot drive concrete nails into your ceiling. There are two reasons for this. First, the concrete, if it has correct quality, is too hard and brittle to accept nails. The main reason is that it is physically difficult to hammer over your head for any length of time or apply enough hammering leverage.

There is only one way to attach sheet rock to the ceiling and it isn't easy. Here is the method that will work: Use a ¼" drill bit, drill a hole approximately 1½" deep and insert the appropriate part of an anchor-bolt assembly. These are available from almost any hardware supply store. I suggest you use 1" × 3" wood strips, 8 feet long for ease of handling. You should first place a bead of panel cement on each wood strip and then put anchor bolts every 2 feet for a typical wood strip installation. Now all you have to do is to continue this procedure throughout the house in each room you want sheet rocked.

If you don't like either of these methods of finishing your ceiling, there is yet another alternative to ceiling decoration.

CREATIVE CEILINGS

This alternative is the method I have on the ceiling of two of my rooms. All that is involved is a little patience, originality and time. The pattern is nothing more than pieces of wood cut at random lengths, widths and thicknesses. The largest piece is approximately 8" long. The reason for the short lengths is that panel cement is the only thing holding them in place. No bolts, screws or nails, only glue. Most likely the smaller pieces will stick without support until the glue sets, especially if you tap it gently with a hammer to force a tight seal. Experimentation on your part will soon develop a style and approach that will make a super ceiling with a personal touch. An additional value of this method is the fact that wood is an excellent insulator and a little extra insulation never hurt anything.

As in previous chapters, I have tried to be honest with you on the pros and cons of each step as I see them. The negative side of this method is the extra wood is looked upon as additional fire hazards by the inspectors. This might cause some contention, so consider this negative possibility.

If you do decide to glue something to your ceiling, remember that almost anything can be glued up if you use a pole brace until the glue dries. The glues on the market used for construction are very strong.

In short summary of ceilings, if you plan on having a conventionally smooth sheet rock ceiling, extra effort will be involved in securing the sheet rock and getting it on a level plane. The easiest and most artistic approach would be to glue something directly onto the concrete or apply a stucco or paint of some type. Keep your imagination working overtime!

19

After Basic Completion

Once the basic construction part of your underground home is complete, you can and should relax for a while before going on to the fine details of finishing.

FINISHING TOUCHES

These details include driveway surfacing other than basic gravel, landscaping other than grass and standing trees and so forth. On the inside these finishing touches may include the shop work bench you've always wanted, or storage shelves everywhere. These are all things that are nice to have and you want them, but they are not essential to a final inspection by the bank or building codes department. As a matter of fact, anything you build is subject to inspection. Therefore, the less there is to inspect, the less chance you have of hitting a snag. Take your time adding these finishing touches.

STORAGE SHEDS

Another subject I want to cover that is particularly pertinent to the underground house is the ever popular outside storage shed. These are the metal sheds that often rust two weeks after erection. It never ceases to amaze me that people will buy a $90,000, 3,006 square foot home with a three-car

Fig. 19-1. Driving up to an underground house.

Fig. 19-2. This long driveway leads to an underground house.

Fig. 19-3. Entrances to an underground house.

Fig. 19-4. An underground home.

garage and full basement, and within six weeks of moving in they find they need outside storage. So they buy one of these storage sheds for a couple of hundred dollars and the tax assessor sees it and up go the property taxes. They continue to pay a premium for having the shed year after year, even after it's rusted beyond recognition. What I'm leading to is this: These sheds seem to be an intricate part of middle-class American homes, probably because almost every neighbor has one. Somehow I can't imagine building an underground house, spending countless hours getting grass to grow on the roof, side slopes, creating that back-to-nature attitude and then methodically plopping an outbuilding of any type nearby. It's not a logical move and is bound to be an eyesore even if it's well constructed. You must remember that your structure is not seen by your neighbors, so the outside shed, garage or outbuilding is the only monument visible to the outside world. Can't you just picture driving up to your underground house (Figs. 19-1 and 19-2) and seeing nothing except a rusty storage shed in the middle of three acres? No way! If your house can be seen from the highway, why make the world look at your storage shed? I'd even go as far as to request that you keep the lawn trimmed and neat. Let's not give opponents of underground homes anything to pick at. We may be an endangered species.

THE ENTRANCE

Another thought I'd like to pass on is why not give your entrance (Fig. 19-3) a distinctive appearance? Maybe an unusual mail box, or just a nice display of evergreen shrubbery. Unless there is a sudden surge of popularity in building underground, your house will definitely be a novelty and the curiosity seekers will drive by to take a look, even though they may not see much from the outside. They will form a lasting opinion of your home by what they see from the road. See Fig. 19-4 for a view of my home.

Getting Used to Living Underground

Building underground is one thing to accomplish, living underground successfully is another. You must realize, as you are building, that there is no way to see if you will like living underground until you actually are. Spending a few hours touring and visiting an underground home doesn't give a true indication. Hundreds of people have been inside my home for a short period of time, but they still don't know for sure what it's like living there. The sad thing about this point is that it costs a great deal of money to find out. If you don't like what you've built, there is a big question as to its value. If you're lucky, you could sell it at a profit, but on the other hand, your potential buyers are few and far between.

NO WINDOWS

Probably the first thing you adapt to easily, as we did, was the absence of windows. You've probably always had a window to look out of or to open. Here is where your dome and indoor garden will save you.

STRANGE SENSATIONS

For the first few months of living in our home we experienced an odd feeling caused by the absense of noise. In a conventional house when you turn the television off late at night and the children are asleep, if you sit still and listen, you might say things are deathly silent. Well they are in comparison to normal activity. The average person would go bananas in an absolutely soundless room.

An underground house is somewhere in between these two extremes due to the fact that these block walls absorb the sounds that most people never realize they hear. Noises such as hot water heaters warming up, or the presence of car noises on the nearest road, or airplanes, or dogs barking are all considered "normal." These are now almost totally eliminated. The strange effect is this: If your daily routine takes you to the outside world, such as shopping or school, your ears become tuned into the sound level around you and your speech level is comparatively higher. However, when you walk into your underground home especially for the first few months, you will find yourself talking louder than necessary by force of the habit from trying to be heard normally on the outside. The absence of background noise isn't noticed and you continue talking as if it were present. This is something you get used to in a short time so it's nothing to get excited about. Also I should add that the layout and configuration of the rooms makes quite a difference as well as the carpet quality and the amount of glass.

RADIO AND TELEVISION RECEPTION

This is something that never crossed my mind as I designed my house. Once we moved in and turned the radios and televisions on, we immediately noticed that in some rooms absolutely nothing could be picked up on the radio. The waves could not penetrate the earth and concrete. Of course, as you get closer to the doors or your dome, if you have one, the television and radio waves will filter in giving some reception. Even close to an opening, the reception leaves much to be desired.

Our solution was to use the aluminum structure of the dome as an aerial for both television and radio. The amount of aluminum available and its configuration make quite a difference. So you may have to get a service man good with television and aerials to stop by and show you the best way to attach and run the wiring.

Bad reception is easily overcome if you run a master aerial lead to each room as you are finishing the walls. This wire is not covered by codes and is harmless to work with.

CABLE TELEVISION

If you live in an area where cable television is available, I would suggest you check into the service to insure good reception, especially if you are an avid television fan.

As you see, things are somewhat of a new experience and quite exciting at times.

21

Alternate Sources of Energy

Alternate energy, now there's a catch-all phrase! Since I began building this underground house I have heard more stories about alternate sources of energy than you would believe.

My definition of alternate energy is any energy source for which you don't receive a bill in the mail. Of course, energy is synonymous with utilities when discussing home use. The two basic requirements are heat and electricity.

HEAT

Some people who have heard unfounded stories about underground homes not needing a heat source are definitely of the wrong impression. Heat most certainly is required. The good thing about building underground is that it only takes about 25 per cent of the heat required for a conventional home. As you can figure, it doesn't take long for a 75 per cent annual fuel bill savings to add up to a substantial amount. Then there's the obvious fact that sometime in the near future fossil fuels, as we know them, will be unavailable to heat your house at any cost. So you can look at the underground idea as doing your part to save energy. Now that I have convinced you that some small heat source will be required, I'll help put into true perspective the alternate methods of obtaining this form of energy.

WOOD STOVES

I have come to discover that this back-to-basic piece of equipment called a wood stove is probably used in over 50 per cent of all underground homes. I base this fact on information given me by other underground home builders that have contacted me. I've taken no scientific survey, but I'm convinced that wood stoves are the most popular heat sources in underground homes.

Like any other commercial product on the market, there are stoves of excellent quality and stoves that are outright dangerous to use. You will only get what you pay for in a wood stove: so be prepared to buy "quality." Most of the brands are sturdily built and have excellent air flow. You will find quite a few manufacturers of wood stoves that distribute regionally. Therefore, they are not available to everyone, everywhere. There are good books written on wood stoves. So I suggest you make up your mind intelligently by reading up on the subject and by physically examining as many brands as possible until you're satisfied that you know what you are buying.

Here is a good example as to why a good stove is important. There are many scientific results available from different manufacturers indicating that one brand burns twice the wood of another brand under similar conditions supplying the same heat. This is a fact. So you see you could end up cutting twice the wood necessary to get through a winter.

As for my underground home, I don't have to buy wood. But I do realize that wood could be a costly fuel if you have to buy cords of wood year in and year out. But even if you paid premium prices, it would still be cheaper than the oil-base fuels. Besides, wood is a replenishable natural resource. If you have to buy wood by the cord over any extended period of time, you're doing something wrong. Wood is everywhere. Some builders will even pay you to clean up the scrap wood after a new house is built. Many people will pay to have a piece of land cleared of the trees, and you keep the wood. All you need is a good chain saw, energy, and the old station wagon mentioned earlier. I won't dwell on this subject since it is only remotely related to underground home building. All that I'm saying is, don't buy wood, just look around because it's everywhere for free.

COAL

Just as I use wood as a fuel, some people use coal. In some sections of the country it is easier and cheaper to obtain than wood. There are problems with the odor and the mess, but it's cheaper and easier to handle than wood. So check the price of coal as compared to the availability of wood.

The important thing to remember if you use a stove is to locate your heating unit centrally. Your chimney is the main part of your natural heating-ventilation system. Put it near the center of the living area. As your hot air rises up the chimney, it draws air from the point of least resistance, and that is out of the living area as long as you provide a method for fresh air to be drawn inside the house.

In an underground house the hot air rises up the chimney. This draws air out of the adjacent room creating a slight vacuum. This vacuum is filled by fresh, colder air from the outside, thus creating a continuous flow of air naturally. This idea of air flow may need mechanical assistance such as a small fan or duct system. The exact size and layout of your home will determine this. You may also use vents or lowered panels in doors to create a flow of fresh air. This pattern of air flow will continue as long as the air temperature is warmer inside than outside or a slight breeze is blowing past the chimney.

Of course your building inspector will ask, "What happens when the wind doesn't blow and it's 100° outside and you have a fire in your stove?" He is technically correct, although not practical. Since this condition will only come up in the summer months, it is safe to say that your doors won't be continually shut for an extended period of time (a week or more). But in case your inspector requires additional assurance of ventilation you can install a small fan and vent from the exterior, or you can draw fresh air from the indoor garden which I hope you included.

This air circulation is a subject that your inspector may harp on or not even mention. It depends on your local inspection system. If it's a big deal to your local officials, rely on your engineer. You probably know him pretty well by now.

For your own information, let me tell you that you can take an underground house the size of mine (2800 square feet of living area), close all exterior doors, burn your stove for at least five days while living normally inside and the atmosphere inside will hardly be stale. The fact that an underground home is more airtight than a conventional home scares some people into thinking they are going to lack fresh air. It just isn't so. Normal traffic opens and shuts exterior doors numerous times a day. I do suggest that a vent of some type be installed on the exposed exterior wall, and that it feed directly to the interior only as a safety precaution. This is a subject that your local code will control probably in great detail. If you have a vented dome, you're even better off.

SOLAR HEAT

Solar heat is another catch-all phrase. Breaking it down, it means any heat from sunshine. This includes a very simple system of simply opening curtains as the sun shines and closing them as the sun sets, or it could be the complex systems of piping, valves and pumps used on conventional houses adapted for solar heat.

It is my opinion from my research that complex solar heat systems will cost much more to build, install and maintain than you could ever retrieve in heat bill savings in a lifetime. Remember, I'm going on the assumption that your heat requirement will be one-fourth that of a conventional home.

I do encourage you to use solar heat and to do all possible investigation if cost is not a major factor. Solar heating is definitely a subject whose time has come, and everyone should support its use and research. The only drawback is the initial cost. Another negative feature about solar is that you lose the homey atmosphere created by a fireplace.

SOLAR ELECTRIC

Please do not be confused with the two terms, solar heat and solar electric. Solar heat is here today. Solar electric cells for domestic use are in the future somewhere, probably five or six years away. Or it's possible a major breakthrough will never be developed in the production of solar electric cells (also photovoltaic cells). The space industry has put these cells to use, but that is about the extent of their availability.

A WORKABLE ELECTRIC SOURCE

There is, however, a source of electrical power that is less expensive than the power company. You should be well versed on electricity and mechanically inclined to pursue this method. I'll describe the basic idea and you can take it from there since it is only a take-off of the philosophy of underground homes by way of encouraging self-sufficiency.

The alternative electrical system is this: With a small diesel engine, such as a four-cylinder Volvo for example, you can couple this with a direct current (D.C.) generator that charges heavy duty storage batteries similar to the ones used in commercial equipment. By a series of regulators and switches you can keep these batteries fully charged with a minimum use of diesel-fuel. The catch is that you will have to wire your house for D.C. use instead of the usual A.C. from the power company. Most of your light bulbs and small appliances will oeprate sufficiently off of D.C. current. Only the big electric appliances require A.C. This system would be somewhat expensive to set up, but it would pay for itself in a short time, especially the way electric costs have gone up recently.

The slight inconvenience might be worth the advantages gained.

211

WIND POWER

What about a wind generator? A really interesting source of electrical energy that is free is a wind generator. There are approximately 10 good manufacturers in this country. Each claims to be the most efficient. All of them work basically the same. Some use storage D.C. batteries, others use inverters without D.C. batteries and provide A.C. current. One thing to be sure of is that your area has an average wind speed necessary to turn a windmill. Since the wind blows at different speeds from day to day and each wind generator's conditions are different, it's hard to be specific about what conditions are required. From my research I have drawn the conclusion that if you had 15 miles per hour winds 50 per cent of the time, using batteries and a 5-foot diameter blade on the appropriate generator, you could probably do away with the electric company. Call the local airport for basic wind information.

22

Underground Home Publicity

There is a fact that you must face when getting involved in any project as big as building an underground house. As with most unusual projects, many people will be interested. It seems that with the energy shortage, underground homes are surely a subject to get attention. Of course, there are many types of attention that you can get—negative, positive, private and public.

POSITIVE ATTENTION

Fortunately for you as the home builder, the people that give you publicity, whether it be by their request or yours, are fairly easy to categorize. As you read on, you will see what I mean.

I have found one fact to be 99 per cent true. The groups of individuals who personally ask to see your house are almost always friendly and not likely to cause you any problem. You very rarely will have a person ask to see your house and then bad mouth it behind your back. If you build your underground house correctly, visitors will go away impressed. They will also become your best moral supporters. You will be surprised by the number of friendships you make that will continue after the house building has been completed. This is reason enough to build an underground house—we all need all the friends we can get.

NEGATIVE ATTENTION

Just as the private citizens who ask to see your house are 99 per cent friendly, you can rest assured that 99 per cent of the public or regulatory personnel who see your house will have a negative opinion. In all fairness to these people, they usually form their opinions through the eyes of their specific jobs—zoning, health, fire, insurance or building inspectors. Don't be surprised if the dog catcher even gets into the act! Let me explain what I mean by seeing an underground house through their job titles as opposed to their personal interest.

In the course of my complicated maneuverings with the county and state officials, I had one inspector who gave me real problems as he acted in the manner and capacity of an inspector. As a matter of fact, he was downright uncooperative. However, a week after the inspection, the same inspector contacted me and wanted to know if he could show my house to his family. This time everyone was as friendly as could be. Once back on the job, he reverted to his old self.

PUBLIC ATTENTION

This is the most critical type of attention you will receive. It can make your adaption into the community smooth, or if the attention the newspaper, radio and television give you is negative, the neighborhood will be convinced that your house is a black spot in the community. At this point, I will put your mind at ease and tell you to relax. When a newspaper reporter or television station contact you for an interview, they are almost always forward-thinking, intelligent individuals who like to see people doing individualistic projects, especially saving energy. The time is right. These reporters can be your best allies if you get into any real hassles with officials. Reporters, by nature, will see that no one pulls the wool over anyone's eyes simply by constant exposure in the media.

I do, however, have some good advice for you as you prepare for your interviews with the media, be it television or newspapers. Know what you are talking about, don't make dumb, specific statements. First of all, they only want general information that the public can relate to. For example, if a reporter asks you how strong your concrete roof is, don't answer that it will hold up exactly 795 pounds per square foot. First of all, no one knows exactly how strong your concrete is and secondly, someone will begin to question your judgment. Whatever you do, don't pin yourself into a corner by broadcasting specific facts about your house that the public does not need to know.

All the reporters I have talked to have been friendly, so be sure to act accordingly. They are great people to have on your side to spread the word about the good points of your underground house.

The one reservation you must have around reporters is to be exact as to what you want to be *on the record* or *off the record*. This, of course, has nothing to do with underground homes, but since you probably are not familiar with interview procedures, I will only tell you that once a statement is made, it cannot be retracted. However, a reporter will not report anything preceded by the words, "This is off the record."

PRIVATE ATTENTION

This is the same as acceptance by or rejection by the neighborhood. The less negative attention you receive publicly, the less private attention you are likely to receive. Accept the fact that building an underground house is an attention-getting project. Use it to your advantage and do not let it cause you a problem.

23

One Year Later

My underground home has been completed for over a year now. For you, the reader and potential underground home builder, my problems will be your gain. In reading the previous chapters, you learned of my experiences dealing with day to day problems. This year has given me time to collect my thoughts and change my opinions on some things. Some of the things I thought to be insignificant were not, and some of the things I thought to be important and critical were no problem at all.

First, I'll go over a few items that gave me a problem or at least some concern during the past year.

DOME ALIGNMENT

As I located my house on the piece of property I had bought, I centered the structure with the front doors facing the only direction feasible. I thought nothing about this layout at the time because I thought if I was totally underground, what difference would it make how the house was situated. For the most part, there was no problem. The slight inconvenience I did discover was caused by the way the sunlight comes through the panes of the dome. As it turned out, I had two corners of my garden area under the dome. About 15 per cent of the total area was never directly hit by sunlight. This doesn't affect the garden in any way, except for losing a small growing area. Needless to say, a real professional could have figured the path of the sun and the shadow it would cast if he had given it the time and concern.

Another little discovery that I made, once I actually settled down to a daily routine in my house, was that the dome sweats year-round. Only in extremely cold temperatures do the droplets freeze to the panes of plastic. Otherwise, the condensation droplets accumulate and cling to the panes. This is fine, and they soon evaporate and dissipate into the air. However, all good things have at least one drawback. These droplets cling to the panes as high as 22 feet overhead. If the wind is blowing slightly, all is well. Only when the wind velocity nears 40 miles per hour in gusts do the panes vibrate, thus shaking the droplets loose to fall to the ground. Still, it is not a big problem unless you are walking through the garden in the early morning around sunrise when the most drastic temperature changes take place. Unfortunately, this is the time we are usually crossing through the garden from the bedroom to the kitchen for the first cup of coffee. If the time is right and the wind is blowing hard enough, you can get a nice shower. This only happens once in a while, so I consider it a unique feature of underground living. I'm not about to do any major construction to eliminate a few drops of water. This is the type of phenomenon that was not expected. Only a year's living experience brought it to light.

DOME FOUNDATION

While on the subject of the dome, I have still another fact to share after one year. The building codes call for any structure similar to my dome to be anchored solidly to the roof structure. If you recall, I did not do this. I stacked concrete blocks on the roof slab using no mortar. The reason for no mortar was to allow normal water seepage for the indoor garden soil. The inspectors said that this would cause a problem, and I was cited for noncompliance. This point has still not been resolved. The fact is that the stacked block works extremely well. Only a limited amount of rain water actually seeps through, and the cracks allow air to filter through into the top of the dome. The statement that the earth will settle against these stacked, unmortared block and cause them to cave in is unwarranted. My block are exactly in the same place I put them 18 months ago. One thing I did do after one year was raise the dome 8" higher by placing another row of block around the perimeter. The reason for this was to allow a build-up of dirt to create more of a slope for rain to run off.

SUN HEAT

Another interesting fact I discovered about having an enclosed garden area is the true power of the sun to heat. Now, one year later, all of the armchair engineers are telling me, "I told you it would be hot in there." Of course anyone could have predicted that, but I don't believe anyone expected the temperature to get as high as 165°F, which it actually did. Do you know that 165°F literally fries tomatoes on the vine? This was a problem that I discovered only after I lost quite a few good yielding tomato and pepper plants. The solution to that problem is simple. If you are in the midst of a hot spell, spread a thin sheet of polyethylene (plastic) over the plants. This is the same plastic you used for waterproofing the walls and pouring concrete. It works well. Additionally, during the extreme hot days of August I used a portable electric household fan directed upward to circulate additional air. It is not practical to install a fan of this size permanently since it will only be used approximately 10 days a year. These are truly little bits of information that only time can reveal.

CRICKETS

Many people ask if I have an insect problem. No, I do not have an insect problem. Specifically, I have a cricket problem. Right! Crickets. Those black grasshopper-like creatures that supposedly make noise by rubbing their legs together. One year later, I can truthfully say that spiders, ants or bugs of any kind are literally non-existent. Not many normal, above-ground homes can say that.

I have been told that an indoor garden like the one I constructed is the perfect living quarters for crickets, and I have verified that fact. Now, before you get excited and conclude that my house is overrun with crickets, I'll be specific. First, they seem to congregate in the garden only. Occasionally one will venture into another room, but a normal house will have that same problem. The fact that they stay near the humid, garden-dome area makes them easy to control. Many of the commercial insect sprays do the job. It doesn't eliminate them completely. It only cuts down their population. A week later they are back. So I spray again. I have to admit, I enjoy the chirping sound at night. It sounds like you're sleeping in a tent sometimes. I even feel cruel when I exterminate these harmless creatures. However, I built the house for humans and not crickets, so one of us has to leave, and I'm the one who pays the mortgage.

Enough about the problems I encountered in the atrium area.

SNOW

As I mentioned in the beginning of this chapter, I could really only set my house facing in one direction—north-northwest. Except for the shadows in the growing area of the garden, this northern, rather than southern, exposure created only a couple of other minor problems.

One of them is drifting snow. Maryland is not known for its fierce snow storms, but we do get a couple of big snow storms every winter. This year was no exception. Since the winds blow directly onto my front door, it will be no surprise to tell you that on a couple of occasions the drifting snow packed against my front door to heights of up to 6 feet or so. Of course, an advantage to these snow storms was that the deeper the snow got, the warmer the inside became. Snow on top of the earth is a good insulation.

The problem with the snow drifting and blocking the doors was relatively easy to solve. When spring descended, I planted shrubs and trees to cause a natural barrier to block the drifting snow. In my case, as in most other underground homes, a good building location is hard to find for many reasons. Trying to find a satisfactory location with a southern exposure is like being on a treasure hunt. Most of you, however, will probably have to sacrifice that southern exposure for other benefits.

VISITORS

Don't draw the conclusion that I'm anti-social. The opposite of this is more my preference. I like to share my project with people who are sincerely interested in saving energy or who are merely curious. The only part about visitors that gets to be unpleasant is that a few, maybe 20 per cent, show up at my front door without any warning whatsoever. Not even a phone call. They just show up at the door. Well this isn't too bad since we try to keep the house presentable most of the time, and for the most part, their timing isn't too bad. If I'm really busy, the children have been very efficient about taking visitors on the "grand tour" and explaining the interesting points. However, there are a few inconsiderate people who not only show up without warning but do it at 7 o'clock on a Sunday morning. It's asking alot to be congenial under these circumstances. If you ever build an underground house, you will see that I'm not joking. The timing of some people is really off and their consideration almost nonexistent. However, I have never refused to show anyone through who has asked to see my house and answer their questions.

There is another type of person that will show up with or without an invitation. They will bring their children and dogs. If the children are well behaved, fine. But more often than not, they are renegades. These visitors are few and far between, but rest assured that if you build an underground house and it's unique to your community, you will have all types of visitors.

Most are considerate. So you see, visitors are another facet of underground living that only a year's experience could reveal.

UTILITY BILLS

Anyone investigating underground home building has checked on the utility savings—less fuel for heat, etc. Well, one year later, I can verify a few actual facts. The truth is that although I don't use a conventional heating system that uses a fossil fuel, I use only wood and a minimum of that. So I have really cut my fuel use by 100 per cent. The only negative side to the energy saving idea of an underground home is that my neighbor's electric bill is running approximately 10 per cent lower than mine. He owns a conventional normal-sized home. So I figure that I actually use only 50 to 55 per cent of the total amount of energy that I would be using if I actually had a conventional fuel bill and electric bill. This statement, however, is made with a slight reservation. Because all the traffic created by this new project has begun to subside and the constant use of power tools has slacked off, I expect my electricity consumption to drop in the coming months.

LACK OF LIGHT

Earlier in this book, I said we adapted well to the absence of windows. That, of course, was my first thought, with only limited experience living without them. I can honestly say that one year later the windows aren't even missed—not one bit. I am fully convinced that even conventional homes could do well by eliminating a few windows. With the right decoration inside, the lack of windows is a blessing. Don't let anyone try to convince you that windows are a necessary part of comfortable home living. You'll never miss them. However, there is one small catch you should be made aware of—oversleeping or losing track of time. This, believe it or not, is easy to do. Remember, once you shut a bedroom door and turn the lights out, it is totally dark. The only savior you have in the morning is the alarm clock.

During the first year, we had several occasions to sleep in one of the three bedrooms without natural light. Since it was a weekend, we didn't have to get up for work. All of a sudden the phone rang, and I grabbed it giving the party on the other end a few choice words not fit for publishing because I thought it was 4 a.m. It turns out it was nearly noon. Oversleeping happened more than once, especially to the children on school days.

PROBLEM NEIGHBORS

If by unfortunate necessity, you had to build your house close enough to neighbors so that they could see your progress, you probably had at least one neighbor give you static over your choice to go underground. The old saying, "Time heals all wounds" is true even in underground homes. You will find, just as I did, that one year later the people opposing your house have become tired of hearing themselves talk, and the neighbors who were questionable have become good friends. The official side mellows just as easily. The building inspectors will be tired of talking to you by now, especially if you haven't let them get you down.

In closing this chapter, I can safely say that the only thing rougher than the actual building construction was the first year of living inside. Things are settling down, and it is almost like living in a conventional house.

Appendix A
Weights and Specific Gravities

WEIGHTS AND SPECIFIC GRAVITIES

Substance	Weight Lb. per Cu. Ft.	Specific Gravity
METALS, ALLOYS, ORES		
Aluminum, cast, hammered	165	2.55–2.75
Brass, cast, rolled	534	8.4–8.7
Bronze, 7.9 to 14%, Sn	509	7.4–8.9
Bronze, aluminum	481	7.7
Copper, cast, rolled	556	8.8–9.0
Copper ore, pyrites	262	4.1–4.3
Gold, cast, hammered	1205	19.25–19.3
Iron, cast, pig	450	7.2
Iron, wrought	485	7.6–7.9
Iron, spiegel-eisen	468	7.5
Iron, ferro-silicon	437	6.7–7.3
Iron ore, hematite	325	5.2
Iron ore, hematite in bank	160–180	
Iron ore, hematite loose	130–160	
Iron ore, limonite	237	3.6–4.0
Iron ore, magnetite	315	4.9–5.2
Iron slag	172	2.5–3.0
Lead	710	11.37
Lead ore, galena	465	7.3–7.6
Magnesium, alloys	112	1.74–1.83
Manganese	475	7.2–8.0
Manganese ore, pyrolusite	259	3.7–4.6
Mercury	849	13.6
Monel Metal	556	8.8–9.0
Nickel	565	8.9–9.2

Substance	Weight Lb. per Cu. Ft.	Specific Gravity
TIMBER, U.S. SEASONED		
Moisture Content by Weight:		
Seasoned timber 15 to 20%		
Green timber up to 50%		
Ash, white, red	40	0.60–0.62
Cedar, white, red	22	0.32–0.38
Chestnut	41	0.66
Cypress	30	0.48
Fir, Douglas spruce	32	0.51
Fir, eastern	25	0.40
Elm, white	45	0.72
Hemlock	29	0.42–0.52
Hickory	49	0.74–0.84
Locust	46	0.73
Maple, hard	43	0.68
Maple, white	33	0.53
Oak, chestnut	54	0.86
Oak, live	59	0.95
Oak, red, black	41	0.65
Oak, white	46	0.74
Pine, Oregon	32	0.51
Pine, red	30	0.48
Pine, white	26	0.41
Pine, yellow, long-leaf	44	0.70
Pine, yellow, short-leaf	38	0.61
Poplar	30	0.48

Platinum, cast, hammered	1330	21.1–21.5	
Silver, cast, hammered	656	10.4–10.6	
Steel, rolled	490	7.85	
Tin, cast, hammered	459	7.2–7.5	
Tin ore, cassiterite	418	6.4–7.0	
Zinc, cast, rolled	440	6.9–7.2	
Zinc ore, blende	253	3.9–4.2	

VARIOUS SOLIDS

Cereals, oats ....bulk	32	
Cereals, barley ....bulk	39	
Cereals, corn, rye ......bulk	48	
Cereals, wheat ....bulk	48	
Hay and Straw ....bales	20	
Cotton, Flax, Hemp	93	1.47–1.50
Fats	58	0.90–0.97
Flour, loose	28	0.40–0.50
Flour, pressed	47	0.70–0.80
Glass, common	156	2.40–2.60
Glass, plate or crown	161	2.45–2.72
Glass, crystal	184	2.90–3.00
Leather	59	0.86–1.02
Paper	58	0.70–1.15
Potatoes, piled	42	
Rubber, caoutchouc	59	0.96–0.9.
Rubber goods	94	1.0–2.0
Salt, granulated, piled	48	
Saltpeter	67	
Starch	96	1.53
Sulphur	125	1.93–2.07
Wool	82	1.32

Redwood, California	26	0.42
Spruce, white, black	27	0.04–0.40
Walnut, black	38	0.61
Walnut, white	26	0.41

VARIOUS LIQUIDS

Alcohol, 100%	49	0.79
Acids, muriatic 40%	75	1.20
Acids, nitric 91%	94	1.50
Acids, sulphuric 87%	112	1.80
Lye, soda 66%	106	1.70
Oils, vegetable	58	0.91–0.94
Oils, mineral, lubricants	57	0.90–0.93
Water, 4°C. max. density	62.428	1.0
Water, 100°C.	59.830	0.9584
Water, ice	56	0.88–0.92
Water, snow, fresh fallen	8	.125
Water, sea water	64	1.02-1.03

GASES

Air. 0°C. 760 mm	.08071	1.0
Ammonia	0.478	0.5920
Carbon dioxide	.1234	1.5291
Carbon monoxide	.0781	0.9673
Gas, illuminating	.028–.036	0.35–0.45
Gas, natural	.038–.039	0.47–0.48
Hydrogen	.00559	0.0693
Nitrogen	.0784	0.9714
Oxygen	.0892	1.1056

WEIGHTS AND SPECIFIC GRAVITIES

Substance	Weight Lb. per Cu. Ft.	Weight Lb. per Cu. Ft.	Substance	Weight Lb. per Cu. Ft.	Specific Gravity
ASHLAR MASONRY			**EXCAVATIONS IN WATER**		
Granite, syenite, gneiss	165	2.3–3.0	Sand or gravel	60	......
Limestone, marble	160	2.3–2.8	Sand or gravel and clay	65	......
Sandstone, bluestone	140	2.1–2.4	Clay	80	......
			River mud	90	......
			Soil	70	
			Stone riprap	65	......
MORTAR RUBBLE MASONRY.					
			MINERALS		
Granite, syenite, gneiss	155	2.2–2.8	Asbestos	153	
Limestone, marble	150	2.2–2.6	Barytes	281	
Sandstone, bluestone	130	2.0–2.2	Basalt	184	
			Bauxite	159	
			Borax	109	
			Chalk	137	
DRY RUBBLE MASONRY			Clay, marl	137	
Granite, syenite, gneiss	130	1.9–2.3	Dolomite	181	
Limestone, marble	125	1.9–2.1	Feldspar, orthoclase	159	
Sandstone, bluestone	110	1.8–1.9	Gneiss, serpentine	159	
			Granite, syenite	175	
			Greenstone, trap	187	
BRICK MASONRY			Gypsum, alabaster	159	
Pressed brick	140	2.2–2.3	Hornblende	187	
Common brick	120	1.8–2.0	Limestone, marble	165	
Soft brick	100	1.5–.7	Magnesite	187	
			Phosphate rock, apatite	200	
			Porphyry	172	
CONCRETE MASONRY			Pumice, natural	40	
Cement, stone, sand	144	2.2–2.4	Quartz, flint	165	
Cement, slag, etc.	130	1.9–2.3	Sandstone, bluestone	147	
Cement, cinder, etc.	100	1.5–1.7	Shale, slate	175	
			Soapstone, talc	169	

VARIOUS BUILDING MATERIALS

Ashes, cinders	40–45
Cement, portland, loose	90
Cement, portland, set	183
Lime, gypsum, loose	53–64
Mortar, set	103
Slags, bank slag	67–72
Slags, bank screenings	98–117
Slags, machine slag	96
Slags, slag sand	49–55

	2.7–3.2
	1.4–1.9

EARTH, ETC., EXCAVATED

Clay, dry	63
Clay, damp, plastic	110
Clay and gravel, dry	100
Earth, dry, loose	76
Earth, dry, packed	95
Earth, moist, loose	78
Earth, moist, packed	96
Earth, mud, flowing	108
Earth, mud, packed	115
Riprap, limestone	80–85
Riprap, sandstone	90
Riprap, shale	105
Sand, gravel, dry, loose	90–105
Sand, gravel, dry, packed	100–120
Sand, gravel, dry, wet	118–120

STONE, QUARRIED, PILED

Basalt, granite, gneiss	96
Limestone, marble, quartz	95
Sandstone	82
Shale	92
Greenstone, hornblende	107

BITUMINOUS SUBSTANCES

Asphaltum	81
Coal, anthracite	97
Coal, bituminous	84
Coal, lignite	78
Coal, peat, turf, dry	47
Coal, charcoal, pine	23
Coal, charcoal, oak	33
Coal, coke	75
Graphite	131
Paraffine	56
Petroleum	54
Petroleum, refined	50
Petroleum, benzine	46
Petroleum, gasoline	42
Pitch	69
Tar, bituminous	75

COAL AND COKE, PILED

Coal, anthracite	47–58
Coao, bituminous, lignite	40–54
Coal, peat, turf	20–26
Coal, charcoal	10–14
Coal, coke	23–32

The specific gravities of solids and liquids refer to water at 4°C., those of gases to air at 0°C, and 760 mm. pressure. The weights per cubic foot are derived from average specific gravities, except where stated that weights are for bulk, heaped or loose material, etc.

Appendix B
Underground House Statistics

- HOUSE SIZE—40′ × 90′ (3600 SQUARE FEET)
- FIFTEEN ROOMS, PLUS GARAGE
- OVER 7500 CONCRETE BLOCK USED
- OVER 250 CUBIC YARDS OF CONCRETE
- APPROXIMATELY TEN TONS OF STEEL USED
- OVER 800 TONS OF DIRT ON ROOF
- WOOD HEAT STOVE ONLY

Appendix C
Weight of Basic Materials Used in Underground Construction

Weight of Basic Materials Used In Underground Construction		
SANDY SOIL	1 CUBIC FT.	65 LB
MUD	1 CUBIC FT.	90 LB
WATER	1 CUBIC FT.	62½ LB
CONCRETE	1 CUBIC FT.	140 LB
4' × 8' SHEET ¼"	ACRYLIC PLASTIC	47 LB
4' × 8' SHEET ½"	SHEET ROCK (GYPSUM BOARD)	65 LB
4' × 8' SHEET ½"	PLYWOOD	55 LB
12" × 8" × 8"	CONCRETE BLOCK	54 LB
6" × 8" × 8"	CONCRETE BLOCK	38 LB

Appendix D
Slump Test

The slump test is used to measure the consistency of the concrete. The test is made by using a SLUMP CONE; the cone is made of No. 16 gage galvanized metal with the base 8 inches in diameter, the top 4 inches in diameter, and the height 12 inches. The base and the top are open and parallel to each other and at right angles to the axis of the cone. A tamping rod ⅝ inch in diameter and 24 inches long is also needed. The tamping rod should be smooth and bullet pointed (not a piece of rebar).

Samples of concrete for test specimens should be taken at the mixer or, in the case of ready-mixed concrete, from the transportation vehicle during discharge. The sample of concrete from which test specimens are made will be representative of the entire batch. Such samples should be obtained by repeatedly passing a scoop or pail through the discharging stream of concrete, starting the sampling operation at the beginning of discharge, and repeating the operation until the entire batch is discharged. The sample being obtained should be transported to the testing site. To counteract segregation, the concrete should be mixed with a shovel until the concrete is uniform in appearance. The location in the work of the batch of concrete being sampled should be noted for future reference. In the case of paving concrete, samples may be taken from the batch immediately after depositing on the subgrade. At least five samples should be taken from different portions of the pile and these samples should be thoroughly mixed to form the test specimen.

The cone should be dampened and placed on a flat, moist nonabsorbent surface. From the sample of concrete obtained, the cone should immediately be filled in three layers, each approximately one-third the volume of the cone. In placing each scoopful of concrete the scoop should be moved around the top edge of the cone as the concrete slides from it, in order to ensure symmetrical distribution of concrete within the cone. Each layer should be RODDED IN with 25 strokes. The strokes should be distributed uniformly over the cross section of the cone and should penetrate into the underlying layer. The bottom layer should be rodded throughout its depth.

When the cone has been filed to a little more than full, strike off the excess concrete, flush with the top, with a

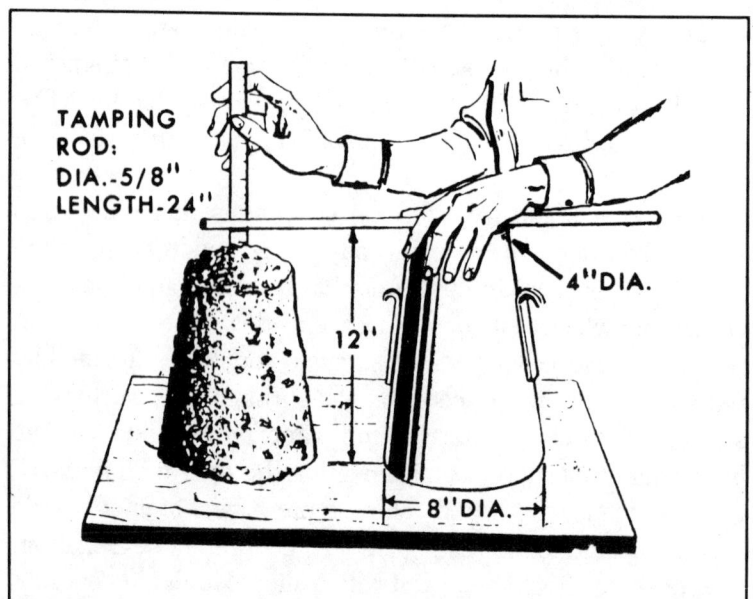

Fig. D-1. Measurement of slumps.

straightedge. The cone should be immediately removed from the concrete by raising it carefully in a vertical direction. The slump should then be measured to the center of the slump immediately by determining the difference between the height of the cone and the height at the vertical axis of the specimen as shown in Fig. D-1.

The consistency should be recorded in terms of inches of subsidence of the specimen during the test, which is called slump. Slump equals 12 inches of height after subsidence.

After the slump measurement is completed, the side of the mix should be tapped gently with the tamping rod. The behavior of the concrete under this treatment is a valuable indication of the cohesiveness, workability, and placeability of the mix. A well-proportioned workable mix will gradually slump to lower elevations and retain its original identity, while a poor mix will crumble, segregate, and fall apart.

Appendix E
Cement Statistics

Table E-1. Age Compression Strength. Relationship for Types I and III Air-Entrained Portland Cement.

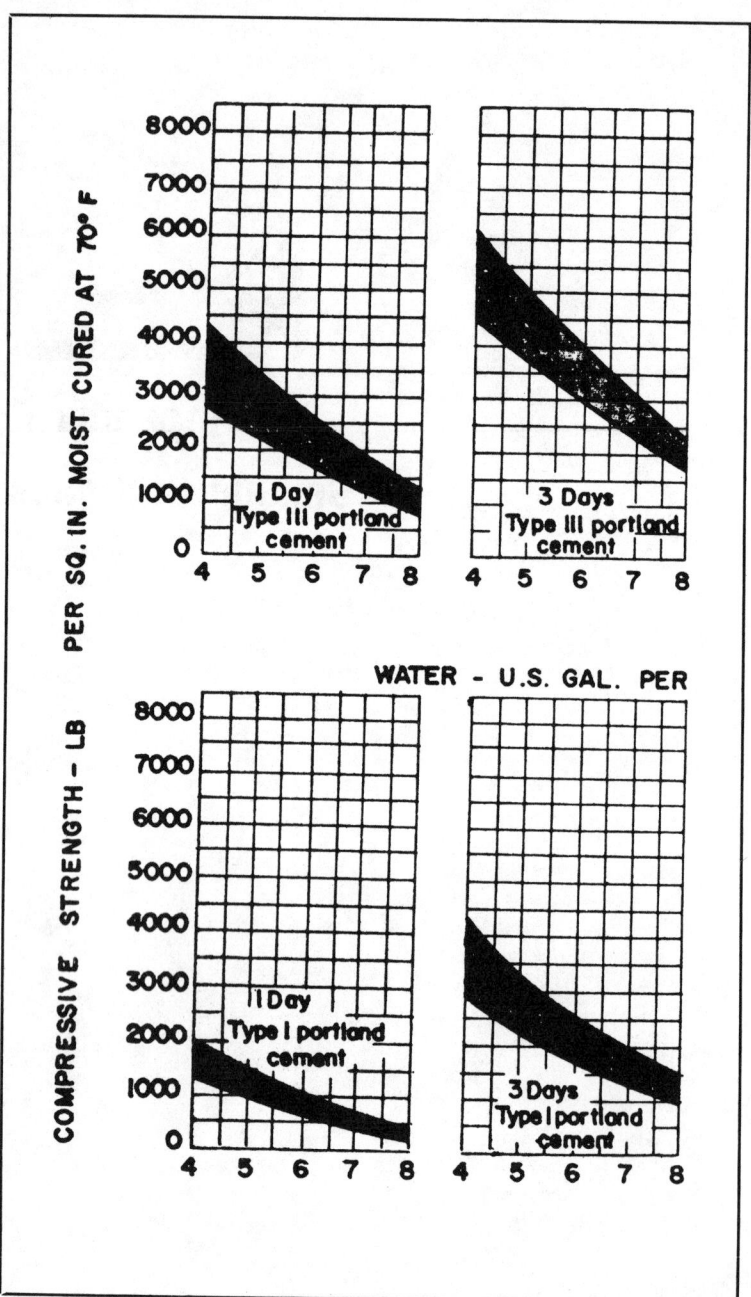

Table E-2. Suggested Trial Mixes for Non-Air-Entrained Concrete of Medium Consistency With 3- to 4-inch Slump.

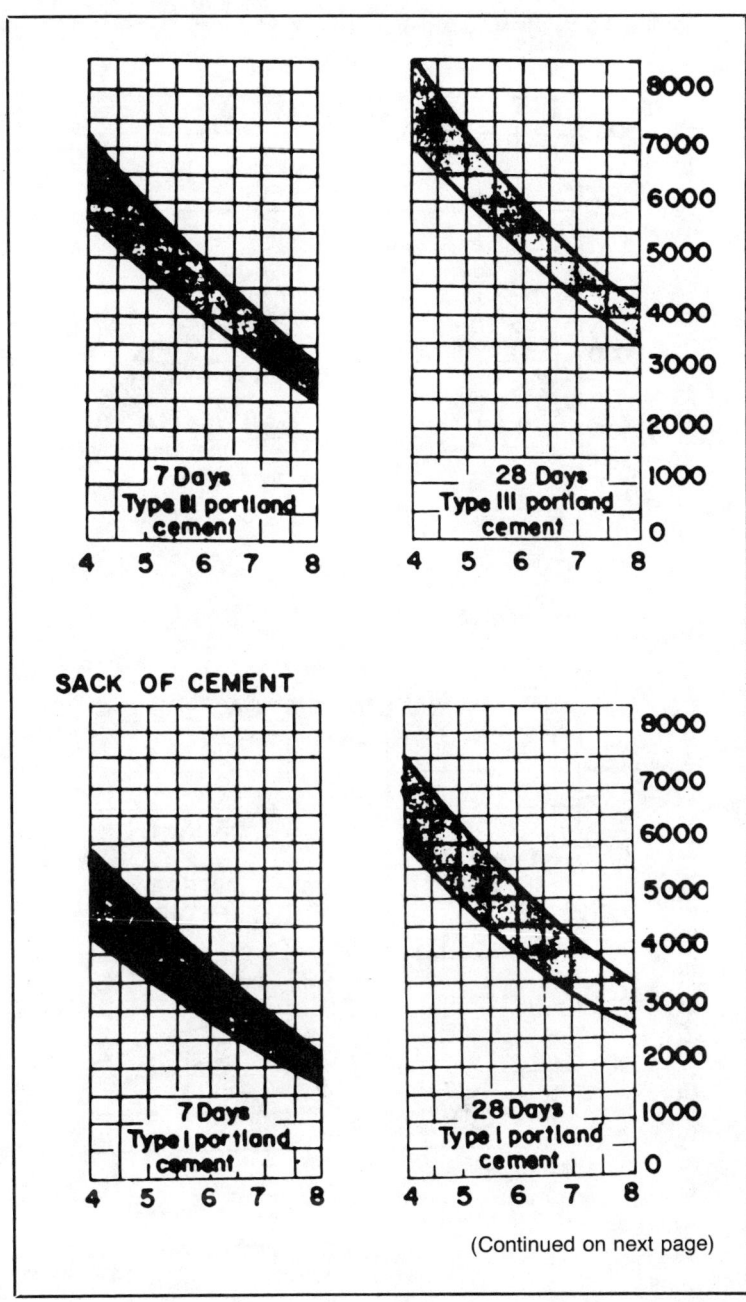

(Continued on next page)

(Continued from previous page)

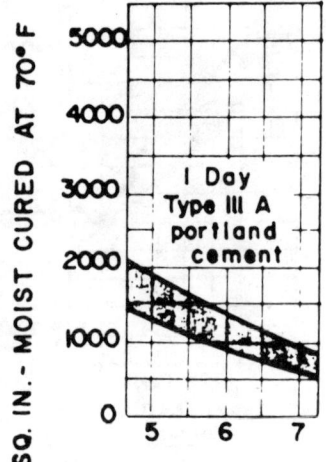
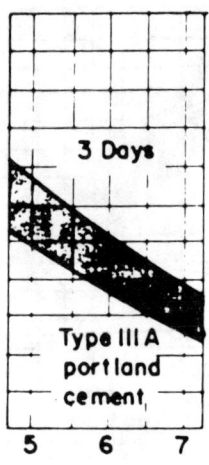
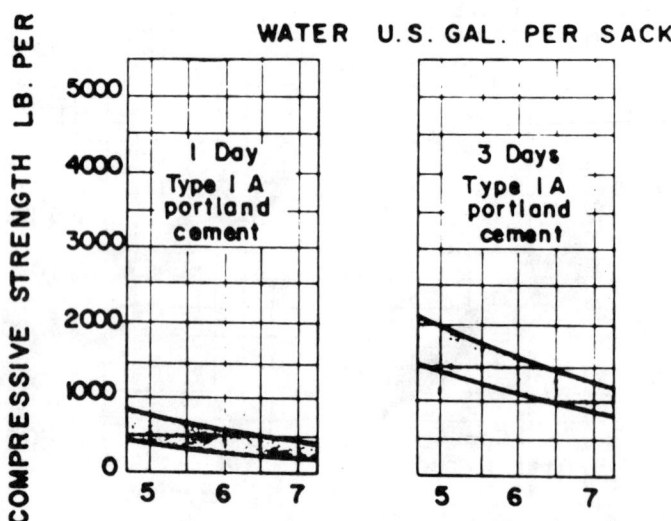

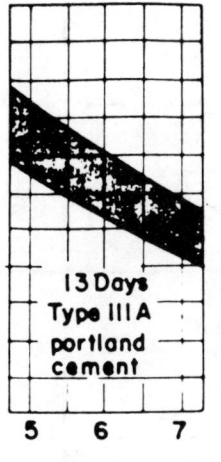
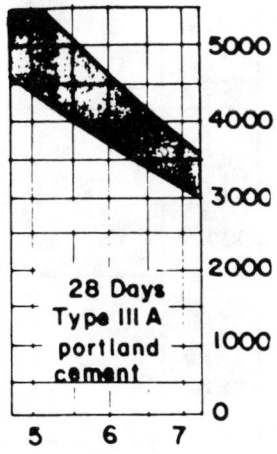

OF CEMENT

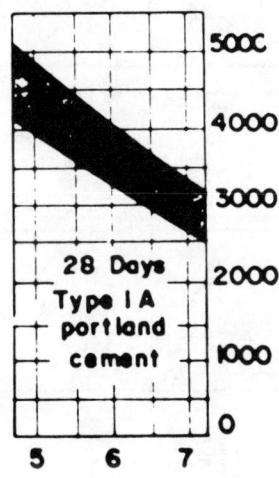

Table E-3. Suggested Trial Mixes for Air-Entrained Concrete of Medium Consistency with 3- and 4-Inch Slump.

Water-cement ratio Gal per sack	Maximum size of aggregate inches	Air content (entrapped air) per cent	Water gal per cu yd of concrete	Cement sacks per cu yd of concrete	With fine sand—fineness modulus = 2.50		
					Fine aggregate per cent of total aggregate	Fine aggregate lb per cu yd of concrete	Coarse aggregate lb per cu yd of concrete
4.5	3/8	3	46	10.3	50	1240	1260
	1/2	2.5	44	9.8	42	1100	1520
	3/4	2	41	9.1	35	960	1800
	1	1.5	39	8.7	32	910	1940
	1½	1	36	8.0	29	880	2110
5.0	3/8	3	46	9.2	51	1330	1260
	1/2	2.5	44	8.8	44	1180	1520
	3/4	2	41	8.2	37	1040	1800
	1	1.5	39	7.8	34	990	1940
	1½	1	36	7.2	31	960	2110
5.5	3/8	3	46	8.4	52	1390	1260
	1/2	2.5	44	8.0	45	1240	1520
	3/4	2	41	7.5	38	1090	1800
	1	1.5	39	7.1	35	1040	1940
	1½	1	36	6.5	32	1000	2110

6.0	3/8		46	3	7.7	53	1440	1260
	1/2		44	2.5	7.3	46	1290	1520
	3/4		41	2	6.8	39	1130	1800
	1		39	1.5	6.5	36	1080	1940
	1½		36	1	6.0	33	1040	2110
6.5	3/8		46	3	7.1	54	1480	1260
	1/2		44	2.5	6.8	46	1320	1520
	3/4		41	2	6.3	39	1190	1800
	1		39	1.5	6.0	37	1120	1940
	1½		36	1	5.5	34	1070	2110
7.0	3/8		46	3	6.6	55	1520	1260
	1/2		44	2.5	6.3	47	1360	1520
	3/4		41	2	5.9	40	1200	1800
	1		39	1.5	5.6	37	1150	1940
	1½		36	1	5.1	34	1100	2110
7.5	3/8		46	3	6.1	55	1560	1260
	1/2		44	2.5	5.9	48	1400	1520
	3/4		41	2	5.5	41	1240	1800
	1		39	1.5	5.2	38	1190	1940
	1½		36	1	4.8	35	1130	2110
8.0	3/8		46	3	5.7	56	1600	1260
	1/2		44	2.5	5.5	48	1440	1520
	3/4		41	2	5.1	42	1280	1800
	1		39	1.5	4.9	39	1220	1940
	1½		36	1	4.5	35	1160	2110

*See footnote at end of table.

(Continued on next page)

Table E-3. Suggested Trial Mixes for Non-Air Entrained Concrete of Medium Consistency With 3- to 4-Inch Slump

(Continued from previous page)

Water-cement ratio Gal per sack	With average sand—fineness modulus = 2.75			With coarse sand—fineness modulus = 2.90		
	Fine aggregate percent of total aggregate	Fine aggregate lb per cu yd of concrete	Coarse aggregate lb per cu yd of concrete	Fine aggregate percent of total aggregate	Fine aggregate lb per cu yd of concrete	Coarse aggregate lb per cu yd of concrete
4.5	52	1310	1190	54	1350	1150
	45	1170	1450	47	1220	1400
	37	1030	1730	39	1080	1680
	34	980	1870	36	1020	1830
	32	960	2030	33	1000	1990
5.0	54	1400	1190	56	1440	1150
	46	1250	1450	48	1300	1400
	39	1110	1730	41	1160	1680
	36	1060	1870	38	1100	1830
	34	1040	2030	35	1080	1990
5.5	55	1460	1190	57	1500	1150
	47	1310	1450	49	1360	1400
	40	1160	1730	42	1210	1680
	37	1110	1870	39	1150	1830
	35	1080	2030	36	1120	1990
6.0	56	1510	1190	57	1550	1150
	48	1360	1450	50	1410	1400
	41	1200	1730	43	1250	1600
	38	1150	1870	39	1190	1830
	36	1120	2030	37	1160	1990

6.5		57	1550	1190	58	1590	1150
		49	1390	1450	51	1440	1400
		42	1240	1730	43	1290	1680
		39	1190	1870	40	1230	1830
		36	1150	2030	37	1190	1990
7.0		57	1590	1190	59	1630	1150
		50	1430	1450	51	1480	1400
		42	1270	1730	44	1320	1680
		39	1220	1870	41	1260	1830
		37	1180	2030	38	1220	1990
7.5		58	1630	1190	59	1670	1150
		50	1470	1450	52	1520	1400
		43	1310	1730	45	1370	1600
		40	1260	1870	42	1300	1830
		37	1210	2030	39	1250	1990
8.0		58	1670	1190	60	1710	1150
		51	1520	1450	53	1560	1400
		44	1350	1730	45	1400	1680
		41	1290	1870	42	1330	1830
		38	1250	2030	39	1280	1990

*Increase or decrease water per cubic yard by 3 per cent for each increase or decrease of 1 in. in slump, then calculate quantities by absolute volume method. For manufactured fine aggregate, increase percentage of fine aggregate by 3 and water by 17 lb. per cubic yard of concrete. For less workable concrete, as in pavements, decrease percentage of fine aggregate by 3 and water by 8 lb. per cubic yard of concrete.

Table E-4. Approximate mixing water requirements for Different Slumps and Maximum Sizes of Aggregates.

Water-cement ratio Gal per sack	Maximum size of aggregate inches	Air Content (entrapped air) per cent	Water gal per cu yd of concrete	Cement sacks per cu yd of concrete	With fine sand—fineness modulus = 2.50		
					Fine aggregate per cent of total aggregate	Fine aggregate lb per cu yd of concrete	Coarse aggregate lb per cu yd of concrete
4.5	3/8	7.5	41	9.1	50	1250	1260
	1/2	7.5	39	8.7	41	1060	1520
	3/4	6	36	8.0	35	970	1800
	1	6	34	7.8	32	900	1940
	1 1/2	5	32	7.1	29	870	2110
5.0	3/8	7.5	41	8.2	51	1330	1260
	1/2	7.5	39	7.8	43	1140	1520
	3/4	6	36	7.2	37	1040	1800
	1	6	34	6.8	33	970	1940
	1 1/2	5	32	6.4	31	930	2110
5.5	3/8	7.5	41	7.5	52	1390	1260
	1/2	7.5	39	7.1	44	1190	1520
	3/4	6	36	6.5	38	1090	1800
	1	6	34	6.2	34	1010	1940
	1 1/2	5	32	5.8	32	970	2110
6.0	3/8	7.5	41	6.8	53	1430	1260
	1/2	7.5	39	6.5	45	1230	1520
	3/4	6	36	6.0	38	1120	1800
	1	6	34	5.7	35	1040	1940
	1 1/2	5	32	5.3	32	1010	2110

6.5	3/8	7.5	41	6.3	54	1460	1260
	1/2	7.5	39	6.0	45	1260	1520
	3/4	6	36	5.5	39	1150	1800
	1	6	34	5.2	36	1080	1940
	1 1/2	5	32	4.9	33	1040	2110
7.0	3/8	7.5	41	5.9	54	1500	1260
	1/2	7.5	39	5.6	46	1300	1520
	3/4	6	36	5.1	40	1180	1800
	1	6	34	4.9	36	1100	1940
	1 1/2	5	32	4.6	33	1060	2110
7.5	3/8	7.5	41	5.5	55	1530	1260
	1/2	7.5	39	5.2	47	1330	1520
	3/4	6	36	4.8	40	1210	1800
	1	6	34	4.5	37	1140	1940
	1 1/2	5	32	4.3	34	1090	2110
8.0	3/8	7.5	41	5.1	55	1560	1260
	1/2	7.5	39	4.9	47	1360	1520
	3/4	6	36	4.5	41	1240	1800
	1	6	34	4.3	37	1160	1940
	1 1/2	5	32	4.0	34	1110	2110

*See footnote at end of table.

(Continued on next page)

Table E-4. Suggested Trial Mixes for Air-Entrained Concrete of Medium Consistency with 3- to 4-inch Slump.
(Continued from previous page)

Water-cement ratio Gal per sack	With average sand—fineness modulus = 2.75			With coarse sand—fineness modulus = 2.90		
	Fine aggregate percent of total aggregate	Fine aggregate lb per cu yd of concrete	Coarse aggregate lb per cu yd of concrete	Fine aggregate percent of total aggregate	Fine aggregate lb per cu yd of concrete	Coarse aggregate lb per cu yd of concrete
4.5	53	1320	1190	54	1360	1150
	44	1130	1450	46	1180	1400
	38	1040	1730	39	1090	1680
	34	970	1870	36	1010	1830
	32	950	2030	33	990	1990
5.0	54	1400	1190	56	1440	1150
	46	1210	1450	47	1260	14000
	39	1110	1730	41	1160	1630
	36	1040	1870	37	1080	1830
	33	1010	2030	35	1050	1990
5.5	55	1460	1190	57	1500	1150
	46	1260	1450	48	1310	1400
	40	1160	1730	42	1210	1680
	37	1080	1870	38	1120	1830
	34	1050	2030	35	1090	1990
6.0	56	1500	1190	57	1540	1150
	47	1300	1450	49	1350	1400
	41	1190	1730	42	1240	1680
	37	1110	1870	39	1150	1830
	35	1090	2030	36	1130	1990

6.5	56	1530	1190	58	1570	1150
	48	1330	1450	50	1380	1400
	41	1220	1730	43	1270	1680
	38	1150	1870	39	1190	1830
	36	1120	2030	37	1160	1990
7.0	57	1570	1190	58	1610	1150
	49	1370	1450	50	1420	1400
	42	1250	1730	44	1300	1680
	38	1170	1870	40	1210	1830
	36	1140	2030	37	1180	1990
7.5	57	1600	1190	59	1640	1150
	49	1400	1450	51	1450	1400
	43	1280	1730	44	1330	1680
	39	1210	1870	41	1250	1830
	37	1170	2030	38	1210	1990
8.0	58	1630	1190	59	1670	1150
	50	1430	1450	51	1480	1400
	43	1310	1730	44	1360	1680
	40	1230	1870	41	1270	1830
	37	1190	2030	38	1230	1990

*Increase or decrease water per cubic yard by 3 per cent for each increase or decrease of 1 in. in slump, then calculate quantities by absolute volume method. For manufactured fine aggregate, increase percentage of fine aggregate by 3 and water by 17 lb. per cubic yard of concrete. For less workable concrete, as in pavements, decrease percentage of fine aggregate by 3 and water by 8 lb. per cubic yard of concrete.

Table E-5. Approximate Mixing Water Requirements for Different Slumps and Maximum Sizes of Aggregates.

Maximum size of aggregate, in.	Air-entrained concrete				Non-air-entrained concrete			
	Recommended average total air content, per cent†	Slump, in.			Approximate amount of entrapped air, per cent	Slump, in.		
		1 to 2	3 to 4	5 to 6		1 to 2	3 to 4	5 to 6
		Water, gal. per cu.yd. of concrete**				Water, gal. per cu.yd. of concrete**		
3⁄8	7.5	37	41	43	3.0	42	46	49
1⁄2	7.5	36	39	41	2.5	40	44	46
3⁄4	6.0	33	36	38	2.0	37	41	43
1	6.0	31	34	36	1.5	36	39	41
1½	5.0	29	32	34	1.0	33	36	38
2	5.0	27	30	32	0.5	31	34	36
3	4.0	25	28	30	0.3	29	32	34
6	3.0	22	24	26	0.2	25	28	30

*Adapted from Recommended Practice for Selecting Proportions for Concrete (ACI 613–54).
**These quantities of mixing water are for use in computing cement factors for trial batches. They are maximums for reasonably well-shaped angular coarse aggregates graded within limits of accepted specifications.
†Plus or minus 1 per cent.

Index

A
Aerial	204
Air	62
circulation	62, 131, 210
pockets	134
Aluminum, cutting	188
Approved	66
Atrium	182

B
Backhoe	44, 78
Backhoe removal	145
Baseboard heat	175
Basement	202
Bedrooms	158
Bearing walls	105
Below-grade-level method	29
Benefits	15
Blacktop	73
Block walls	88
Bookcases, wall	160
Brick, old	164
Building	66
Building codes	19, 56
appeals board	66
Building underground methods	27-30
Bulbs, colored	171
Bulldozer	44

C
Cable television	205
Capillary draw	134
Carpet	165
Caulking gun	154
Ceilings, creative	194
Cement mixer	46
Chimneys	117, 209
Clay as a water barrier	122
Coal	209
Concrete block	45, 188
filling holes	104
Concrete	46, 73, 80
footers	80
forming	110
mat	108
precast	116
prestressed	116
pump	112
truck	46
Condensation	132
Conduit	117
Cooling	177
Copper pipes	95
pipe cutter	148
Corridors	58
County regulations	23
Crane spread	142
Crickets	219
Crusher run	72

D
Decoration	157
ideas	173
Dehumidifier	133, 135, 177
Dew point	137
Domes	18, 60, 179, 181
alignment	217
constructing	182

foundation	218
sweating	218
Door openings	66
Doors, hanging	154
prehung	154
Drain pipe	86
Drawings	72
Driveway	67

E

Electric wiring	149
Electricians	150
Electricity, roughing-in	150
Electrical codes	65
Electrical power	211
Engineers	56
construction	106
professional	56
Entrance	202
Erosion	140
Excavating	22, 44

F

Fan, in-line	134
Fences	75
Fiberglass tub & shower unit	95
Financing	23
Finishing touches	197
Firing strips	154
Fixtures	170
hanging	170
side-mounted	170
Floor slab	48
Foam	116
Footers	46, 77
level & square	77
raking	84
shoveling	81
Formed walls	87
Foyer arrangement	133
Fuel savings	15
Furnace	176-177
Furniture	164

G

Garage	202
Gardens, indoor	18, 60, 168, 179
Gas	151
lines	31
Geothermic heat	16
Grading	131
final	144
Grass seed	145
Gravel	72
Ground breaking	36

H

Hacksaw	148
Half-and-half method	30
Hand railings	60
Heating	175
Heating-ventilation system	209
Heat	207
sun	219
Houses	18
shape	18
size	18
Humidity	135
Hydrostatic pressure	22

I

Insulating pipes	137
Insulation, earth	12
Insurance	38
Interior walls	51, 105
Into-the-hill method	27
Ivy, clinging	169

J

Jack hammer	86
Jacks	110

K

Kitchen	160

L

Land	19
mowing	74
restrictions	33
site	19
Lawyer's fees	42
Layout	157
Level-ground method	28
Level pegs	49
Lighting	170
Light, lack of	222
Lights, exterior	172
ground-level	170
Living requirements	105
Lot size	26

M

Macadam	73
Maintenance, exterior	17
Masonry	47
nails	154
Materials, availability	39
recycled	160
Means of egress	57
Mental preparation	12
Mirrors	157
Moisture treatments	120
Mortar	218

N

Nails	153
cut	154
masonry	154
Neighborhood restrictions	19
Neighbors, problem	223
Noise	204

P

Padding	165
Paint	165
Panel cement	154
Paneling	102
Panes	182, 217
acrylics	191
plastic	182
plexiglass	191
tinted	191
Perc test	32
Permanency	17
Physical preparation	12
Pipe fittings, buying	148
Plants	169, 219
Plastic	104
pipe	148
Plenum chamber	176
Plumbing	65, 147
inspector	85
maintenance	149
Plywood	98
Polyethylene	120
layers	120
sheets	134
Poured walls	87
Power air hammer	91
Pressed insulation board	122
Private attention	215
Property	18
conservation	18
cost	42
layout	41
lines	75
Public attention	214
Purchase, sample	42
PVC	148

Q

Quarries	72

R

Radio reception	204
Railroad ties	60
Real estate tax	43
Rebar	107
cutting	107
term "used"	107
Reception	204
radio	204
television	204
Regulators	211
Retaining walls	59
Roads	31
Roof	112
pouring	112-116
slab	193, 218
smoothness of	130
Rough lumber	98
Roughing-in electricity	150

S

Sandpaint	165
Saw, radial-arm	52
Scaffolding	110
Sensations, strange	203
Septic-sewer system	69
Setback	68
Sewage disposal	32
Sewer	65
drain vent pipes	65
pipe	85
Sheet metal duct systems	175
Sheet rock	100
attached to ceiling	194
Shelves, room-length	160
Shoring	97-104
Skylights	18, 179, 182
Smoke detectors	57
Snow	220
Soil testing	22
Solar	16
electric	211
heat	210
power	16
Solder	148
Sponge effect	134
Spread	140
crane	142
tractor	140
trailer	142
Sprinkler system	57
Stairs	65
Stakes	79
Steel	107
placement	110
posts	87
rod	107
Stone, old	164
Storage sheds	197
Sump pump	29
Surveying	71
Switches	211
dimmer	170

T

Tar baby	120
Telephone cables	31
wiring	151
Television reception	204
Theft factor	17
Timers, electric	172
Top soil	76
Torch outfit	51
Transit	71, 78

U

Utilities	151
bills	222

V

Vacuum	65, 209
Vents	175
Vibrator	115
Visitors	213, 221
negative attention	214
positive attention	213

W

Walls	51
bearing	105
block	88
formed	87
interior	51, 105
retaining	59
poured	87
Wall murals	158
Water	22
pipes	148
problems	22
Welder	181
Well	21
depths	21
drilling	32
Wind	212
generator	16, 212
power	212
Windmills	16
Windows	18
no	203
Wire mesh	108
Wiring	150
electric	149
telephone	151
Wood	63, 208
beams	110
old barn	160
stove	63, 208
Working hours, best	38

Z

Zoning regulations	19

How To Build Adobe Houses . . . etc.

Other TAB books by the author:

No. 2262 *How the Air Traffic Control System Works*
No. 2266 *Night Flying in Single-Engine Airplanes*
No. 2274 *The Illustrated Encyclopedia of General Aviation*

No. 1147
$12.95

How To Build Adobe Houses . . . etc.
by Paul Garrison

BLUE RIDGE SUMMIT, PA. 17214

FIRST EDITION

FIRST PRINTING—SEPTEMBER 1979

Copyright © 1979 by TAB BOOKS

Printed in the United States of America

Reproduction or publication of the content in any manner, without express permission of the publisher, is prohibited. No liability is assumed with respect to the use of the information herein.

Library of Congress Cataloging in Publication Data

Garrison, Paul.
　How to build adobe houses.

　Bibliography: p.
　Includes index.
　　1. Building, Adobe. 2. Adobe houses. I. Title.
TH4818.A3G37　　693.2'2　　79-17293
ISBN 0-6306-9755-1
ISBN 0-6306-1147-9 pbk.

ISBN 0-8306-9755-1
ISBN 0-8306-1147-9 pbk.

Contents

Introduction	...9

1 What is Adobe? ...11
    History of Adobe ...18
    Adobe Relics ...20
    Monumental Adobe Buildings ...26
    Modern Adobe Dwellings ...40

2 Doodles of Your Adobe Home ...53
    Doodling in Future Terms ...53
    Perfecting Your Doodles ...54
    Floor Plan ...55
    Professional Advice ...57
    Unconventional Designs ...58

3 A Little About A Lot ...61
    Where to Build ...61
    Practical Considerations ...62
    The Neighborhood ...63
    Legal Restrictions ...64

4 Strengths and Weaknesses of Adobe ...69
    Its Uses ...69
    Adobe Bricks ...70
    Taking it Step-By-Step ...70
    Becoming a Brickmaker ...72

5 From the Bottom Up ...79
    The Foundation ...79
    Digging the Trench ...80
    The Walls ...81
    The Second Story ...81

6 Building Your Adobe Home 87
- Walls 87
- Windows and Doors 88
- Are Walls Really Necessary? 98

7 Under Foot 101
- Floors 101
- Brick Flooring 101
- Floor Pattern 103
- Concrete Floor 105
- Ceramic Tile 106
- Vinyl Materials 107
- Wood Floor 108

8 Over Head 109
- Vigas 109
- Ceilings 114
- Interior Finish for Your Ceilings 116
- Keeping Dry 118
- Your Roof 118
- Roof and Ceiling Options 123

9 Entering Your Home 125
- Entry Hall 125
- Other Hallways 126

10 Main Living Quarters 129
- Living Room 129
- Den 132
- Kitchen 136
- Dining Area 140
- Bedrooms 144
- Bathrooms 152

11 Hobby Rooms 157
- Workshops 157
- Studios as Workshops 158
- A Painter's Studio 158
- A Photographer's Studio 160
- A Sculptor's Studio 161
- A Musician's Studio 161

12 Areas of Moderate Dimensions 163
- Utility Spaces 163
- Closets 166

13 Fireplaces 171
- Foundation 176
- Stem 178
- Firebox 182
- Throat 183
- Smoke Shelf 183
- Flue 183
- Shell 184
- Face 184
- Hearth 184

14 Outdoor Projects 187
- The Garage 187
- Patios 190
- Outdoor Barbeques 202
- Hornos 203
- Swimming Pools 208

15 Utilities and Plumbing 211
- Heating 211
- Cooling 213
- Electricity 214
- Gas 214
- Plumbing 214

16 Remodeling an Old Adobe 217
- Foundations 220
- Walls 221
- Floors 222
- Doors and Windows 222
- Ceilings 224
- Roofs 224
- Removing Walls 228
- Repairing Exterior Walls 229
- Reinforcing Old Foundations 230

17 Solar Adobe 231
- Solar Collectors 231
- Passive Solar Homes 238
- Greenhouse System 239
- Solar Home Costs 242

Glossary 245

Additional Reading 251

Index 253

Introduction

This book is not intended to miraculously transform the reader into a first-rate architect or an efficient contractor. Rather it will deal with the inherent beauty and flexibility of adobe as a building material which, to a much greater degree than any other such material, permits individual artistic expression in the planning and execution of a home or structure, while reducing the need to deal with such hard-to-handle modern building materials as steel and cement.

The potential adobe builder should think of himself as a sculptor designing a three-dimensional work of art which, incidentally, is also intended to serve as a comfortable dwelling for himself and his family. He will, of course, have to remember that it must include such prosaic necessities as bathrooms, kitchens, means of providing heat and ventilation, closets, storage space and so on. But all of these are part and parcel of any structure intended for human habitation and should in no way inhibit the degree of artistic expression used in the design of the basic exterior shape.

What this book will try to do is to dwell on the excitement of adobe building. There are endless possibilities in terms of form and shape which can and should be a delight to the eye when approached from any direction under all conceivable light conditions. There are chapters on the basic techniques involved in working with adobe, but the serious builder who will get his hands dirty and turn his dream sculpture into reality should get advice and help from men experienced in the actual back-breaking job of doing the real building. Advance research and listening to the experiences of others will prevent getting caught in time consuming and often costly mistakes. It will also help give the do-it-yourself builder a reasonably accurate estimate as to the amount of time and money he will have to devote to the project.

No matter how ambitious the builder, and no matter how outwardly simple the project to be built, the amateur architect-contractor is bound to overlook necessary and important details. He is likely to make mistakes in the consecutive order in which each individual task should be started and completed. He is likely to be overly optimistic with regard to the amount of time needed which tends to run from 2,000 to 3,000 man hours even for those who are skilled in the trade. Probably more than twice that amount will be needed for anyone undertaking such a job for the first time and planning to use the absolute minimum of expert and paid assistance.

While a detailed analysis of all the myriad of tasks involved may cause the project as a whole to appear staggering, it is, in fact, simply a large succession of small jobs. Each of them is a minor achievement, eventually adding up to the envisioned whole.

But enough of all this talk of time and money and aching muscles or calloused hands. Let's look at adobe itself, its history, its beauty and the visual excitement which it is capable of at the hands of a talented designer.

That, then, is one part of the purpose of this book. The other is to serve as a primer for amateur builders.

Paul Garrison

Chapter 1
What Is Adobe?

The word itself is commonly used to denote a number of different meanings. It stands for the clayey soil which, when appropriately treated, turns into a hard and weather resistant building material. It stands for the buildings made from this material and in some cases for structures made from other materials but conforming to what is generally referred to as the adobe style. And it also is used to describe the individual bricks made from dried adobe soil and constituting the primary structural ingredient in most adobe buildings (Fig. 1-1).

It is of a somewhat uncertain origin, described by Webster as having derived from the Arabic *at-tub* and the Coptic *tobe*, both meaning brick. On the other hand, the *Encyclopedia Britannica* claims it to be a derivative of the Spanish word *adobar*, meaning to plaster.

But be that as it may, adobe is simply plain ordinary mud, found in most of the more arid regions of the globe, consisting in varying proportions of clay, sand and a variety of organic matter. When mixed with water and subsequently dried it turns rock hard, though frequent exposure to excessive amount of moisture may cause it eventually to crumble and subsequently disintegrate (Fig. 1-2).

Primitive peoples, finding it readily available underfoot and easier to work with than lumber or rock with their simple or often no tools, started to use it thousands of years ago to build uncomplicated conical or round mudhuts as protection against the elements and enemies.

Fig. 1-1. Adobe bricks, made from adobe mud and sun-dried, are the primary building material in most adobe buildings.

Today, in many areas where the appropriate soil is readily available, adobe can be commercially purchased, usually in the form of adobe bricks. It is widely used in combination with lumber, cement blocks and other materials which permit maintaining its esthetic advantages (Fig. 1-3) while minimizing the detrimental qualities with reference to permanence. This is especially true in locations where frequent precipitation or sub-freezing temperatures would otherwise result in the need for frequent and annoying repairs.

Not everyone finds the adobe look pleasing (Fig. 1-4). It does not readily lend itself to the so-called California ranch-style houses with their immense expanse of picture windows and sliding glass doors (Figs. 1-5 through 1-8). Similarly no one in his right mind would think of using adobe to build a New England *saltbox*, and it is certainly not the ideal material for a high-rise structure, the multi-storied adobe "apartment house" at the Taos Pueblo in New Mexico not withstanding.

It is ideal for the single-family dwelling which will, if designed and constructed with love and the eye of an artist, look like no other anywhere and be one of a kind—a monument expressing the taste of its creator (Fig. 1-9).

Fig. 1-2. Adobe needs protection and constant attention. When left indefinitely exposed to moisture it will gradually disintegrate.

Fig. 1-3. Adobe, to a greater degree than any other building material, permits individual artistic expression in the planning and execution of a home.

Fig. 1-5. This home along the Camino del Monte Sol in Santa Fe maintains the typical adobe character.

Fig. 1-6. Older adobe homes such as this one often include carved wooden doors, vigas and row wood beams for lintels above windows and garage doors.

Fig. 1-4. The adobe look does not appeal to everyone.

Fig. 1-7. This home includes the typical adobe characteristic of rounded surfaces rather than sharp corners.

Fig. 1-8. Adobe walls often surround the property of an adobe home.

Fig. 1-9. Adobe offers endless possibilities in terms of form and shape which delight the eye when approached from any direction under varying light conditions.

Fig. 1-10. A carefully sculpted adobe wall encircles a small front patio in the front of a home on Camino del Monte Sol in Santa Fe.

Adobe means no sharp corners and no glass-smooth flat planes. It lends itself to all manner of sweeping curves, meandering lines and walls with just a sufficient suggestion of topography to catch the light (Fig. 1-10).

In the old days, when it was used without the addition of strengthening materials, it often resulted in massive structures with three or four-foot-thick walls and immense exterior buttresses blending into the outer surfaces. Then its superior insulating qualities kept outdoor cold and heat from seeping into the interior. Windows were kept small and doors to a minimum. Few examples of this kind of construction remain today with the possible exception of some of the more exciting churches erected by the Spaniards during the time of their occupation of much of the southwestern United States (Figs. 1-11 and 1-12).

HISTORY OF ADOBE

And that brings us to the history of adobe architecture in North America as originated by the Pueblo Indians many centuries before Columbus conned Queen Isabella into financing his westward trip to what he expected to be India; to the subsequent influence on style and construction by the Spanish conquerers and missionaries; and to the changes wrought by the gradual introduction of a variety of additional building materials and the acceptance of more modern construction methods.

Fig. 1-11. An excellent example of the massive building style often used in the construction of churches by the Spanish missionaries with the help of their Indian converts. This church is located near the Nambe Pueblo north of Santa Fe.

Fig. 1-12. The side view of the church in Nambe Pueblo shows how abutments have been built into the thick walls to give them extra strength. The canales stick out several feet from the roof to prevent draining rain water or melting snow from running down the side of the walls and impairing the adobe plaster.

ADOBE RELICS

The oldest remaining adobe structures in North America are the ruins (Fig. 1-13) of extremely complicated and apparently highly sophisticated Indian settlements, whose occupants, for no known reason, either died out or simply abandoned their homes to go elsewhere some two thousand years ago. No one knows where they went.

Chaco Canyon National Monument, an area of some 16 square miles in northwestern New Mexico, contains the ruins of thirteen great pueblos plus several hundred smaller ones, most said to date back to around 500 A.D., the time when the Anasazi Indians are said to have gradually relinquished their earlier nomadic existence in favor of agriculture and communal living. Using a combination of native rock and adobe, they built immense structures, housing the entire tribe in what was, in fact, one continuous building (Fig. 1-14). Of those in the Chaco Canyon area, Pueblo Bonito is the most famous and best preserved. Once, centuries ago, it rose five stories high, covered more than three acres and contained close to a thousand rooms including 34 kivas, circular ceremonial chambers devoted to religious functions.

What caused these people to one day simply walk away from their cities is not known. What is known is the fact that during the thirteenth century there was a period of little rain and prolonged drought, and other Indian tribes, those known today as the Apaches

Fig. 1-13. An aerial view of the ruins of the nearly 2,000 year old pueblos at Canyon National Monument, considered the cradle of the Indian pueblo civilization.

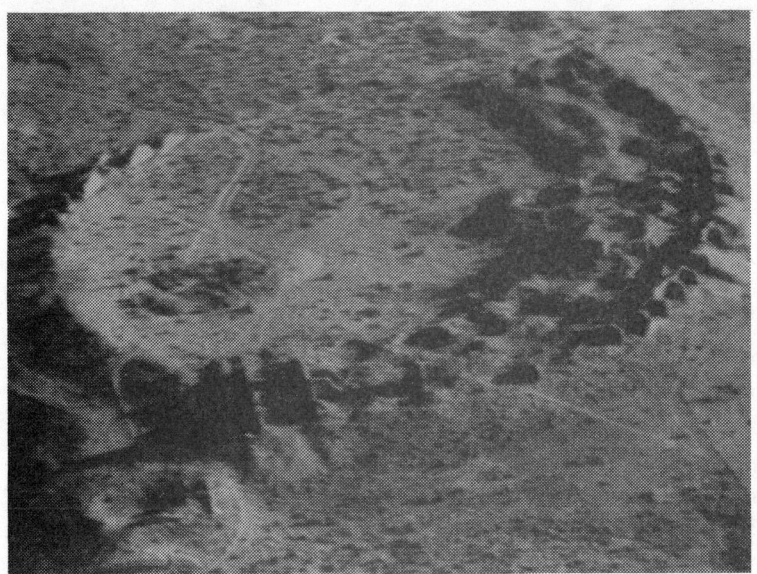

Fig. 1-14. More ruins of the nearly 2,000 year old Indian pueblos.

and Navajos, attracted by the apparent wealth of the Anasazi began raiding the pueblos for food. They were later renamed Pueblo Indians by the Spaniards—the Spanish word *pueblo* meaning town or village.

Fig. 1-15. A typical structure of the mesa built atop an outcropping against the side of the cliffs.

The Puebloans, in turn, searched for safer places in which to live, places which could more successfully be defended. Today the entire Four Corners area—the place where Arizona, Colorado, New Mexico and Utah meet—is dotted with cliff dwellings and intricate rock and adobe structures built into the near-vertical sides of sandstone cliffs and atop virtually inaccessible mesas. The best known among them are those at Puye Cliffs and in Bandelier National Monument, both near Santa Fe, New Mexico; in Mesa Verde National Park in southwestern Colorado; and in the still inhabited Acoma Pueblo, known as the Sky City, some 60 miles west of Albuquerque. Some miles west of Espanola in northern New Mexico the mesa known as Puye Cliffs rises steeply out of the surrounding terrain (Figs. 1-15 through 1-19). In centuries past, the forebearers of today's Santa Clara Pueblo Indians built veritable fortresses against and into the sides of the cliffs as a means of protection against roving nomadic Indian tribes and, in later years, the conquering Spaniards and Anglos. Using adobe bricks they constructed multi-storied dwellings, using vigas to separate the stories and to support the adobe roofs. The vigas were at one end, set into the relatively soft rock. Depending on the length used, they were left sticking out of the walls on the other end. Ladders were used to climb from one level to the next. They were pulled up in the event of an enemy attack. Figure 1-15 shows a typical two-story structure built atop an outcropping against the side of the cliffs. In Figure 1-16 you can

Fig. 1-16. Cliff dwellings are practically inaccessible. Note the top of a ladder at the far left leading into a natural cave.

Fig. 1-17. Some structures were built between natural rocks and were partially supported by them.

visualize the inaccessability of such cliff dwellings. The top of a ladder at the far left leads into a natural cave. Figure 1-17 shows a tall, narrow adobe brick structure built between natural rocks and partially supported by them. Note the round holes in the cliffs above which once held vigas for long-ago disintegrated dwellings. In Figure 1-18 all that is left to indicate past inhabitation is a ladder, leading from one narrow ledge to another. Again you can see the round holes which once upon a time supported vigas. The typical remains of what once was a sizeable cliff dwelling are seen in Figure 1-19. You can clearly see by the viga holes where the outer buildings stood in front of an entire series of natural caves.

This mesa originally had no natural access from the surrounding areas. Today a somewhat precipitous road leads to the top, making it possible to drive up. An acre or more is covered with the ruins of what once must have been a veritable adobe city. Stripped of the protecting plaster by centuries of weather, the adobe bricks show where hundreds of rooms housed the Peublo Indians (Fig. 1-20). Several circular kivas were excavated and constructed underground. Some are still in fair shape. Among the rubble there still

Fig. 1-18. A ladder led from one narrow ledge to another.

remains a two-story structure, bearing witness to the fact that this was once a multi-story peublo (Fig. 1-21).

Though each of today's pueblos represents an independent tribe with its own individual language or dialect, they do all share a mutual history and tradition. Thus it is easy to see why the architectural styles, having survived to this day, are of common imagery and methods of construction (Figs. 1-22 through 1-25). They have rounded corners, flat roofs serving as terraces for upper stories and rough-hewn outdoor ladders instead of indoor stairs. The rooms themselves are small with ceilings of vigas and latillas supporting the roof. Small corner fireplaces provide a degree of warmth during the long New Mexico winters.

In Indian tradition applying the outer finish to a dwelling was the work of the women. Close examination of the sculptured walls often still shows where loving female hands smoothed the adobe surface (Fig. 1-26). It is this peculiar characteristic of adobe—the fact that it permits itself to be shaped and formed by hand rather than inanimate tools—which gives it its unique appearance.

While much of what we think of today as adobe architecture is derived from the work of the North American Indians, adobe is by no means exclusive to this part of the world. It has been and still is widely used in some of the more arid regions of Africa where the

Dogon people of Mali used adobe to sculpt incredibly intricate temples. Farther north the Arabs used it to build entire towns and villages, many of them strikingly similar in style to those of the Indians. Mexico, too, as well as Central and South America are dotted with fine examples of using adobe in combination with native rock and other conveniently available matter as building material.

There are entire adobe cities in India and as far away as China. The famous lamaseries in Tibet are built of adobe. As a matter of fact, historians who have made a study of the subject claim that to this day close to half the population of the entire world is living in adobe-type structures.

As far as North America is concerned, it is only logical that with the arrival of the white man in the new world, the traditional style of Indian architecture underwent much adjustment and change.

For over three hundred years, from 1539 to 1848, much of the southwestern United States was either under Spanish occupation or a part of Mexico. Thus the Spaniards exerted a strong, and to some degree lasting, influence on architectural styles. Much of it is due to the individual desire to express personal success and wealth through magnificent mansions. This was an idea which had been entirely foreign to the Indian culture which believed that each being was as an

Fig. 1-19. Typical remains of cliff dwellings.

Fig. 1-20. Adobe bricks show where hundreds of rooms housed Pueblo Indians at this mesa.

integral part of the overall environment with neither right nor desire for land ownership or personal possession.

MONUMENTAL ADOBE BUILDINGS

Adobe did continue to be the primary building material, and in the early days of the Spanish occupation the basic Indian style was reasonably faithfully followed. One good example of this includes the Government Palace in Santa Fe, built entirely of adobe in 1609. It is the oldest public building in the United States. Erected atop an old pueblo, it incorporates some of its original walls in its structure (Figs. 1-27 through 1-29).

Another example is the so-called Oldest House, also in Santa Fe (Figs. 1-30 and 1-31).

The many churches built by Spanish missionaries with Indian labor offer more examples. Buttresses of adobe and rock were built to strengthen the walls of the San Miguel in Santa Fe (Fig. 1-32). This church is considered to be the oldest church in the United States.

Some of the most magnificent examples include the church at Racho de Taos (Figs. 1-33 and 1-34) and the massive adobe church at Nambe, New Mexico (Fig. 1-35).

Fig. 1-21. Among the rubble of this mesa, there still remains a two story structure.

Fig. 1-22. The multi-story Indian pueblo near Taos, New Mexico. This pueblo is known to have been continuously inhabited for over 700 years. It is still in regular use today.

Fig. 1-23. Another view of an Indian pueblo in New Mexico that is still in use today.

Fig. 1-24. Flat roofs serve as terraces for the upper stories of this Indian pueblo.

Fig. 1-25. Indian pueblos used rough-hewn outdoor ladders instead of indoor stairs.

Fig. 1-26. The outer finish of a dwelling was usually smoothed by the hands of women.

Fig. 1-27. The oldest public building in the United States is the Governor's Palace in Santa Fe.

Fig. 1-28. The Governor's Palace in Santa Fe was built in 1609 atop an old Indian pueblo.

Fig. 1-29. Some of its old walls are still incorporated in the structure of the Governor's Palace in Santa Fe.

Fig. 1-30. This very old adobe in Santa Fe is claimed to be the oldest house in the United States.

Fig. 1-31. This so-called oldest house in the United States is often visited by tourists in Santa Fe.

Fig. 1-32. The San Miguel Church in Santa Fe is considered to be the oldest church in the United States.

Fig. 1-33. A magnificent example of adobe architecture includes the church at Taos Pueblo.

The Santuario de Chimayo which is halfway between Santa Fe and Taos in northern New Mexico is one of the finer examples of early Spanish use of adobe in church construction (Fig. 1-36). Facing a cemetery surrounded by an adobe wall with a beautiful old wooden gate (Fig. 1-37), the Santuario is built atop a place where the earth is

Fig. 1-34. The adobe church at Taos Pueblo has recently been restored.

Fig. 1-35. The adobe church at Nambe, New Mexico is massive.

said to have miraculous healing qualities. An opening in the floor inside the church permits worshippers to dig up small quantities of this earth which is then used in order to try to cure a number of ailments.

Fig. 1-36. This old Spanish adobe church is still in regular use today.

Fig. 1-37. The Sanctuario de Chimayo faces a cemetery surrounded by an adobe wall with this beautiful old wooden gate.

Fig. 1-38. The construction of this church at Las Trampas included massive walls.

Fig. 1-39. A close look at the turret of the church at Las Trampas shows the deteriorating effects of weather.

Figures 1-38 through 1-41 are four views of the church at Las Trampas, located on a back road leading from Santa Fe to Taos. The massive walls, thickened further by repeated applications of more and more plaster, in their not quite straight lines bear witness to hand work done over the years. A close look at the turrets shows the deteriorating effects of weather and the impending need for one more coat of plaster. Wood was used effectively to create simple but pleasing designs. As is typical of most of the churches of that period, this one is also surrounded by an adobe wall with a wooden gate.

Fig. 1-40. Wood was used to create simple but pleasing designs on the adobe church at Las Trampas.

El Cristo Rey, located on Canyon Road in Santa Fe, is said to be one of the largest adobe structures of its kind. Awe-inspiring in its massive simplicity (Fig. 1-42), it bears witness to the beauty of line, lights and shade which is one of the unique qualities of building with adobe. The covered walk to the rear door of the church uses raw vigas to support an adobe-mud roof, using flat lumber in a herringbone design as decking (Figs. 1-43 and 1-44).

An elegantly carved front door brings you inside (Fig. 1-45). The interior of the El Cristo Rey church combines simplicity of form with intricate wood carvings. The high viga and latilla ceiling with its handcarved corbels on either side helps to effect the hushed quiet which we expect of a church interior (Fig. 1-46). An early Spanish handcarved crucifix is the sole decoration on one of the walls inside El Cristo Rey (Fig. 1-47).

Also included here should be the monumental church at Acoma (Figs. 1-48 and 1-49), not because of any particular architectural distinction but because it seems quite incredible to us today how its builders were able to bring the huge quantities of building material up that torturous crevice which served as the only means of getting from the valley floor to the top of the mesa. The torturous narrow path was the only access to the Acoma Pueblo atop the mesa in the old days (Figs. 1-50 through 1-53). All materials to build the huge church as well as the dwellings had to be carried by hand up this path.

Fig. 1-41. The church at Las Trampas was surrounded by an adobe wall with a wooden gate.

Fig. 1-42. El Cristo Rey is awe-inspiring in its massive simplicity.

Fig. 1-45. The elegantly carved front door to the Cristo Rey Church.

A final example is the Fine Arts Museum on Palace Avenue in Santa Fe, generally considered one of the finest examples of the use of adobe in a public building (Figs. 1-54 and 1-55). In order to maintain its beauty and structural integrity it, too, needs frequent attention. On the shaded part of the wall in the center of the

Fig. 1-43. A covered walk brings you to the rear door of El Cristo Rey.

Fig. 1-44. Flat lumber is used in a herringbone design as decking for this adobe church.

Fig. 1-46. The interior of the El Cristo Rey church combines simplicity of form with intricate wood carvings.

photograph of Figure 1-54 we can see where a section of plaster has weathered away, and will soon have to be repaired in order to prevent water from seeping into the walls themselves.

MODERN ADOBE DWELLINGS

As time passed tools began to replace human hands and the pleasantly rounded surfaces of the older adobes were replaced by sharp corners. Instead of vigas throwing their slanted shadows across the walls, roof edges were lined with fired red brick, arranged

Fig. 1-48. This immense adobe and rock church is at the Acoma Pueblo.

Fig. 1-49. The Acoma Pueblo church turret.

Fig. 1-47. An early Spanish crucifix decorates El Cristo Rey.

in all manner of intricate designs. Thus a style was born which still remains popular today, known as *Territorial* (Figs. 56 and 57). Though originally also built primarily of adobe, its basic character had been lost and by now few would think of using that word with reference to a territorial home.

By now, with the continuing migration of people from all parts of the country to the Southwest, things seem to be coming full circle. Brand new homes are being built in large numbers by amateurs and professionals (Fig. 1-58) not only using adobe as the primary building

Fig. 1-50. This narrow path led to Acoma Pueblo.

material (Fig. 1-59), but also closely imitating the style of the traditional Indian dwelling.

An example of an older Indian dwelling is found in Figure 1-60. This small corner deep inside the Taos Pueblo illustrates how each room or group of rooms opens onto a small outdoor balcony. During

Fig. 1-51. At one time the only access to Acoma Pueblo was by this tortuous path.

the warmer seasons the balcony serves as the primary living area. There are no indoor stairs, therefore ladders are everywhere, providing access to the upper stories. In centuries past they provided protection from enemies since the ladders could be pulled up, making assault on the inhabitants of the pueblo difficult. The adobe-clad chimneys bear witness to the profusion of fireplaces inside. Through the opening between the two walls at the bottom we see a corner of a *horno*, still used today for the purpose of baking bread.

Fig. 1-52. Huge quantities of building material were carried up this path to build Acoma Pueblo atop the mesa.

Modern adobe buildings naturally vary from the original designs slightly. The rooms are now large and there are more and bigger windows. Also, instead of outdoor ladders, indoor staircases lead to upper stories. Poured cement or cement blocks are used for foundations, and in many instances lumber is incorporated with the adobe bricks in the construction of walls. But both inside and out most builders use much care to do away with sharp corners and angles, replacing them with the pleasantly rounded sculptured look of the ancient adobes (Fig. 1-61).

Fig. 1-53. Hand and footholds are worn into the rock from generations of use.

Figures 1-62 through 1-65 are perfect examples of how modern architects and builders have been able to adapt modern building materials to reproduce the traditional adobe style with a considerable degree of faithfulness. Figure 1-62 shows the multi-story Taos Pueblo, which is known to have been continuously used as living quarters by the Taos Pueblo Indians for over seven centuries, dating

Fig. 1-54. The Fine Arts Museum in Santa Fe is generally considered one of the finest examples of the use of adobe in a public building.

Fig. 1-55. Intricate carving distinguishes the balcony above the front entrance to the Fine Arts Museum.

Fig. 1-56. The Sena Plaza in Santa Fe is one of the more outstanding examples of the Territorial style of building with adobe. Note the intricate brickwork along the roof.

Fig. 1-57. A modern home which copies the traditional Territorial style.

Fig. 1-58. New adobe homes are being built by amateurs and professionals.

Fig. 1-59. Many new homes are using adobe as the primary building material.

Fig. 1-60. Groups of rooms upon rooms are remnants of old Indian adobe dwellings.

Fig. 1-61. Liberal use of adobe permits the builder considerable liberty in the design of an individual home, as is obvious in this large hillside dwelling being built north of Santa Fe.

Fig. 1-62. The multi-story Taos Pueblo has been kept in excellent repair by the Indians.

back to the thirteenth century or possibly earlier. Rising in places up to five stories, it has been kept in excellent repair by the Indians by constantly replastering the walls to replace the adobe washed away by rain and melting snow.

Fig. 1-63. A brand new condominium complex, built to resemble the adobe style, is actually constructed of conventional concrete block, lath and plaster.

Fig. 1-64. A modern adobe style condominium complex can be found in New Mexico.

Even commercial buildings, hotels, apartment houses and condominiums, though, in fact using little or no adobe in the construction, are painstakingly finished to look like traditional adobes (Figs. 1-63 and 1-64).

Figure 1-65 is of the newest, most elegant, most expensive hotel in Santa Fe, the Inn at the Loretto. Built in 1974 and 1975, it is constructed of concrete, lathband plaster, rises to four stories (the maximum permitted in Santa Fe) and carefully copies the traditional Indian style. In Santa Fe, the Historical Society has been eminently successful in maintaining a pleasing harmony of architectural style

Fig. 1-65. A new and elegant hotel in Santa Fe is constructed of concrete and lathband plaster.

Chapter 2
Doodles Of Your Adobe Home

Bill Lear, the famous designer of airplanes and inventor of the car radio, eight track stereo and a great variety of other electronic marvels, once said that the most important part in designing anything is the time spent doodling. "You do a good job doodling, and chances are you'll come up with a good design."

While, at the time, he was talking about designing an airplane, the advice is just as valid when it comes to designing a home.

From the moment you first start thinking in terms of building a new home, it's a good idea to keep a pencil and paper handy to write down anything that comes to mind that might be a desirable feature. The number of bedrooms, guest rooms, full, three-quarter or half baths, living room, dining area, den, closets, work room, storage space, entry hall, pantry, the size and kind of kitchen, patios and other outdoor areas such as balconies or verandahs, garage or carport, flower gardens, lawns, etc. The list of things which may be important to one person and meaningless to another is endless.

DOODLING IN FUTURE TERMS

Think not only in terms of today, but tomorrow and five and ten years from now. Today's young children soon grow into teenagers and young adults with different needs. You aren't going to get any younger either and steps which may be fine today could turn into a chore a decade from now.

Think in terms of convenience. Can the groceries be unloaded from the car and brought into the house on a rainy day without you and them getting soaked? Are there going to be enough closets not only for clothes, coats and hats, but for linens, for liquor, and above all for all the junk that tends to accumulate over the years while a house is being lived in?

With all of this in mind, start to doodle. For this you don't need a ruler and you don't have to worry about exact measurements. Just make rough drawings. Don't be satisfied with the first, second or even third. Make dozens, hundreds. The more you doodle, the clearer a picture you'll start to get in your head as to the kind of house that would really be right for you and your family.

PERFECTING YOUR DOODLES

When you think you've got something that feels right, then is the time to get a ruler. Buy yourself an architect's scale and use it to transpose the result of your doodling into an actual plan. Use a scale of a ¼ inch to 1 foot and you'll be able to get a plan for the entire house and its surroundings on one reasonably sized sheet of paper.

The Basics

Certain basics must be kept in mind. No room should be wider than 20 feet regardless of length, or structural problems will develop. The smallest bathroom size for a full bath, including the tub, sink, and toilet, is about 8 by 5 feet. Standard tubs measure 5 feet and nonstandard tubs, whether larger or smaller, tend to cost nearly twice as much. Closets for clothes should be 2 feet deep, hallways should not be narrower than 3 feet and standard kitchen counter tops are 25 inches wide. Standard doors are 30 inches wide. But remember, appliances and large furniture will have to be brought into the house; and the doors the larger pieces will come through must be of adequate size. If stairs are involved, each step should be not less than 7 and not more than 8 inches high. They should be 10 inches deep. If you have or plan to buy oversized pieces of furniture or a larger than normal refrigerator or freezer, be sure to allow for the space needed to accommodate them.

Grouping Rooms

Where possible, keep in mind that it saves money to group rooms which require plumbing in relative proximity to one another, but don't ruin the whole plan with such considerations. A few hundred dollars spent on extra plumbing is going to be a drop in the bucket in the overall scheme of things.

Fig. 2-1. Windows in a restored old adobe catch the rays of the setting sun and offer an always exciting view of the ever-changing sunsets.

Orientation

Think in terms of orientation. Some rooms will receive the morning sun, some the evening sun and some will have a view (Fig. 2-1). It would be foolish to have the morning sun hit the garage and the best view outside a guest room window.

Separation of Activities

Think in terms of separation of activities. You may want the children's area, which usually means clutter and noise, separated from the rest of the house. Will it be possible to contain the smell of cooking in the kitchen area or will it permeate the entire place? Do you enjoy eating outdoors and, if so, is it going to be easy to take the food out to the patio without dragging it all across the living room rug?

FLOOR PLAN

The overall floor plan may, of course, vary considerably with the size of your lot, your own personal preferences and, last but by no means least, the amount of money you can afford to spend. In days past, when settlers had to worry about protecting themselves and their families from the dangers associated with the absence of law enforcement as we know it today, many homes took on the character of a veritable fortress. The house would be built like a rectangular wall of rooms around a large patio with only one entrance, large enough to admit horses, wagons and livestock. Outside

Fig. 2-2. The Sena Plaza, originally a family home built around a large rectangular patio, today houses stores, offices and a restaurant.

windows were kept to a minimum and all family living took place within the confines of the house and patio. An excellent and rather spectacular example of this type of home is the Sena Plaza in Santa Fe (Fig. 2-2). Today, instead of being a family home, it houses a variety of stores, offices and a restaurant. Another is the Governor's Palace, built in the early 17th century atop an old Indian pueblo and incorporating some of the original adobe walls (Figs. 1-27, 1-28, and 1-29).

Today this kind of floor plan would be excessively wasteful in terms of space, not to mention its impracticality. Still, the idea of spreading the house over a large area may be very appealing to some people. Others prefer to think in terms of a compact unit with all rooms in close proximity to one another. An important consideration in this respect is the climate. In areas with long summers and mild winters it might be perfectly feasible to think in terms of a sleeping unit, a cooking and eating unit, a play and entertainment unit and so on. To use an extreme example, they could all be connected by covered outdoor walks. Or, alternately, several wings could be devoted to the different activities, extending from a central connecting area with individual patios between them. The overall square footage needed for such a plan may not be much greater than for one in which all rooms adjoin each other. Also, since the overall cost of construction depends largely on the total amount of square footage, it might only be slightly more expensive.

PROFESSIONAL ADVICE

In any case, whatever type of floor plan appeals to you, it would be advisable to take your ideas to a professional architect or builder, preferably the former, and discuss them at length. The past experience of such professionals is worth whatever it may cost in terms of

Fig. 2-3. Adobe lends itself to many unconventional designs and shapes.

Fig. 2-4. There are round adobe homes and oval ones and others with multi-story towers.

preventing you from making expensive and impractical mistakes.

Use their advice and knowledge with reference to practical things, such as heating, plumbing, building code requirements and so on. However, don't let them talk you out of the individuality in terms of design. Many commercial builders and some architects seem to be incapable of thinking in terms of anything except the thoroughly conventional. Faced by a lot with an unusual topography, the first thing they're likely to do is hire a bulldozer to flatten the whole thing into a characterless city lot and then put up a house that looks like a million others.

UNCONVENTIONAL DESIGNS

The whole charm of using adobe as a primary building material is that it lends itself to unconventional designs and shapes (Fig. 2-3). There are round adobe homes and oval ones (Fig. 2-4), some partially underground and others with multi-story towers. Just by driving around Santa Fe and the surrounding countryside one can find dozens of entirely different design concepts, each representing the individual taste and needs of the person or family for whom it was conceived (Fig. 2-5).

Fig. 2-5. Each adobe home represents the individual tastes of the family living in it.

Some are the expression of a desire for communal family living with privacy for the individual reduced to a minimum. They might consist of a large space with cooking, eating and living areas, but a minimum of separating walls or doors. Some will have large window areas to bring a feeling of the outside into the house, while others have reduced the size and number of windows to a minimum, preferring to shut out the outside when living indoors. Some are all on one level and in others each room is a step or two above or below the level of the next. In still others a desire for individual privacy produced a multitude of individual rooms, studios, workshops, dens and possibly separate guest houses.

This is going to be your home, and the way you design and build it is going to strongly influence you and your family's life style for years to come. The idea is to make the home fit the life style you are comfortable with. You shouldn't have to adjust your life style to the house. Otherwise you might as well buy a ready-made house and eliminate the bother of planning and building.

Chapter 3
A Little About A Lot

Wanting to build a house is one thing. Finding the right piece of land to build it on is something else. The selection of a building site is probably the most important single decision that has to be made. A house, even after it has been built, can be enlarged, renovated and even changed to some degree, but the location of the lot, its relation to the surroundings, its topography, and in most cases, its size cannot be changed.

WHERE TO BUILD

What kind of lot appeals to you is a matter of personal preference, coupled with a variety of purely practical considerations. There are nice, orderly rectangular building sites on level ground, or there are odd-shaped plots on hillsides or lots sliced in half by an arroyo which is probably dry all year except for a day or two when the melting snow turns it into a churning river.

Figure 3-1 illustrates a large hillside home under construction. A mixture of adobe, concrete blocks and lumber is being used. The walls are up, door and window openings are in place and the vigas are in place. The chimney at the right, sticking up above the yet unfurnished roof, bears witness to the location of one of several fireplaces in this building.

In the construction of the home in Fig. 3-2, which is located against a steep hillside, the concrete-block stem was built up to an unusual height since it has to double as a retaining wall. One story is more or less complete with a second story in the early stages of being built. Note the wooden pole nailed to the side of the wall to assure that the upper wall surface remains perfectly vertical.

There are other lots bordering on paved streets and others stuck away somewhere in the boondocks which require the building of a road in order to be accessible. Or it may be located on a narrow, steep road which becomes impassable during the snow season, except by means of a four-wheel drive vehicle or by using chains (Fig. 3-3). There are lots with spectacular views and others stuck in little valleys surrounded by hills or mountains. And then, of course, there are those which fall within your budget and those which you may fall in love with but can't afford.

PRACTICAL CONSIDERATIONS

First, let's look at the practical considerations. If you have school age kids, or if you and your wife must be at an office or place of business five days a week, you may prefer to think of a location reasonably close to your town or city, rather than one which involves having to drive long distances day after day.

Fig. 3-1. A large adobe home is under construction on a hillside.

Fig. 3-2. Often the concrete-block system is built up to an unusual height for homes built on a hillside.

THE NEIGHBORHOOD

If that is the case, look at the surroundings, the other homes in the area and the people who will be your immediate neighbors. Whatever you see you'll be stuck looking at for years to come because the basic looks and character of a neighborhood aren't likely to change. Also check on such things as utilities, sewers and the like. The ease or difficulty with which access to these can be achieved may make a multi-thousand-dollar difference in the cost of your home. Even the quality of television reception is a major importance to a lot of us these days.

Fig. 3-3. Some lots are located on narrow steep roads which can become virtually impassable during rain or snow seasons, except by four wheel drive vehicles.

LEGAL RESTRICTIONS

Check on easements and restrictions which affect the potential orientation of the house on the lot. There may be minimum distance requirements which would prevent you from building as close to the lot line as you would like. And be sure that the seller will guarantee a clear title. You don't want to take a chance of getting involved in some sort of legal hassle over some ancient and obscure dispute involving the lot of your choice.

Regardless of whether you want to buy close to town or miles away from the madding crowd, the following is a simple checklist of subjects to keep in mind.

Location. This includes privacy; distance from schools, markets, office, etc.; and traffic problems, if any.

Size and shape. Knowing roughly the kind and size of home you have in mind, is the lot large enough and of the shape which will permit you to build the house you are envisioning?

Surroundings. Are the surroundings to your liking? Remember that even if you are planning to enclose the entire area with an adobe wall (Fig. 3-4), you'll have to look at the surroundings every time you come or go.

Access. Is the place easy to get to, or will you have to spend a small fortune to build an access road or driveway which will remain passable under all weather conditions?

Utilities. Are water, electricity and gas readily available? Bringing in an electric line from some distant spot can cost thousands of dollars. Water is a must. If no water connection is available, are you prepared to drill a well? Do you have the right to do so? If no gas line is nearby, are you prepared to operate with LPG, and if so, is it available at an acceptable price?

Sewers or septic tanks. Is there a sewer and, if so, what will it cost to be connected to it? Will you be stuck with the cost of tearing up a portion of the pavement of the street and then having it replaced? If no sewer is available, is there adequate space somewhere on the lot to bury a septic tank and room for the associated leach field? Septic tanks do have to be pumped out from time to time, therefore there must be some kind of access for the pump truck.

Topography. Is the ground flat or on the side of a steep hill? How easy or difficult and in turn, expensive, will it be to bring all the needed building materials to the site and to pour the foundation? Will there be a need to erect retaining walls? Is the ground undisturbed and thus capable of supporting the foundation and the structure? Is there fill which would require digging deep down to get to firm ground?

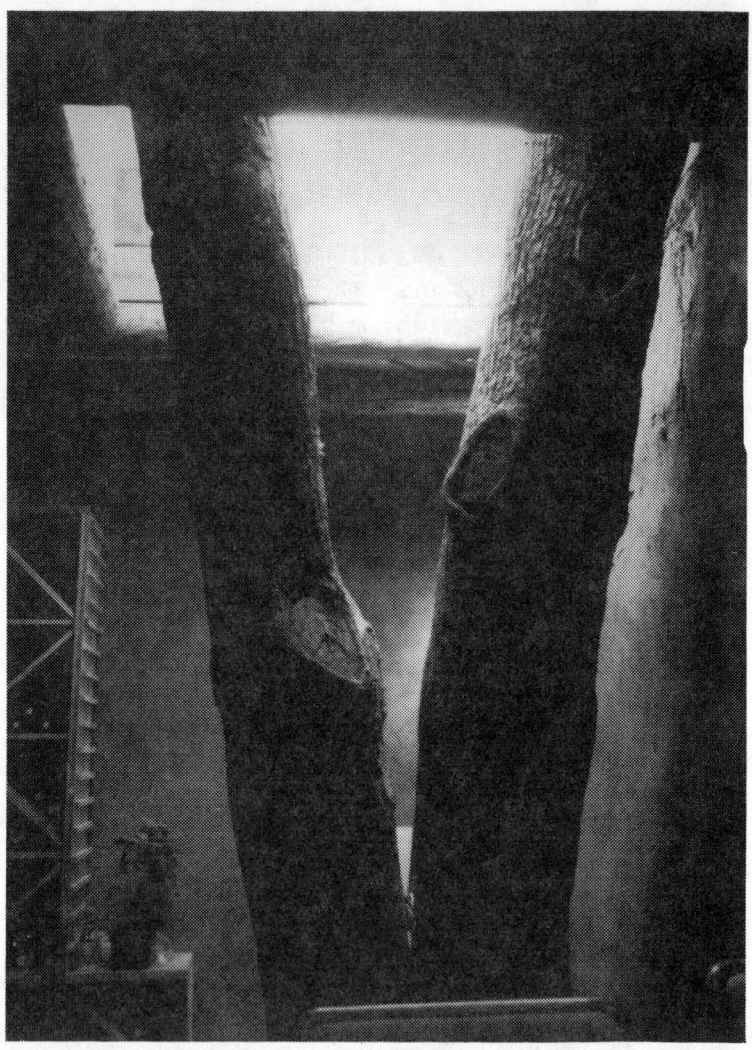

Fig. 3-5. Even if there is a tree in the way of the house, you might wish to consider building around it. This huge tree happily grows right through the dining room at the Periscope, a Santa Fe restaurant.

Trees and shrubs. Remember that it takes years for trees and shrubs to grow to any respectable size. Any greenery which isn't in the way of the actual house should be left undisturbed. Most commercial builders seem to love to totally denude a building site, resulting in houses sitting sort of naked on an ugly piece of bare earth. It is often worthwhile when planning the house to keep in mind existing vegetation and to take full advantage of it.

Fig. 3-4. An adobe wall offers privacy for the inhabitants of this small adobe home.

Legalities. Deal with a reputable real estate agent and a lawyer. Be sure you know all zoning restrictions and what you can and cannot do. Ascertain the exact wording and meaning of easements and other covenants which affect your property. Sometimes, if it's important, they can be changed or modified. However, that usually involves lawyers and considerable time and expense.

Resale value. Since the lot hasn't yet been bought or the house built, the idea of the resale value may be far from your mind. Still, unless you are absolutely certain that you'll want to spend the rest of your life in the place, the subject should at least be thought about. Granted, real estate values have been steadily rising for years and the trend is not likely to be reversed in the foreseeable future. But much of this increase in value is offset by the constantly rising inflation. If the time should come when, for one reason or another, you would want to or have to sell, is it the kind of place for which a buyer can readily be found?

Chapter 4
Strengths And Weaknesses Of Adobe

Remember when on visits to the sea as a child you built sand castles with all manner of turrets and carefully sculptured balconies, only to see all of your magnificent handiwork collapse upon itself with the first wave of the incoming tide?

Well, the same thing can happen to your adobe home unless you study and learn to understand the peculiarities of this unique building material, its strengths and its weaknesses.

ITS USES

Since time immemorial adobe has been used in a wide variety of different ways, but basically the methods of use can be divided into three classifications. One such method, probably the oldest and least satisfactory, is to simply mix the soil with sufficient water to produce a sticky paste and then to pour and shape that paste into long, narrow mounds. You let them dry and then repeat the process until something resembling a wall rises from the ground. This may have been a workable process when building a primitive igloo-type of shelter, but it is totally unsatisfactory for the kind of construction we think of today for even the simplest dwelling.

Another method known to have been used by the Indians and others is to prepare some sort of form from wood, branches or animal hides. Then fill this form with adobe mud and let it harden. Afterwards, the cast-form is removed. This is basically the method used in pouring premixed cement in the construction of modern buildings. A variation on the same idea, also used by some of the

Indians in centuries past, is to weave basket-like containers and pour the adobe mud into them. Let them dry and harden in the sun and then pile these more or less ball-shaped building blocks upon one another, smearing adobe over the whole thing to hold them together.

ADOBE BRICKS

This last method is, of course, the precurser of today's preferred method, namely the use of precast adobe bricks of a given size. The generally accepted dimensions of these bricks are 14 × 10 × 4 inches. They are produced by pouring the adobe mud into a wooden frame, removing the frame and then letting them dry in the sun. There is no particular reason why these bricks should be of the dimension noted above, except that smaller sizes would require vastly greater numbers of bricks to construct a given size wall and larger ones would be simply too heavy to be easily moved. As it is, a 14 × 10 × 4-inch adobe brick weighs 30 pounds.

No one knows how this particular proportion of the adobe brick was arrived at. It simply was the accepted size and brickmakers continued to use it as a standard, not worrying about the reason why. Interestingly enough, during some excavations in Egypt, adobe bricks were unearthed showing the same 14 × 10 × 4-inch dimension. Scientifically tested for age, they proved to be over 5,000 years old.

The adobe brick is the basic ingredient of any adobe structure built today. It can be purchased commercially from various companies. Most of these companies are located in New Mexico around the Santa Fe area. The price for the number of bricks needed to construct a given-size wall is comparable to the cost of standard bricks needed for a similar amount of square-footage.

Alternately, you can make them yourself and they won't cost you a thing, except the price of some rather basic tools and a transition period during which your muscles have to get used to working harder than they are likely to be used to.

TAKING IT STEP-BY-STEP

Before doing anything else, spend much time talking to people, people who are either in the process of building, or those who have done so. Also read all available material on the subject and get your head thoroughly filled with anything related to adobe. Not everyone you talk to or who's work you read will agree with everyone else. Concentrate on the ones who seem to make the most sense to you

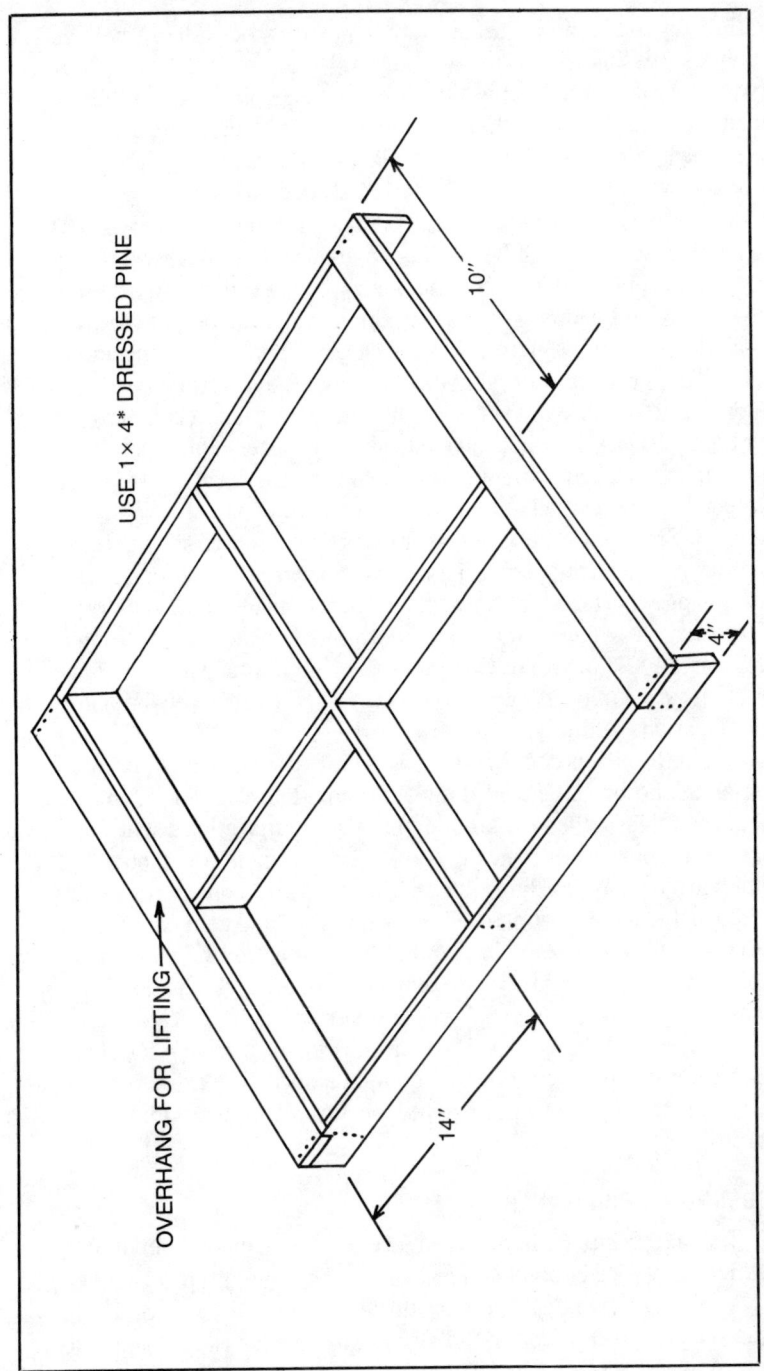

Fig. 4-1. Form for pouring adobe bricks.

and then try to follow whatever method has worked well for them as closely as possible.

Also spend some time kibitzing. Go to a place where abode bricks are being made, either commercially or by an individual, and just simply stand around and watch. Seeing is learning. If whoever is doing the work seems willing to talk, ask questions.

Eventually you'll be convinced that you know as much as you need to know, and you'll be getting anxious to get your own hands dirty. At this point get hold of someone with experience and take him to your chosen building site and let him get a good look at the soil. Not all the mud under your feet is necessarily ideal for making adobe bricks. Too much clay content will cause excessive shrinkage during the drying process, while too much sand may cause crumbling. It may be necessary to mix the soil available on your plot of land with some other soil from some nearby or even distant location. If you're not certain, mix a small amount of the selected soil with water and make just a few bricks, possibly using several different soil mixtures to arrive at a means of comparison. The more time you spend at this testing stage learning just how much water it takes to get the right consistency, learning to make a smooth mix and seeing how long it takes for the test bricks to dry under the temperature and humidity conditions at your location, the less likely it will be that you'll run into miscalculations and mistakes.

You have now come to a critical juncture in your transformation from an adobe dreamer and doodler to an adobe builder. Don't be stubborn. Making these tests may have been more hard work and more time consuming than you had anticipated. If the thought of multiplying this by the huge factor that must be considered when thinking in terms of an entire building seems beyond your capabilities in terms of either time or brute muscle power, you might be a lot better advised to dig into your savings account, pick up the phone and simply order the appropriate number of adobe bricks from a commercial supplier. You also better start looking around for some help, preferably people who have done this sort of work before and are either temporarily unemployed or want to earn some extra income.

BECOMING A BRICKMAKER

If, on the other hand, you are still willing to become a brickmaker before becoming a bricklayer, the next step is to make sure you've got whatever tools and materials are needed. Don't skimp on the quality. Lousy tools result in poor work and you'll be using them for months, if not years.

The Hardware

First you need something with which to level the piece of ground on your plot on which the adobe bricks will be poured and dried. A good rake will usually do the trick, although if the ground is quite uneven, you may need a shovel to remove protrusions, rocks or what have you.

You need a saw, a hammer, nails and some preferably dressed pine, to make the form into which the adobe is to be poured. A standard such form for homemade adobe bricks is usually designed to cast just four bricks at a time (Fig. 4-1). The reason is that it can be lifted off by one person. Any larger form would require two or more people.

A small hatchet or similar implement will come in handy later to trim irregularities from the nearly dry bricks.

Fig. 4-2. Adobe bricks piled up and drying at the Pecos National Monument. They will be used in the faithful restoration of the church ruin.

Get a heavy-duty wheelbarrow with a sufficiently large wheel to cause it to roll easily over uneven ground, even when fully loaded.

If running water is available at the site, fine. If not, you need a sufficiently large container to enable you to wash off the wooden form after each casting.

You'll need a hoe to work the mixture and possibly a pitchfork. So much for the hardware.

The Labor

Now you take your shovel and dig a pit. Whether it is round, square or any shape makes no difference. It should be about 2 or 3 feet deep and maybe 6 or 8 feet across. Into this pit goes your selected soil or mixture of soils. Water is poured on top of it in sufficient quantity to wet the whole mess. It is obvious by now that the availability of a nearby water supply of ample proportions is a virtual necessity. A lot of water is used in making adobe bricks and if all that water has to be carried for any appreciable distance, the chore could become too enormous to suffer.

The best advice is to let the soil soak in that water overnight. This is not absolutely necessary, but it is mandatory that all of the soil become thoroughly saturated. No dry clumps should ever find their way into the forms.

Once this saturation process is complete, a thin layer of straw may be sprinkled over the whole works. Then using the hoe, or bare feet if you happen to be a frustrated winemaker, the straw should be

Fig. 4-3. Air and wind continue the drying process of adobe bricks.

worked thoroughly into the wet mess. The use of straw in making adobe bricks has for some time been a matter of argument among the so-called experts. Some say it is unnecessary. Others insist on using it. The Indians traditionally used horse manure with its high content of very fine undigested straw fibers, but with horse manure rarely readily available these days, that idea should be shelved. Suitable substitutes for straw could be any number of tough-fibered grasses or other fibrous material. Generally speaking, it takes over one 100-pound bale of straw to make about 1,000 bricks.

If you've been reasonably thorough when making all those test bricks, you'll have found that the amount of water used to moisten the soil is fairly critical. It should be wet enough to be handled with the pitchfork. However, if it is too wet it will refuse to retain its shape when the form is removed, will buckle or "belly" at the edges and, in extreme cases, start to run.

You should now have a mixing pit full of adobe mud of the right consistency. You fill your wheelbarrow and pour it into the form which is lying on the smoothed-over piece of ground. A light layer of sand spread on the ground beforehand will help prevent the mud from sticking to the ground. The mixture should now be firmly

Fig. 4-4. Sun-dried adobe bricks are stacked and ready to use.

Fig. 4-5. Adobe bricks should be stacked where the ground is dry.

pressed into the form, making sure that it fills all corners. It is then smoothed across the top and any excess is removed.

It is usually a good idea, unless you have gone to the extra length of lining the form with tin, to have it thoroughly soaked in water before using it. This will help prevent the mud from sticking to the wood.

Okay. You're ready. Lift the form carefully and vertically off the ground. What remains are four adobe bricks. Wash the form with water and if you have a sufficient amount of level ground to work on, place it down again and cast another four.

The next step is transforming what is lying on the ground into usable bricks is up to the sun, weather and time. Even in dry climate with the sun shining every day, they will have to remain flat on the ground for several days until they are sufficiently dry and hard enough to be moved. If the weatherman predicts rain or if an anvil cloud in the far sky indicates the possibility of a thunderstorm with a sudden downpour, you may want to spread a plastic sheet over all of the bricks to keep them from getting any wetter than they are. But be sure to remove it as soon as the danger of rain has passed. Free air circulation is a must.

Fig. 4-6. It takes months for stacked adobe bricks to be thoroughly cured.

Once they have dried to the point that they can be picked up, they should be placed on edge, preferably with a little space between each one (Figs. 4-2 and 4-3). This will permit air and wind to continue the drying process. They will have to remain in this position for several more days, the longer the better. Like wine, they improve with age. In fact, it takes months for them to be thoroughly cured.

Two thoughts of precaution:

■ Stack the bricks somewhere where the ground is dry and where no water will collect in the event of rain (Figs. 4-4, 4-5 and 4-6).

■ Cover the top of the rows of stacked bricks with some waterproof material in a manner which will prevent water from running down the sides of the bricks, but don't envelop them so completely that the drying process will be inhibited.

So you're now an expert brickmaker. The next step comes in Chapter 5 and as we will explain, it is probably the most important in the whole process of building yourself a lasting and comfortable home.

Chapter 5

From The Bottom Up

In the same way in which water helps to make adobe, it also will eventually destroy it. In other words, the adobe brick which you will be using to build your house will have to be protected from contact with moisture to the greatest degree possible. Obviously, the greatest danger of moisture contamination is at ground level where the soil tends to be soaked every time it rains. It remains wet there for extended periods of time and water may collect in actual puddles, especially on the side of the house least exposed to the rays of the sun. In other words, your adobe house will have to be elevated above ground level. To accomplish this you need a foundation of material which is impervious to moisture.

THE FOUNDATION

Foundations serve a dual purpose. One, as already mentioned, is to keep the adobe away from the ground. The other is to support the not inconsiderable weight of the entire house. In order to accomplish the first, all that is needed is to build a foundation high enough to keep the bottom of the lowest adobe brick at least 10 to 15 inches above the surrounding surface. Accomplishing the second purpose is somewhat more difficult and before we go into some of the more complicated details, it might be well to suggest that consideration be given to having the foundation constructed by a professional. It may cost a bit more than doing the work yourself, but at least you can be reasonably certain that the whole thing isn't going to one day collapse around your ears.

Table 5-1. Number of Adobe Bricks Needed for Walls of Varying Thicknesses.

```
10-inch thick wall ..................................................................... 257 bricks
14-inch thick wall ..................................................................... 360 bricks
20-inch thick wall ..................................................................... 514 bricks
24-inch thick wall ..................................................................... 617 bricks
28-inch thick wall ..................................................................... 720 bricks
```

Two types of materials are suitable for foundations, rock and concrete. Rock foundations—masses of reasonably flat rock piled one atop the other and secured with cement mortar—are esthetically more pleasing but unless extremely well constructed, could prove to be somewhat less durable. Concrete is less attractive but the more trouble-free of the two. For this reason, it is also by far the most popular in modern construction.

DIGGING THE TRENCH

Regardless of the material chosen, the first question which must be answered is: How deep down must a foundation go? If the ground is undisturbed, meaning that there is no fill anywhere in the area covered by the foundation, it must reach down far enough to be safely below the freezing level of the worst winter cold that can reasonably be expected in your area (Fig. 5-1). The reason is simple. When water freezes it expands, and if the moisture under the foundation should suddenly freeze, it might succeed in raising the foundation. A shift of as little as ⅛ inch can result in unpleasant cracks in the plaster all over the house. Any local contractor should be able to give you a fair estimate of the depth to which the foundation trench must be dug.

The digging of the trench itself is best done by a trench-digging machine. You can hire a man who owns one to do the job for you, or you can probably rent one from one of the local equipment rental places. Be sure to let the man show you how to use it because they are a bit complicated.

The trench itself should be about 8 inches wider than the planned thickness of the wall. It must be dug everywhere where a load-bearing wall is to be erected. Special consideration should be given for fireplaces and such, but more about that later. If there are soft spots or any areas of fill in the way of the foundation line, they must be excavated down to the level of undisturbed earth. Or later they must be bridged by a separate concrete beam of greater strength than the concrete used for the basic foundation. This beam will have to extend far enough to be supported on both ends by undisturbed soil.

THE WALLS

How thick should you build a wall? In trying to answer this question, a number of considerations should be kept in mind. The most basic has to do with the bearing strength which is required. Most of the weight of the entire structure must be supported by the outside walls. Experts seem to differ on what they consider an adequate thickness, but using the bricks lengthwise, which results in a 10-inch wall, is thought by some to be insufficient for outside walls. By turning them the other way we end up with a 14-inch wall which is adequate for a single-story structure.

THE SECOND STORY

If a second story is planned, or even just thought about as a possible future addition, walls of greater thickness may be indicated. Depending on how the bricks are layed, walls of 10, 14, 20 (Fig. 5-2), 24 (Fig. 5-3) or 28 inches (Fig. 5-4) can easily be built. The only prerequisite is a foundation of the appropriate thickness to carry the wall and, of course, the availability of the required number of bricks.

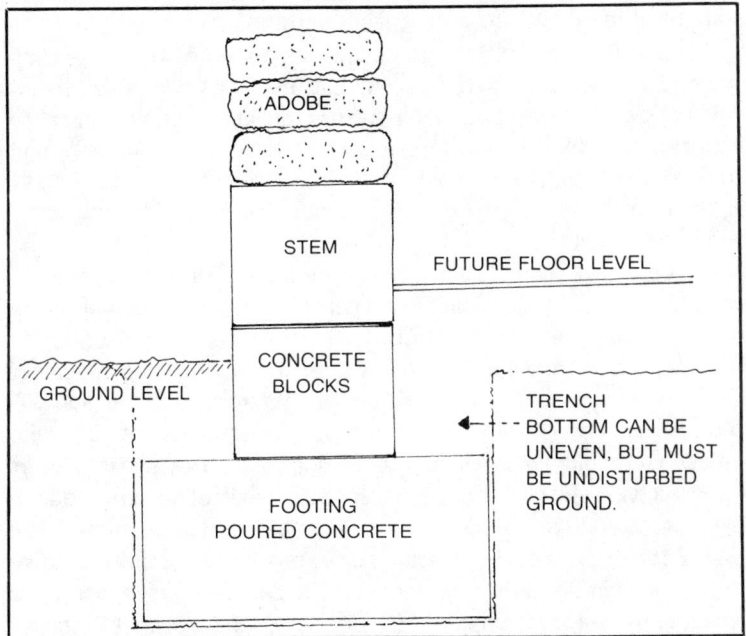

Fig. 5-1. Digging and pouring a foundation for your adobe home.

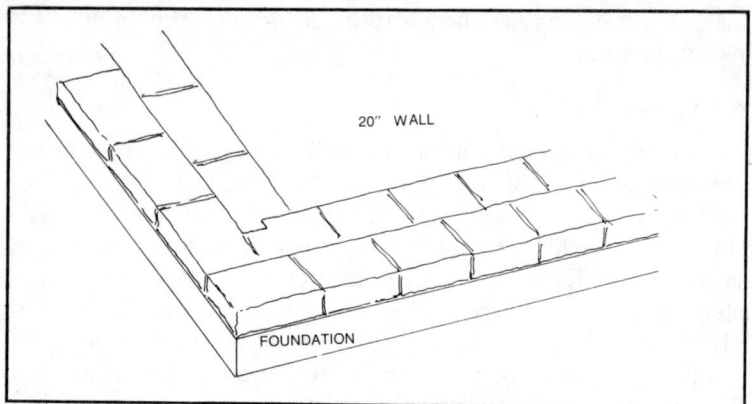

Fig. 5-2. A 20-inch thick foundation wall.

To figure out the number of bricks needed, divide the horizontal measure of the wall(s) by the width (length) of the bricks and then multiply by the number of 4-inch layers needed to reach the required height.

Table 5-1 offers a general guide to the number of adobe bricks needed for a 10 × 10-foot section of wall of varying thicknesses. Don't worry about windows and doors. There is always a certain amount of breakage and waste from cutting.

Aside from the purely practical considerations of the bearing strength of the walls, a greater wall thickness has two other advantages. One is the exceptional insulating quality of adobe. In areas with considerable temperature extremes during hot summers and cold winters, the extra cost of a thick wall will eventually pay dividends in terms of greater indoor comfort and lower heating or air conditioning bills.

The other consideration is purely esthetic. Thick walls are quite beautiful and much of the unique charm of traditional old adobes is the result of their massiveness (Fig. 5-5).

When the trench is ready it is time to start pouring concrete. Concrete is a mixture of cement, sand, gravel and water and different proportions will result in differing bearing strengths. Again, unless you really know what you are doing, don't be proud—let an expert advise you as to the strength needed and let an expert do the pouring. If your plot is adequately accessible, you can contract with one of those people who operate ready-mix trucks. They will drive the truck right up to the site and pour the concrete through a chute which is part of the equipment included with the truck. If for some reason that is not possible, the concrete will have to be off-loaded into wheelbarrows and transported by hand. This is not an easy job, to put it mildly, especially if it involves an uphill grade.

Steel reinforcing bars, called *rebars*, must be embedded into the concrete and stick out far enough to subsequently hold the cement blocks in place. The concrete portion of the foundation simply consti-

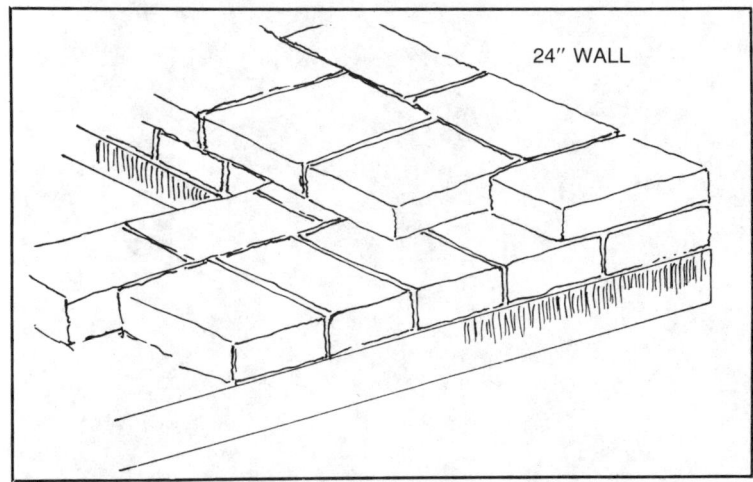

Fig. 5-3. A 24-inch thick foundation wall.

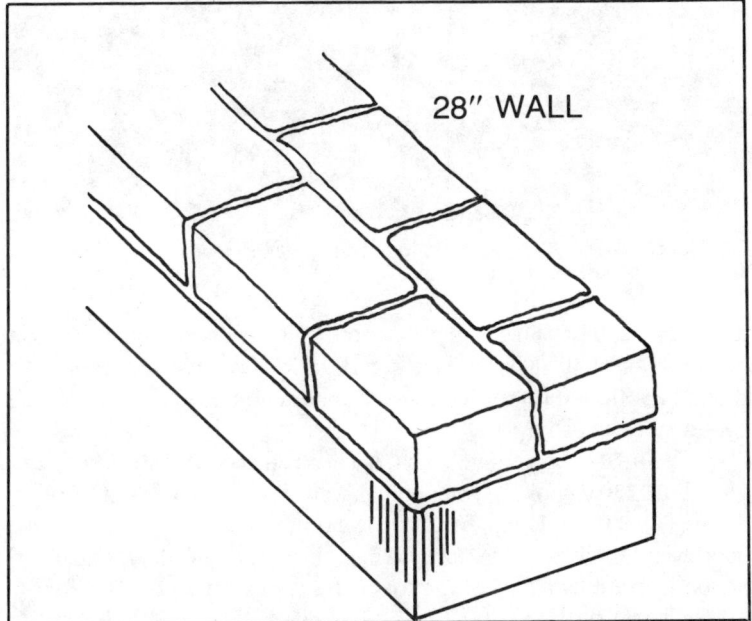

Fig. 5-4. A 28-inch thick foundation wall.

Fig. 5-5. The extra thickness of the double-brick wall is clearly visible in this view through a window of the north patio.

tutes the footing. This is the base on which the whole structure is going to rest. Once it is in place you're still not ready to proceed with those beautiful adobe bricks which have been patiently hardening somewhere nearby.

The next step involves what is referred to as the stem. It is the very bottom portion of your actual wall. It usually consists of two rows of concrete blocks, one atop the other. When in place they are filled with concrete. They are held in place by the rebars inside and become an integral part of the foundation. The top of the upper row of these concrete blocks should be 10 to 12 inches above the ground. This represents the base for the actual adobe wall. Since this is likely to be somewhat above the level of the eventual interior floors, you may want to remember to omit the upper cement blocks in places where doors are planned, or you may subsequently have to chip them down to the level of the floor.

An alternate means of constructing a foundation is to pour a solid concrete slab under the entire house, or at least part of it, such as the area which will eventually be the garage. Before such a slab can be poured, the ground must be prepared by clearing it of grass and all manner of vegetation which might gradually decay or permit the slab to settle and possibly crack. A wooden form must be built to the height to which the concrete is to be poured. The upper edges must be level because they will serve as a means of smoothing the concrete and removing excess.

Again, this is really a job for an expert. Most amateur builders would be best advised to pay to have it done by someone who knows what he is doing. Skilled concrete contractors are not that expensive. Remember, you'll have to live with the final result for a very long time.

Chapter 6
Building Your Adobe Home

Now we finally get to the part we've been preparing for all this time. We're going to build a house. What is really meant by this is that we're ready to start piling all of those adobe bricks one on top of the other. But this too, isn't quite as simple as it sounds. First we need mortar to glue the bricks to one another.

To make mortar we use the same soil mixture that was used to prepare the bricks. Bits of rock and extraneous matter were of no particular importance in making the bricks, but it must be removed from the mortar mix. To do this the mix should be strained through a sufficiently fine screen to eliminate any such matter exceeding a ¼ inch in size. Once that has been accomplished the mortar is spread in a thickness of approximately ½ to ¾ of an inch atop the foundation stem and the first row of adobe bricks is layed on top. Then comes another layer of mortar and the second row can be started.

WALLS

Be sure to offset the bricks in such a way that the vertical cracks between bricks are at least 4 or more inches away from one another (Fig. 6-1). Do not fill these vertical spaces with mortar. Later on, when you apply the outer coating of adobe or some other kind of plaster, it will seep into these vertical spaces and thus adhere to the wall without the need for wire mesh.

While it is relatively simple to lay the first few rows of bricks in a straight line, the higher the wall gets, the easier it becomes to cause a slight lean in one direction or another. Unless corrected early, the immense weight of the wall will eventually cause it to collapse. To avoid this, drive wooden stakes vertically into the ground at both ends of the wall. Use a plumb line to make sure that they are truly vertical. Then tie a string between the two stakes at the level at which you happen to be working. Lay the bricks along that string.

Don't lay more than five or six rows of bricks on top of one another at any one point on any one day (Fig. 6-2). If you do, the still-wet mortar may be squeezed together before it has a chance to harden and your wall may end up being a mess of unsightly wavy lines. In addition, such compression of the mortar and the resulting unevenness will be detrimental to the bearing strength of the wall.

As long as the top of the wall on which you are working is no more than about waist high, the work is relatively easy. This is assuming that you consider lifting hundreds of 30-pound blocks easy. However, once it gets higher than that, the task should really be handled by two people. One should prepare and spread the mortar, the other should climb up and down ladders with the bricks.

WINDOWS AND DOORS

But a house, in order to be livable, must not have only walls. There are doors and windows to be considered, places where one

Fig. 6-2. Do not lay more than five or six courses of bricks at a time. The mortar in the lower courses has to dry somewhat before it can support the weight of additional bricks.

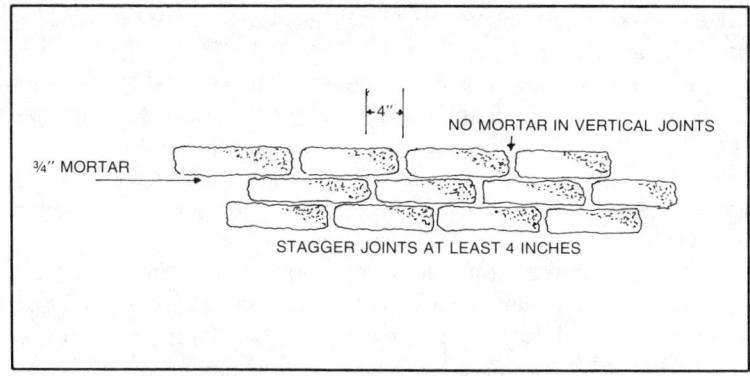

Fig. 6-1. Bricks must be offset by 4 or more inches.

may eventually wish to secure cabinets to the wall and so on. Contrary to many other building materials, you can't nail anything to an adobe wall. For this reason, anything that is to be attached to the wall must be thought of and planned for in advance.

The material best suited for this purpose is wood. It is therefore logical that in the appropriate places, wood sections must be incorporated into the wall. These can be flat 1-inch thick pieces inserted horizontally between the layers of bricks. Or they can be so-called *gringo blocks*, pieces of wood of the same thickness as the adobe

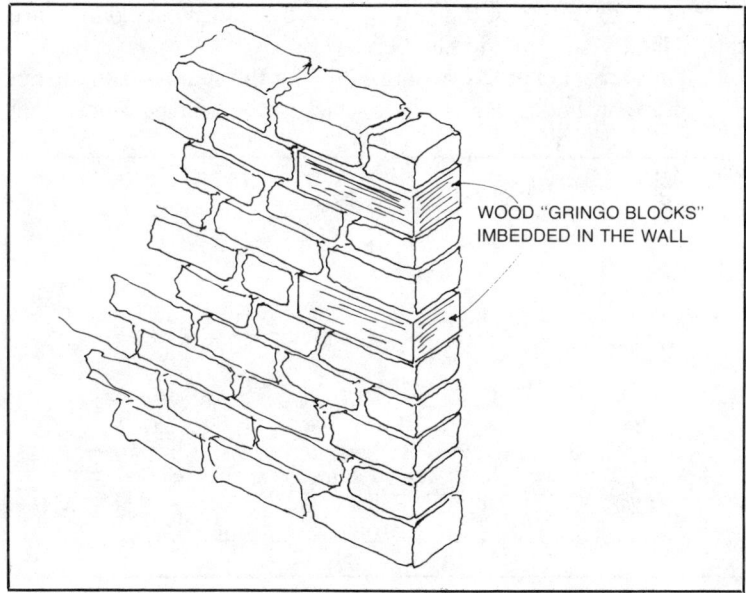

Fig. 6-3. Gringo blocks are often embedded in the walls of an adobe house.

bricks which replace some of the bricks in places where the need for nailing is anticipated (Fig. 6-3).

A frame for the door and window must be constructed from lumber. Be sure to nail some diagonal pieces across these frames (Fig. 6-4) to assure that they remain rectangular and don't start leaning in one direction or the other. Build the adobe blocks up against the frame four or five courses (rows) high and then continue the wall building away from the opening.

Any such opening for a door or window requires *lintels*. Lintels are horizontal wooden beams across the top. These must be of sufficient strength to carry the load of the wall and the roof portion that will be built up above them (Figs. 6-5 through 6-9).

Back to the lintels. Usually 6 × 8-inch planks are used. Two of them stand on edge side by side, with at least 1 foot on each end resting on the wall itself. They may either be placed in a manner which will keep them exposed after the structure is finished (Fig. 6-10) or their combined width may be as much as 4 inches narrower than the wall. This would permit you to subsequently cover them with narrow strips of adobe brick.

Traditionally, windows in the old adobes were small. They were simply tiny ventilation holes with no covering except possibly some animal hides in the winter. Then when first mica and later glass became available, the Indians built somewhat larger windows into their adobes. But even those windows, by modern standards, are rather limited in size and number.

Today most of us like a lot of light. But the summer sun can get uncomfortably hot in most areas in which adobe building is prevalent

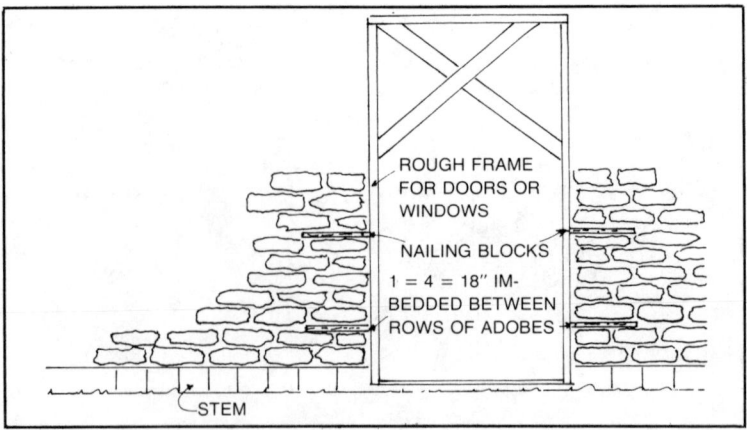

Fig. 6-4. Door and window frames must be built of wood and the adobe walls built around them.

Fig. 6-6. A solid wooden beam is used as the lintel.

Fig. 6-7. Lintels are shimmed on one side with left-over pieces of plywood in order to attain a perfect level.

Fig. 6-5. An opening is left for the future window in this adobe home currently under construction.

and the cold winters of the high-altitude desert and mountain regions bring their cold into the house through the windows. The windows also offer considerably less insulative effect than the thick adobe walls.

It doesn't much matter at this stage of building whether you will eventually opt for single- or double-pane windows because either will fit into the frames set into the wall. But if you like a lot of light and want large and numerous window openings, the extra cost of double-pane windows may pay meaningful dividends in the long run.

Fig. 6-8. Nailing blocks have been incorporated into the wall to hold the future window frame.

Fig. 6-9. A completed window opening awaits its window frame.

Fig. 6-10. In this photograph of a window opening in an adobe wall, the lintels are left exposed. Note the pieces of screening nailed over spots where non-adobe material, such as wood shims, would cause the adobe-mud plaster to fail to adhere to the wall surface.

They are a bit harder to keep clean, but then, nothing is perfect.

Once all bearing walls have been built up to the height of the future indoor ceiling, provisions must be made to support the vigas. The vigas support the ceiling material on which the roof will eventually be built. Adobe has only minimal resistance to compression and therefore the vigas cannot simply be placed on top of the highest course of adobe bricks. What is needed is a continuous support which will distribute the weight of the vigas, ceiling and roof evenly across the entire length of the walls. This can be accomplished by either pouring a concrete beam (Fig. 6-11) or by placing a heavy wooden beam along the top of all bearing walls.

In order to pour a concrete beam (Fig. 6-12), a wooden form has to be constructed and held in place by some sort of brackets (usually metal). The concrete is then poured into the form. A rebar should be incorporated into the concrete for extra strength. Once the concrete has sufficiently cured, vigas can be laid atop it, and adobe bricks built up on top of it around the vigas to a height of about twelve or more inches above the top of the vigas (Figs. 6-13 and 6-14).

Most adobe structures have flat roofs. This means that the ceiling and roof are built up directly on top of the vigas, with no open space in between (Fig. 6-15). It goes without saying that such roofs must have a sufficient grade in one direction or the other. This will cause water and melting snow to run off and not stand on the roof in puddles which would eventually cause even the best constructed roof to begin to leak. It does not have to be much of a grade. A few inches will do.

In many instances this grade is achieved as a logical result of the fact that vigas, being actually tree trunks, are thinner on one side than on the other. By laying then all with the thin side in the same direction, a certain amount of slope will be created at the top while the bottom remains level. If this degree of slope should appear to be insufficient, or if finished round, square or rectangular beams are to be used, the slope will have to be provided for in the supporting concrete beam. The form into which the concrete is to be poured must also allow for it.

While more attractive wooden beams can be used in place of the concrete, they may be less satisfactory. All wood continues to shrink for very long periods of continuous gradual drying. This could possibly result in some cracks long after the house is finished. Also, unless beams of sufficient length can be found to go from one end of

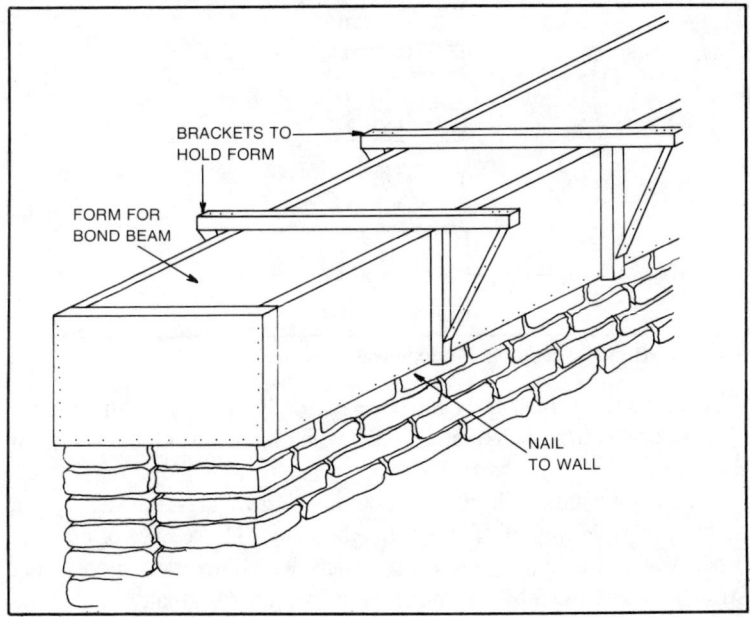

Fig. 6-12. Form for a concrete bond beam.

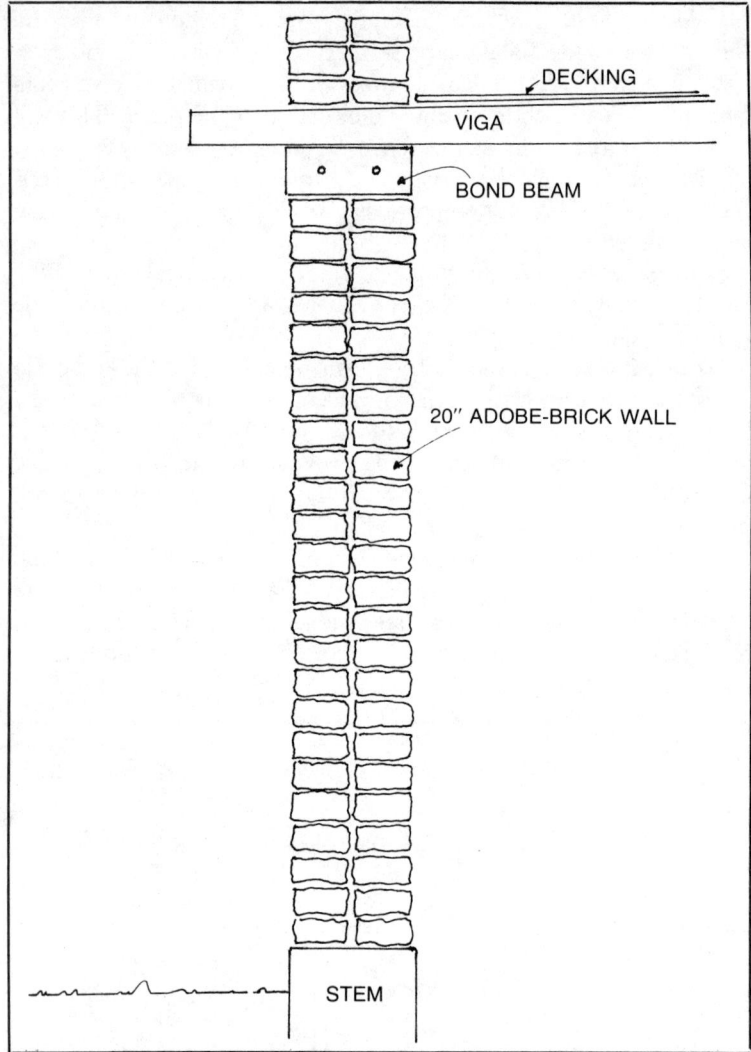

Fig. 6-13. Cross section of an adobe wall.

the wall to the other, they must be carefully spliced to turn pieces into several continuous beams which won't have a tendency to sag at the joint.

So far we have talked only about bearing walls—the walls which must carry the weight of the entire building. There are, of course, other walls in a home. There are walls which are designed to act strictly as partitions between individual rooms. Originally all of these walls were also constructed of adobe, usually of a somewhat thinner

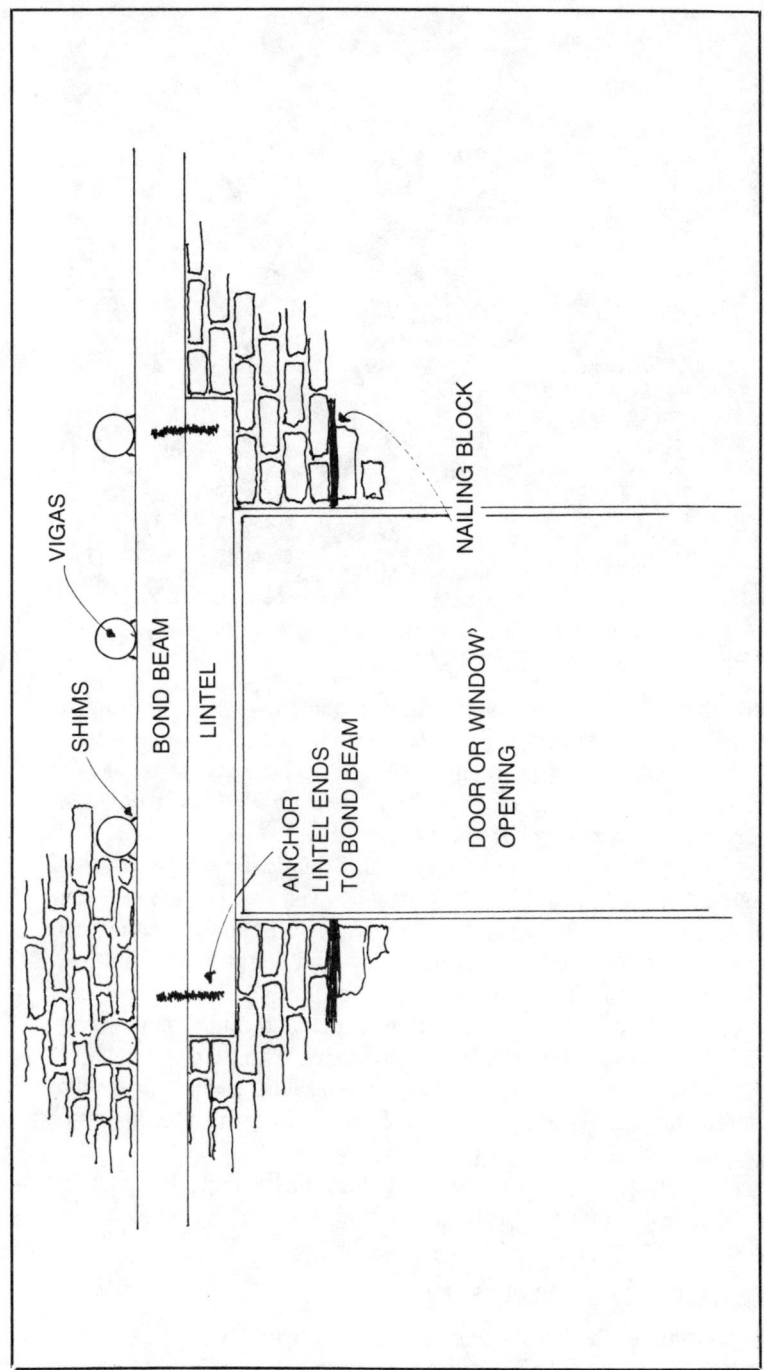

Fig. 6-14. Bricks are built up atop the bond beam to form the parapet.

Fig. 6-11. Although adobe brick is used in the construction of this home, concrete blocks are used for the top of the walls.

width than the outside walls. Using adobe throughout the house gives a pleasant effect of unity of construction. It also results in effective sound proofing, a characteristic which may be especially desirable if certain parts of the home will be children's quarters where an inevitable racket can be expected.

On the other hand, expediency may demand a simpler type of construction for these walls. Curtain walls, which are wooden frames covered with plaster board or some other such material, can be easily constructed lying flat on the ground. They are then raised into their appropriate position and subsequently bolted to the floor and ceiling. Such walls are easier and quicker to build, cost somewhat less and take up a little less floor space. With a large number of such partitions, this can add up to a considerable amount. They also simplify the installation of electrical wiring and the placement of electrical outlets and switches.

The choice is yours. If sound proofing and the unity of structural appearance are more important than time and money, by all means use adobe throughout the house.

ARE WALLS REALLY NECESSARY?

In a currently popular television series called "Vegas", the hero lives in what appears to be a converted warehouse. It consists of one

Fig. 6-15. The vigas are in place atop this immense future living room. The large picture window in the back wall has necessitated angling the bond beam over its top. It is the same case with the large fireplace which is constructed of concrete blocks and set into the wall at the right.

huge room, divided by plants and groups of furniture, where he works, lives, sleeps and keeps his car. It is also where his assistant spends her days answering the phone. There isn't a wall in this whole combination living, working, sleeping and garage area, yet it all looks rather charming.

Some younger couples building adobe homes in outlying areas seem to find a similar arrangement attractive and livable. They'll simply build the outside walls around a large space which is divided by furnishings and possibly different floor levels for sleeping, living, cooking and eating areas. There are no interior walls except possibly one to shut off the bathroom.

Frequently the owners of such homes will find that sooner or later they will want to add other rooms to this one-room complex, especially if children are born. They will require a place in which to take their naps and sleep at night while the rest of the family is still up and about.

The initial advantage is that such a one-room enclosure can be built rather cheaply and in comparatively little time. It can then be lived in while the rest of the house begins to grow as the need arises. The disadvantage is that there is no privacy. Certainly not everyone can stand being around other people, even loved ones, all day and all night.

Chapter 7
Under Foot

Every home has to have some sort of floor finish and the character of adobe construction lends itself to a wide variety of such finishes (Fig. 7-1).

FLOORS

Traditionally the Indians didn't bother to build floors at all. They simply leveled and smoothed the floors by tamping the earth down with moccasined or bare feet. They wet it repeatedly with water or animal blood (for color) or a mixture of the two until it became a solid surface of adobe.

In such houses one would step across a threshold and down into the room, rather than continuing on a level with the base of the door opening. While this method is by far the cheapest and easiest, it is no longer considered adequate in the context of modern living.

BRICK FLOORING

In the modern adobe one of the most attractive types of floor covering is brick. Although not exactly cheap, it is easy to lay and if treated correctly, easy to maintain.

In order to produce a satisfactory brick floor, the surface beneath needs some preparation. First you should gather all of the left-over dirt from the excavation of the foundation channel and pile it inside. Usually that will be sufficient to raise the surface to a level which, when the bricks are added, will bring the floor level with the base of the door openings.

Fig. 7-1. Adobe construction lends itself to a wide variety of floor finishes.

The desired level of the subfloor is some 3½ inches below the level of the final floor. It should be scribed on the inside of the foundation stem. Then the dirt should be wetted repeatedly, raked to an even surface and stamped down in order to eventually have it compact into a reasonably smooth, level and hard surface. It will probably require repeated shaving of protrusions and filling of spaces which have sunk below the desired level. It is important that this be done with patience and care since the weight of the bricks and that of the people walking on them will cause them to settle unevenly if the subsurface is not hard enough and insufficiently smooth.

All soil, no matter how hardened, is full of all kinds of bugs and other potentially living matter. To prevent these beasts from deciding at one point to start crawling up through the cracks between the bricks, the entire surface should now be sprinkled rather liberally with some kind of insecticide, such as chlordane (Fig. 7-2). Don't be chintzy with that stuff. Be sure that there is at least some of it everywhere.

The next step is to spread a plastic sheet over the entire area. This will act as a vapor barrier. Such material is available in rolls of widths sufficient for even the largest room area, even up to 40 or more feet. Ask for four-mil thickness when buying it. The width to select when buying the roll should be the width, not length, of your largest room. Preferably it should be a few inches wider. The edges need not be cut to the exact dimensions, but may be lapped a few inches.

The next material you need is dry sand. Spread dry sand to a thickness of about 1 to 1½ inches over the entire surface. Damp sand is no good because it tends to fail to fill small depressions and can therefore eventually result in an uneven floor. This sand should be leveled quite carefully. One method to use would be to lay two pipes from one end of the room to the other and then slide a 2 × 4 or other screed across them. Later, when the pipes have been removed, the narrow channels left can be filled by pouring sand into them.

FLOOR PATTERN

Now we are ready for the bricks. The bricks to use are referred to as *solids* or *patio type*. Regular common building brick is full of holes which help to hold mortar. This would not be desirable as a floor because it would become a receptacle for all manner of dirt. Before putting down the first brick, you may want to think about the pattern to be used (Fig. 7-3). Most bricks are not exactly twice as long as they are wide, therefore it might be a good idea to use any old

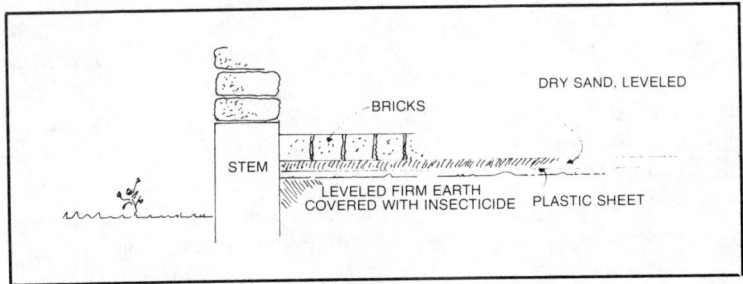

Fig. 7-2. This cross section of a brick floor illustrates the leveled firm earth covered with insecticide.

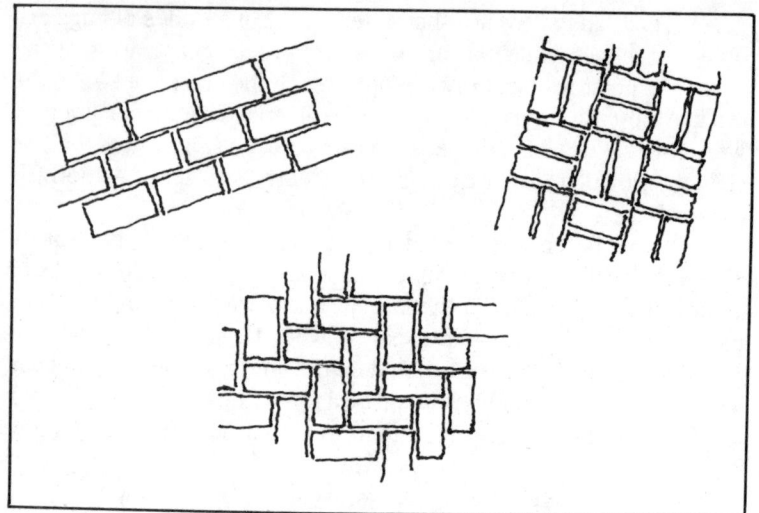

Fig. 7-3. Various patterns for brick floors.

flat surface outside and put down a few bricks in a variety of patterns. See how it works and how you like the looks of the results.

Then, once you have decided on a pattern, start in the center of a door opening and work forward and outward. Most likely, when getting to the wall, you will find that you need to cut some bricks in order to fill spaces into which they won't fit. There are brick chisels and either dry or wet masonry saws to do this job, but it requires patience and care.

Handling bricks eventually becomes murder on the hands. Some kind of covering may be needed unless you've got the skin of an elephant. Some people like to work with gloves. Another method I have heard about is to tape the inside of the fingers with surgical tape. Unless you are a confirmed masochist, you're sure to figure out a means of protection that suits you best.

It is a good idea to plan your time so that you can finish one room in a day and not let it sit there half done throughout a night or two. Once it's done, keep walking on the new floor to a minimum, because it is necessary to sweep fine sand into the cracks between the bricks. This firmly locks them into one another, especially in the areas which will eventually receive the maximum amount of traffic. If that is not done the bricks will tend to shift slightly, resulting in uneven spaces between them and an unsightly overall appearance.

Now the floor is technically ready to be used, although most home owners prefer to add a sealer. Without sealing, the brick floor retains a dull appearance and is exceedingly difficult to keep clean. It may *be* clean, but it won't *look* clean. When mentioning sealers you are likely to get all kinds of contradicting advice as to the ideal product and method to be used. Try anything that appeals to you, but there is a product called Floor Hardener by the Standard Oil Company which can be applied with a paint roller. Bricks are porous and you'll be using considerable quantities of this hardener. A gallon will barely be sufficient for a first coat in a 12 by 15-foot room. It will take two coats at least to effect good sealing of the floor, but you can repeat the process as often as you like. Each additional coat will darken the color of the floor by a small degree (Fig. 7-4).

Subsequently the floor can be kept shiny and clean with standard wax or liquid plastic available in any supermarket. Wax eventually builds up into unsightly yellowish white spots or streaks. Clear liquid plastic products seem to avoid or, at least, lessen that problem.

CONCRETE FLOOR

If you don't like brick, there are a number of alternate choices. The simplest, of course, is a solid concrete slab. It can be poured directly on the undisturbed ground below. It should be of approximately a 4-inch thickness except at places where it has to carry heavy loads, such as the location of a future fireplace. Twelve inches or more may be needed there.

Fig. 7-4. A brick floor in a semicircular den, referred to as the kiva room. Note the fireplace in the far wall, the bench-type seating arrangement built into the wall and the double-brick thickness of the wall itself.

Concrete floors aren't exactly a thing of beauty and no matter how much care was taken in the preparation and pouring, they will eventually crack in a few places. A raw concrete floor is fine in a garage or carport, but it is really unacceptable in living spaces. If most of the area is to be covered by one or a collection of carpets or rugs, there should be sponge-rubber or other padding under the rugs to reduce that feeling of hardness that comes with concrete. Not only is that unpleasant, it is eventually tiring to walk on.

On the other hand, a concrete slab can serve as a base for all sorts of alternate floor coverings. It can be used under a brick floor, although this would seem unwarranted unless the slab is already in place. If that is the case, the portion of the floor to be covered with brick may end up being a shallow step higher than the rest of the floor. Flagstone can be used to create a good effect in areas which border on sliding doors leading to a patio or other outdoor areas. I suppose one could lay wood across a concrete slab, but that, too, seems to be a rather silly way of constructing a wood floor.

CERAMIC TILE

One type of covering that is particularly decorative and lends itself well to the overall style of adobe is ceramic tile (Fig. 7-5). It can be beautiful and it is durable. Its major drawback is its expense. Ready-made tile in all conceivable designs and colors is available from many sources in the United States or it can be imported from Mexico.

When using tile the subfloor is of particular importance because any unevenness or softness will result in a buckling of the floor and possible cracking of some of the tiles. A concrete slab is by far the most desirable type of underfloor, although a well prepared and thoroughly hardened mud floor can be used. Whatever is used as a base, its top should be just a sufficient distance below the base of the door openings. This should allow for the thickness of the tile and the mortar-material used to attach the tile to the surface beneath. This mortar, usually a damp four-to-one mixture of sand and portland cement, is spread over the base. Cover a reasonably small area at a time. It dries rather slowly, giving you time to level the top surface to an even smoothness and then to set the tiles, one at a time. The tiles must be tapped firmly into place with some sort of resilient instrument, preferably a rubber hammer. Some mortar should be put into the joints between the tiles and the excess should be carefully wiped away with a damp rag to avoid stains which will be difficult to remove later on. For several days after laying the tiles the joints should be dampened over and over again in order to prevent

Fig. 7-5. Ceramic tile makes an elegant floor in a bathroom.

the mortar from drying too fast. If it dried too quickly, it would weaken the bond between it and the base.

While it would probably be excessive to plan on doing all floors in a house with ceramic tile, they do lend a rich decorative touch to areas around fireplaces, in bathrooms, entrance halls or other spaces of moderate dimensions.

VINYL MATERIALS

Other types of covering, often preferred in kitchens, bathrooms and possibly children's playrooms, are the various vinyl materials. They are available in a wide variety of colors and patterns, either in the form of individual vinyl tiles or in continuous rolls of adequate width. Some vinyl tiles even come with self-adhesive backing. This makes application easy as well as reduces messiness to an absolute minimum. While laying individual tiles on a smooth and carefully cleaned base is an easy matter that can be accomplished by any amateur with a minimum of problems, laying down entire sheets is an extremely ticklish operation and should really be left to a professional. In either case, the importance of the smoothness of the base cannot be emphasized too strongly. These materials are thin and quite flexible and any indentation or protrusion, no matter how slight, will eventually be reproduced in the surface of the covering.

WOOD FLOORS

Wood floors tend to give the impression of being softer and warmer than any of the hard materials mentioned so far. But a good wood floor is an expensive undertaking and requires a considerable amount of preparation. Usually wood floors are found in houses with basements or at least crawl spaces beneath. They are rarely found in houses set directly on the undisturbed ground. To construct a wood floor, a subflooring must first be built with supports leading to the undisturbed ground below. This will support the actual floor and those who will eventually walk on it. This subfloor can be made of plywood of adequate thickness (5/8 to 3/4 inch) or 1-inch lumber laid diagonally across the joists. Subsequently the lumber to be used in the actual hardwood flooring is then nailed directly to the subfloor, preferably at 90- or 45-degree angles to the boards used in the subfloor. Of course, this would not apply if the subfloor is plywood. Most hardwood flooring can be purchased with tongue-in-groove sides. They provide a tight fit which is made even tighter by toenailing through the groove.

Much of the cost of such a floor depends on the quality of the wood selected. If eventual wall-to-wall carpeting is anticipated, the surface appearance of the wood is of no great consideration. If, on the other hand, large areas of the floor are going to be in plain sight, the texture and grain of the wood can add immeasurably to the beauty of the room. The extra expense for fine woods would be money well spent in that case.

Chapter 8
Over Head

Where there is a floor there is usually a ceiling and ceilings in adobe buildings can be works of true beauty (Figs. 8-1, 8-2 and 8-3). The most beautiful, in my opinion, are those which most closely resemble the ceiling construction used by the Indians in the early days of adobe building.

VIGAS

Once having built up their walls, they would hoist *vigas*—tree trunks from which all branches and bark had been stripped—to the top of the walls (Fig. 8-4). They would place them a given distance apart from one another and then cover them with *latillas*. Latillas are slim tree branches placed quite close together. Together, the vigas and latillas formed the base for the roof which was usually simply a several foot thick layer of adobe mud.

Today this same basic principle is still being used in modern adobe structures. A number of shortcuts have been introduced to simplify and speed up construction, although in many cases, this also reduces the visual beauty of the ceiling.

Vigas can be purchased from commercial suppliers in varying lengths and thicknesses. Depending on the distance from bearing wall to bearing wall which they must cover, they should be adequate thickness to support the weight of the roof itself. Vigas with an average diameter of 6 inches are considered sufficient for a 10-foot span. Longer spans require greater thicknesses: 8 inches for 15 or 16 feet; 10 inches for 20 feet; and so on.

Fig. 8-1. A ceiling in an adobe home is often a work of great beauty.

Moving the vigas from the ground to the top of the wall can be a bit of a chore because of their not inconsiderable weight. Self-propelled lifting machinery that are used in warehouses and in the loading of trucks are called *forklifts*. Some of them are capable of raising their loads to a sufficient height. Forklifts can be rented, but be sure that they are capable of lifting the vigas to a height several inches above the top of the wall. Also, the ground around the building has to be sufficiently level to permit maneuvering the forklift.

If an adequate forklift is not available, or if the surrounding terrain does not permit using one, there are a number of other means of getting the vigas up there. One possibility would be to erect wooden hoists. These are wood beams vertically set into the ground and firmly supported by guy wires. Across the top of these beams another beam is placed horizontally and firmly secured. Two winches are attached to it. Then, using heavy rope, the vigas can then be winched up to the required level.

If that seems too complicated, there is another and simpler way, but this one must be handled with a bit of extra caution since there are certain inherent dangers involved. Two vigas or other strong, smooth beams are layed at an angle against the side of the wall (Fig. 8-5). The longer the viga or beam used for this, the shallower the angle at which it rests against the wall and the easier the work. The next step is to firmly anchor two ropes at the top of the wall.

Fig. 8-2. The ceiling in this adobe home helps to accent the chandelier.

Fig. 8-3. Unique ceilings are frequently found in adobe homes.

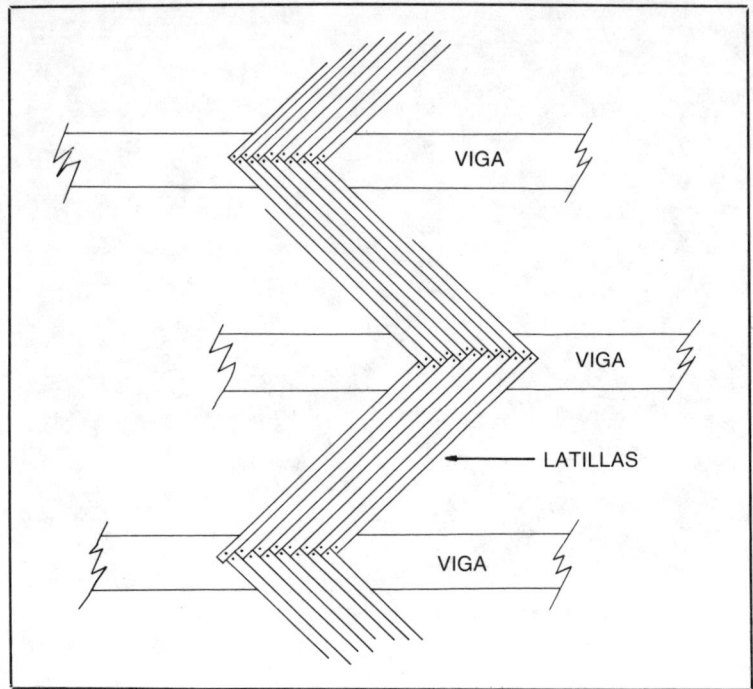

Fig. 8-4. Details of a ceiling as seen from the top.

The first of the vigas to be raised is then placed at the bottom of the two beams, at right angles to them. The rope is dropped down from the top of the wall where one end is anchored. It is fed underneath the viga to be raised. The loose end is then thrown back up to the men atop the wall. The two workers stationed on top of the wall then pull the loose ends of the two ropes, making sure that each pulls at the same speed. The viga will gradually roll up the angled beams.

The dangers mentioned are these:
- Don't stand too close to where the viga will eventually drop off the top of the angled beam and onto the top of the wall. If you do, you are in danger of having it drop on your foot. Needless to say, that could be less than pleasant.
- Don't sit on top of the wall or you may end up with a lap full of viga.
- Persons below, helping to push and guide the viga up the incline, should be aware that there is always the possibility of a rope breaking, an anchor coming loose or one of the men at the top suddenly having to sneeze or losing his footing.

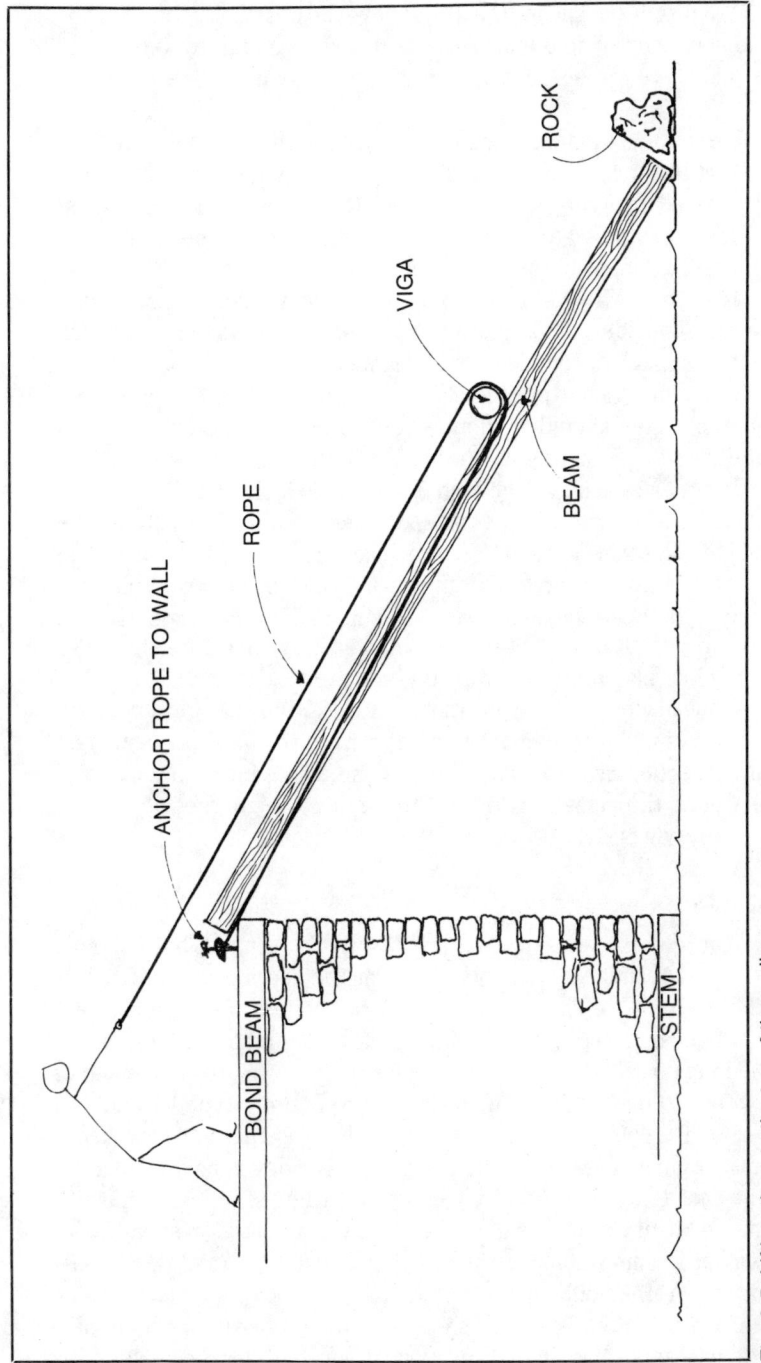

Fig. 8-5. Lifting vigas to the top of the walls.

Whatever the cause, there is always the possibility that the viga could come tumbling down. Anyone unlucky enough to stand in its way is likely to remember that experience for longer than he will care to.

Remember that all vigas have a thicker and a thinner end. Be sure that they are placed with all the thin ends in the same direction. They should be in the direction in which the roof is supposed to slope in order to permit water to run off. Once they are up there, it would be virtually impossible to turn them around.

If all that will eventually go on top of the vigas is the roof, it is generally considered adequate to space them 3 to 4 feet apart. On the other hand, if a second story is planned, they should be placed at 2 to 3-foot intervals to potentially form a firm base for the upper floor (Fig. 8-6). This should be done even if the second story is only a vague idea for some distant future addition.

In order to achieve the traditional adobe look, the vigas should stick out a foot or more beyond the outside wall, especially on the thin side. The thin side is where the vigas will eventually support the *canales*. The canales are the drains that permit the water to run off of the roof. If these canales and their supporting viga ends are too short, the wind may blow the run-off water against the side of the house, thus playing havoc with the adobe wall.

Once placed at the appropriate intervals, they can be secured in place with small shims to prevent them from rolling short distances in one direction or the other. The next step is to build up the adobe wall around the vigas to a level of three or more courses above the top of the vigas.

CEILINGS

You now have the base for a beautiful ceiling. What happens next will determine its true beauty for all the years you intend to live in the house. The choice which must be made is a matter of what type of decking to put on top of the vigas. The simplest might seem to be long boards, layed at right angles to the vigas, from one end of the room to the other. Tongue-in-groove flooring-type lumber can be used for this purpose, but employing this method may seem simpler than it actually is. The problem which develops immediately is the fact that virtually all vigas are not ruler-straight. Some will stick up an inch or more while others may have a slight bend downward. This will make the job of nailing long, straight boards to their tops rather difficult.

An alternative is to use short lengths of board. Cut them at a 45-degree angle at each end and place them at 45-degree angles atop

Fig. 8-6. If a second story is planned, the appropriate spacing of vigas takes on added importance.

the vigas. This creates a kind of herringbone effect. It is not only more attractive to look at, but also eliminates most of the problems caused by the unevenness of the vigas. The fact that the resulting ceiling is not perfectly level is of no importance because it will be virtually impossible to see that from below.

To my mind the most beautiful ceiling can be constructed by using a slightly improved version of the old Indian method. In other words, use latillas. You may be able to purchase reasonably straight, thin branches from about 1 inch to 1½ inches in diameter that are already cleaned of bark, branches and other protrusions. Or you may have to get a permit and go out into the woods and cut them yourself. It takes many individual pieces laid at a 45-degree angle across the vigas to achieve what will appear as a solid ceiling. Whether purchased commercially or gathered and prepared by yourself, they should be thoroughly treated with some sort of effective insecticide to kill and eliminate whatever living organisms may exist in the various cracks.

Today few builders bother with this method, but exceptionally beautiful examples of it can be found in old adobes, especially in some of the old Indian-Spanish churches.

Fig. 8-7. Ceiling detail from a home, still under construction, in which the builder is making greater than average use of concrete blocks in addition to adobe. Here the bond beam has been cast, topped by concrete blocks into which the roof beams have been embedded. High quality tongue-in-groove finished lumber has been used for the decking.

Many builders today prefer finished rectangular beams to the raw round vigas. To lift them to roof height requires either a hoist or a forklift. Obviously. They cannot be rolled up some angled incline. Aside from that, they are used in the same way as vigas and require approximately the same dimensions and distance from one another. The big advantage is that they are perfectly straight and smooth. They can be decked with long boards with no difficulty. In conjunction with such beams, long boards placed at right angles to them produce a perfectly satisfactory effect.

Whether the ceiling atop the vigas or beams consists of standard board lumber, or of latillas, it requires considerable build-up on top to produce a lasting and weather-proof roof (Fig. 8-7). There will be more about this shortly.

INTERIOR FINISH FOR YOUR CEILINGS

The eventual interior finish of such a viga or beam ceiling is a matter of individual taste. In most cases they are simply stained with

Fig. 8-8. Viga ceilings simplify the hanging of planters or other decorative items.

some sort of varnish that brings out the color and texture of the wood itself. Some people like to paint the spaces between the vigas or beams, while others have been known to paint everything. Only remember, once painted, it is an incredibly difficult, time-consuming, frustrating and expensive job to strip the paint away.

I have seen some older adobe homes in which owners or former owners for some incomprehensible reason decided to cover a perfectly good viga ceiling with flat ceiling boards. This makes it look on the inside like any old house. Personally I think that is sacrilege, but then there is no accounting for individual tastes.

One of the marvelous advantages of a viga or beam ceiling is the ability to hang things from it, such as planters or chandeliers (Fig. 8-8). Hooks can be screwed into the beams or vigas with ease. Even if they are removed at some later date, the holes are likely to not show at all. If they do, they can easily be filled with a dab of plastic wood. This same method can be used on the walls to hang heavy

Fig. 8-9. Few things are as important in building a home as a well-constructed roof.

pictures, cabinets and the like. This is an important advantage since nailing adequate supports for such free-hanging weights into an adobe wall may be difficult, if not impossible.

KEEPING DRY

Few things can make life quite as miserable as a leaking roof (Fig. 8-9). That sudden drip-drip in some obscure corner of a room, or just where you have placed your favorite chair, is the sort of thing that can drive you up your adobe wall. Once it starts there isn't a thing that can be done about it except to put a bucket under the leak. A few ounces of prevention are worth several tons of cure. In other words, build a good roof to start with. You'll keep comfortably dry throughout the heaviest downpour and even while those 4 or 5 inches of accumulated snow melt away in the spring sun.

YOUR ROOF

Even the best constructed roof is not completely permanent. Usually, sometime after the 10th year and before the 20th, leaks begin to develop and repairs have to be made. Sometimes an entirely new roof must be built.

Traditionally, the old adobes were covered with a foot or more of an adobe soil mixture with a heavy clay content. It takes a lot of water and considerable time to get clay soaked through. As long as efficient run-off is provided, no water will seep through such a

Fig. 8-10. An extreme example of what can happen to an adobe building when the roof is not cared for.

thickness of clay-rich adobe. However, like all adobe, water tends to wash it away, small amounts at a time (Figs. 8-10, 8-11 and 8-12). Such a roof will need to be built up again year after year.

Obviously none of us would want to be bothered with such frequent and annoying chores. Therefore, we might as well take advantage of whatever modern materials are available. The most commonly used material is asphalt roofing felt, available in a variety of thicknesses. But because this is also affected by weather, especially sun and heat, it needs to be adequately protected.

Since a good roof is so important and since subsequent repairs tend to be costly and often frustrating, it would seem advisable to have the roof built by a professional roofer. Some of them may be willing to guarantee the integrity of the roof for a reasonable period of time.

Regardless of who does the actual work, a good roof consists of several layers of material:

- ■ The decking, a layer of at least 4-inch insulation material.
- ■ An additional roof deck above the insulation, usually constructed of ½ inch plywood and supported by joists so that it won't compress the insulation material.
- ■ Above that, several layers of roofing felt.
- ■ These should then be topped by gravel. Use light colored in hot desert areas and darker gravel elsewhere. Pour it on

Fig. 8-11. If the roof is not taken care of on an adobe building, it collapses.

top of hot asphalt which, when it hardens, will hold the gravel in place.

The space between the two decking layers that is filled with the insulation material should be vented to the outside. The vents need to be covered with a fine wire screen to prevent birds from building nests in the space.

Gabled Roofs

Gabled roofs, atypical of adobe structures, offer greater areas to be used for insulation. If money is no object, the roofing felt can be covered with and protected by Spanish tile. If properly installed, this tile will produce a roof that will last practically forever. Be sure that the tiles extend far enough outward to avoid the water runoff from leaking down the adobe walls and ruining the plaster.

Fig. 8-12. Once an adobe roof collapses, the building soon becomes a ruin which is beyond saving.

Fig. 8-13. A close look at a small section of the Taos Pueblo shows the small windows and the stubs of the vigas separating the various stories and supporting the roof. It also shows canales which drain the water off the roof far enough from the walls to protect them from excessive water damage.

Fig. 8-14. Icicles are hanging from the canales of this adobe home.

Flat Roofs

Flat roofs, in addition to what has been said earlier, need a *parapet*. A parapet is continuation of the walls above the level of the roof, rising approximately a foot or so. This assures that the water will run off through the canales which must be built into the parapet. They must also extend outward far enough to keep the water run-off

Fig. 8-15. Snow is piled up on the vigas of this adobe home.

clear of the walls (Fig. 8-13). Be sure to place the canales in a place where prolonged run-off and dripping doesn't get in the way of traffic or the view out of a window. When several inches of snow start to melt, water is likely to keep running from these canales for several days. This often freezes at night, producing spectacular icicles (Figs. 8-14, 8-15 and 8-16). The canales are U-shaped metal drains and should be supported by extended vigas or the weight of those icicles will cause them to break off.

ROOF AND CEILING OPTIONS

Chimneys, vent pipes, skylights and the like must be specially treated with flashings of extra heavy roofing felt or metal. This will cause the water to run away from them and not start to gradually leak through the space where they are sticking out through the roof.

Skylights are especially vulnerable to leaks. There is a saying in Santa Fe that there isn't a single skylight in that town (and there are thousands) that doesn't start to leak eventually. The trouble is that once such a leak occurs, the only effective way to stop it is to remove the skylight. It can be put back while the entire section of the roof where it is located is being rebuilt.

I have lived in a house with two such leaking skylights. Over a period of three years the roofer came five times to try and correct

Fig. 8-16. Snow and ice can do extensive damage to an adobe home.

the problem. It never worked. Every time there was a heavy rain or snow started to melt on the roof, we had to cover practically the entire room with plastic sheets because the water would seep into the decking and start to drip in several dozen places at once.

Chapter 9
Entering Your Home

Think of the immediate first impression one gets from walking into a house for the first time. There is something comforting and friendly about walking into a foyer-type space first rather than finding oneself immediately in the living room. It facilitates the greeting of guests and the process of removing overcoats and galoshes. It also prevents outdoor dirt from being dragged all over the house. There should be a fair-sized coat closet with a shelf for hats, gloves and such.

ENTRY HALL

The foyer, or entry hall, doesn't have to be a huge space. It should be large enough for four or five people to greet one another simultaneously. It can lead directly into the living room or it may be separated by bookshelves used as a divider. A row of planters often makes a nice divider also.

In climates with cold winters the foyer also prevents gusts of freezing air from blowing through the living room every time the front door is being opened. In such locations it is important to make provisions for a radiator or an outlet for the forced-air heat in the entry hall. This keeps it at a reasonably comfortable temperature even at times when the front door is being opened at frequent intervals, such as might be the case when guests arrive for a party.

A great added convenience, though certainly not a necessity, would be a half bath accessible directly from the entry hall. It keeps

Fig. 9-1. In this home hallways were virtually eliminated by having rooms run into one another, connected by adobe archways.

visitors out of the primary bathrooms and gives women a convenient place to touch up their makeup before being introduced to the other guests.

OTHER HALLWAYS

One typical problem facing the amateur architect in designing his dream house is that he frequently ends up with one or, worse yet, several long hall-ways in his effort to connect all of the individual rooms. A certain amount of hall may be unavoidable, especially if

Fig. 9-2. A relatively narrow hallway can be made pleasant by imaginative decorating.

there are three or more bedrooms and the appropriate number of baths to go with them. But, as a general rule, halls are a waste of space and should be kept to an absolute minimum. Long, narrow halls with doors on either side leading to different rooms tend to result in a hotel effect which is less than desirable. A certain amount of improvement can be achieved by running the hall along an outside wall, with windows on one side and doors leading to the rooms on the other. At least then the hall will be light in the daytime, reducing that unpleasant tunnel effect.

Whenever halls are unavoidable, their dimensions are of significance in making them as pleasant as possible (Fig. 9-1). The absolute minimum width should be not less than 3 feet. It must also be sufficiently wide enough to move furniture in and out. A little extra width, say 4 feet, is a lot better. But don't go over-board. More width becomes a useless waste of space unless you can go all the way to 7 or 8 feet. In that case the hall becomes another room which can be furnished with a chair or two, a cupboard or a chest of drawers and decorated with pictures (Fig. 9-2).

Of course, not all hallways are necessarily ugly or undesirable. One of the more spectacular homes, situated atop a hill in the north section of Santa Fe, is built around a central patio. It is a modern version of the fortress-like homes popular in the early days of the affluent Spaniards. All the way around that inner patio—a thing of beauty in itself with flowers, trees and shrubs—there is an 8 or 10-foot wide passageway.

The patio side of this passageway is glass enclosed with several sliding doors for access. All of the rooms of the house open onto the other side of that passage. In this instance the hall is a thing of beauty, offering easy access to all parts of the house without compromising whatever privacy may be desired.

Chapter 10
Main Living Quarters

No matter what you have done with your hallways, they will eventually lead to several major rooms in your house. Most homes include a living room, a dining area, a kitchen, one or more bedrooms and at least one bathroom.

LIVING ROOM

The living room may not be the primary area for family activities, depending on whether or not your plan also includes a den or family room. One way or the other, the living room can be of any size or shape that appeals to you. However, if the width exceeds 18 or 20 feet, you may have to include some type of structural supports. Wooden pillars or a partial wall could serve as the supports as well as add to the charm of the room. Or a multi-directional fireplace can be built somewhere into the middle of the room, serving the dual purpose of supporting the ceiling and roof as well as providing heat for the room.

Figure 10-1 offers a number of interesting details in its view of an unfinished living room or den. Note the concrete lintel poured above the window and door portion of the right wall. It has been extended across the rear wall and the top of the fireplace. A second bond beam can be seen at the top, supporting the vigas. Electrical wiring has been attached to the wall, but it will eventually be plastered over. Judging by the vents on both sides of the fireplace, it appears to have been constructed with a heatilator type of interior for better distribution of heat. The floor is a solid concrete slab which

Fig. 10-1. The living room is being built in an adobe home.

will probably be covered with either brick, wood or some other floor covering.

You may wish to drop the floor of the living room below the level of the rest of the house (Fig. 10-2) or raise it above that level by a step or two. You may want to combine the room with the primary patio by using sliding double-width glass doors, thus creating the effect of much more space than is actually allotted to the room itself.

Lighting is important both in the daytime when most of the light will be provided by the windows or glass doors and at night when artificial light should create a comfortable and intimate atmosphere. It is certainly advisable to plan dimmers for all electric light in a living

Fig. 10-2. Placing different rooms at different levels often provides added charm. Note the use of aged wood in the door and steps. The inside of this adobe wall was covered with only a very thin coat of plaster to retain the adobe-brick look.

room so that the level of available light can be adjusted to fit any particular occasion.

In planning the layout and the best location for the fireplace, think in terms of being able to create groupings of furniture which will permit small numbers of people to carry on a conversation without having to sit on the floor or to shout at each other all the way across the room.

If there is going to be a television set and a stereo system in the room, you might want to think in terms of recesses in the walls for built-in speakers or for the television. Bookshelves, either built-in or separate, are an important consideration. There is something sterile about a room without books, therefore ample wall space must be available to accommodate them.

Also arrange for a space to keep a supply of logs for the fireplace. You don't want to have to run outdoors in the middle of a snowstorm every time a new log is needed. Logs are placed vertically on the base of the fireplace in the kind that are normally used in adobe homes. You will have little trouble starting the fire if you use reasonably dry pinon or juniper logs. On the other hand if you prefer the more conventional type of fireplace in which logs are burned horizontally on a grate, you may want to include a gas outlet to minimize the need for kindling. Kindling tends to be messy and is a real pain.

Thought should also be given to the height of the ceiling. There is something particularly attractive about a high ceiling, but the room has to be large enough. A small room with a too-high ceiling is just as uncomfortable as a very large room with a standard eight-foot ceiling. Remember that a viga ceiling has actually two heights, the distance from the floor to the bottom of the vigas, and the distance to the decking above the vigas. A beautifully executed viga ceiling is an important part of the ambience of such a room, but it must be the right height in order to not be either oppressive or so high as to be out of proportion.

DEN

A den or family room is a nice luxury, especially for those who like to maintain a degree of formality in the living room (Fig. 10-3). The den should be large enough to accommodate all members of the family for joint activities, but it need not rival the living room in size. It might be planned as an extension of the kitchen or dining area separated by planters or a breakfast counter. Or it can be an entirely separate room.

Think in terms of informal comfort for your den. It should be a place to read magazines and keep those which are of lasting value. It can be a place to watch television or listen to music. It should be furnished with informal but comfortable couches and easy chairs (Fig. 10-4), a large coffee table (Fig. 10-5) or several smaller ones and possibly a desk. Lighting should be arranged to provide individual pools of light, preferably on individual dimmers to control the intensity of the light in different portions of the room.

A fireplace would seem to be a virtual must to create that atmosphere of cozy warmth during long winter afternoons and evenings.

Fig. 10-3. A rounded wall for a den is being built for this hillside home. All the construction details are clearly discernible at this stage.

Fig. 10-4. When planning a den, think in terms of informal comfort.

Depending on your personal preference, a den may be square, or round, or triangular or of any other shape that might fit into the floor plan. Less conventional shapes often add a feeling of intimacy. This feeling may be further heightened by dropping the level of the floor a step or two below that of the rest of the house. Consider a brick floor covered with incidental Indian or other rugs and some throw pillows for sitting on the floor.

In the final analysis, what is being done with a den depends to a great degree on a variety of factors:

- Do you work at home and, if so, do you want to use the den as the place in which to work during the day? If that is the case, it will definitely need to be separate from other rooms in the house.
- Do you and possibly the rest of the family want to be close by while your wife is busy in the kitchen preparing meals? In that case the idea of building the den as an extension of the kitchen or dining area may be preferred. This also comes in handy if you like the idea of informal meals or snacks in front of the television set.
- Do you have a hobby of some sort? Some hobbies such as stamp or coin collecting require little space and produce no

Fig. 10-5. An informal couch and a large coffee table offer a relaxing atmosphere in this den.

mess. Others need lots of room, may involve the use of tools and create all manner of unavoidable disorder. Thus, if the den is to also serve as a hobby room, you may want to proportion it in a way which will permit separating one end or corner from the rest of the room by planters, bookshelves or some similar arrangement.

- Do you have a guest room or will the den occasionally have to accommodate overnight visitors? If that is envisioned, it would again seem preferable to plan it as a separate room which could be closed off. It would also be nice if it wasn't too far away from the nearest bathroom.

KITCHEN

Designing a kitchen would, on the surface, seem to be a cut-and-dried affair. Certain appliances such as a refrigerator, range, oven, sink and dishwasher are basic necessities and of fairly standardized proportions. Appropriate space must be allotted for each. Standard counter tops are 25 inches in width, plus about 1 inch for the splash guard along the back.

But remember that whoever does most of the cooking in the family will most likely spend a great deal of time in the kitchen. It should therefore be efficient, comfortable, attractive and laid out in a way that will minimize the amount of walking needed to get from one appliance to the other.

In addition to the basic appliances there must be cabinets to store dishes, pots, pans and foods. In most standard kitchens some of these cabinets tend to have shelves which are too high to be reached by a woman of average height without climbing on a footstool. They are useless except for the storage of items which are used most infrequently.

In trying to work out a practical layout for a kitchen, first decide on the type of appliances you will want to use. Does a standard range with one or two ovens underneath suit your taste? Or would you rather have the ovens built into the wall where they can be placed at a more convenient level? Refrigerators can have doors opening in either direction or have two doors. If you already have a good refrigerator, then the direction in which its door opens must be taken into consideration.

Many families like their kitchens to be open to the dining area or the living room. Others prefer them to be separate and closed off with a wall and door. In the latter case you might want to consider an opening in the wall with a sliding door through which dishes and food can be handed into the dining area without the need to constantly walk back and forth. In either case, an exhaust fan and a vent are need to draw kitchen odors and smoke from the kitchen to the outside (Fig. 10-6). Some stoves come with built-in vents which draw the smoke over some sort of charcoal filter and then blow it back into the room. They are to be avoided like the plague, because no matter what is being prepared, the whole house will smell of it.

Quite a few newer adobe homes have what is referred to as an *island kitchen*. (Fig. 10-7). An island is built into the center of what is usually a rather large kitchen area (Fig. 10-8). Quite often they have a built-in oven range and a fairly sizeable workspace (Fig. 10-9). Such an arrangement is particularly attractive and practical when the kitchen area includes the dining room.

Fig. 10-6. Exhaust is provided through a flue which goes through the cabinets above the range.

Fig. 10-7. An island kitchen with the range built into the island. The island also serves as a breakfast counter.

Fig. 10-8. An island kitchen adds to the uniqueness of this adobe home.

Fig. 10-9. In this kitchen, the range and the sink are built into the island.

Do you like to have your breakfast or other meals outdoors on a patio? Do you plan to do a lot of entertaining outside? If so, you'll want to consider the ease or difficulty with which food, dishes and drinks can be brought from the kitchen to the patio (Figs. 10-10 and 10-11). If it requires dragging everything through half of the house, the patio is likely to be ignored most of the time.

Pantries, once very popular, virtually disappeared from the scene in recent years. But they are making a comeback and are a most desirable feature especially in homes which are located some distance from markets and shopping areas. In such locations, the additional storage space provided by a pantry can be a great convenience.

Don't forget a service sink. It is impractical and unappetizing to have to wash out cleaning rags and mops in the kitchen sink. Ideally, the service sink should be in a separate room with storage space for brooms, mops and the like. It could also house the washer and dryer, in which case there has to be a vent to the outside for the dryer.

DINING AREA

The formal dining room seems to be a thing of the past. It was popular during the era when there were cooks and maids to prepare

Fig. 10-10. A small patio directly outside the kitchen makes having breakfast and other meals outdoors an easy pleasure.

Fig. 10-11. The patio should be an easy walk from the kitchen.

and serve the meals and when families dressed for dinner, making each meal a formal and festive ocassion. No more. Today we don't normally dine. We simply sit down and eat. The entire process usually takes no more than 30 minutes.

What has developed in place of the dining room is often found at one end of an L-shaped living room. It joins the kitchen where a dining table can be quickly and informally set and meals served with a minimum of fuss. There is nothing wrong with this, but if space and budget permit, a separate dining room can be a beautiful luxury to have.

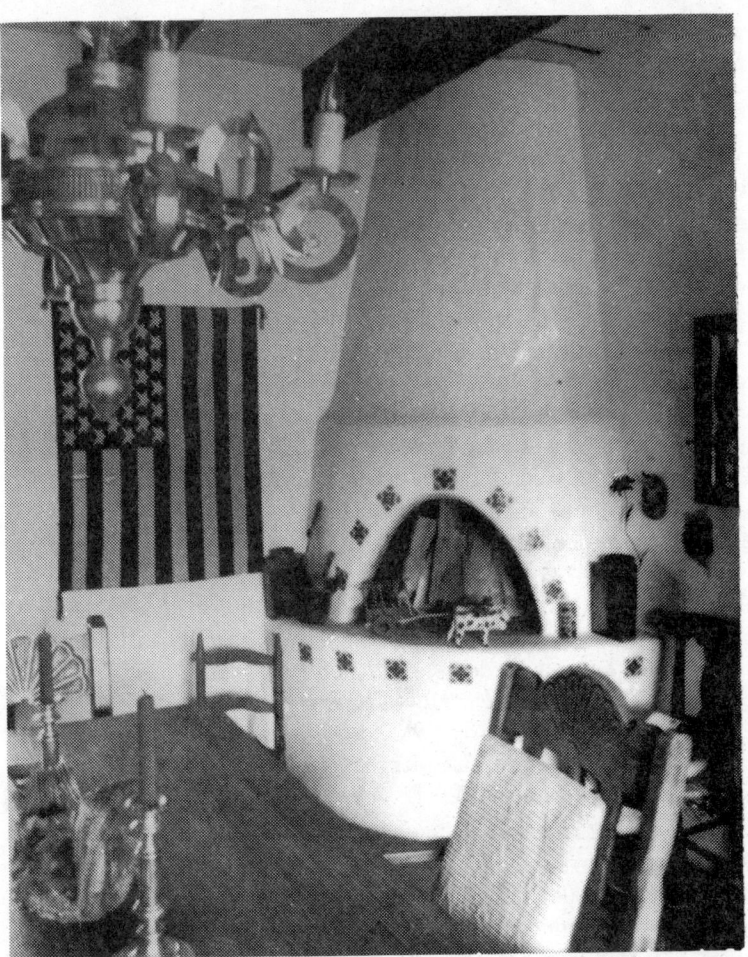

Fig. 10-12. This dining area is next to the island kitchen and features a small corner fireplace.

If you decide to include such a room in your plans don't forget that it requires appropriate furnishings to gain a graceful setting for dinner parties which will certainly be its primary purpose. You need a large and elegant dining table with chairs to match. There should be sideboards, preferably glass-fronted, to hold the better china and crystal. End tables or cupboards are also handy additions.

Lighting is important. There should be enough light to see what is being eaten, yet too much light will ruin the atmosphere. You may like eating by candle light, but even then a certain amount of extra illumination will be necessary. Usually a candelabra of some design which fits into the overall decor is an ideal solution. Put it on a dimmer to be able to control the amount of light you may want at any given time.

Logically the dining room should be next to the kitchen (Fig. 10-12). If the appropriate wall space is available, an opening in the wall through which dishes and food can be handed from the kitchen into the dining room is a great convenience. It should be equipped with shelf space on either side and with a sliding or other type of door which can be closed when the opening is not in use.

As a general rule the desired formality of such a dining room will be enhanced if the floor is of high quality hardwood. Such a floor gives a feeling of warmth and elegance. And it is relatively easy to keep clean. Rugs are a poor idea in dining areas because it is virtually impossible to prevent food from occasionally falling on the floor, causing rugs to become spotted and stained.

Unlike other rooms, a formal dining room can rarely be used for any other purpose. Therefore, unless you are in the habit of serving formal dinners or giving dinner parties with considerable frequency, the room is likely to be used infrequently. But don't think that simply because it will rarely be used, it might as well take up as little space as possible. Too small a dining room defeats the purpose for which it is planned. The whole idea of festive formality requires ample space. A proportion of 12 by 15 feet would seem to be about right, unless the planned parties are quite large. That would require a longer, though not necessarily wider room.

Windows are relatively unimportant, considering that the room will nearly always be used with artificial light. One window on the narrow wall should suffice to provide light in the daytime and the ventilation needed to clear out food odors. With plenty of wall space left over, this might be an ideal place in which to hang valuable paintings.

BEDROOMS

How many bedrooms will you need? First of all, there is the so-called master bedroom for you and your wife. There should be a second bedroom even if the family only consists of the two of you, just in case one of you comes down with a bad cold and you want to save the unaffected spouse from catching it. Such a second bedroom might double as a study, reading or sewing room. In that case, the bed itself should probably be one of those convertible sofas. An additional advantage of such a second room is that it can be used as a guest room, if a separate guest room is not part of your plan.

Fig. 10-13. A fireplace in the bedroom is a pleasant luxury.

In additon, if there are children, they too need room in which to sleep, play and work. Ideally, each should have his or her own room because privacy becomes increasingly important as they grow older. The number of children in your family and the available budget will definitely affect your decision.

Let's take one bedroom at a time.

The Master Bedroom

The variety of preferences when it comes to the place to sleep is virtually unlimited. Some people like a relatively small room with

Fig. 10-14. A double door leads from the bedroom to a small patio area.

just enough space for a bed, the necessary chest of drawers and ample closet space. Others prefer to wake up in a large room, comfortably furnished with easy chairs, a sofa, incidental tables and possibly a fireplace in which the ashes from last night's fire are still glowing (Fig. 10-13). Still others like to build a mezzanine type of area above part of the living room and use it for sleeping. Or one might consider a small private patio outside the master bedroom with large sliding glass doors to be able to enjoy the view of the early morning sun on the trees and shrubs (Fig. 10-14).

Regardless of personal preferences as to size, shape and location, certain basic requirements are an absolute must. Ample closet space is one. Preferably one entire wall should be set aisde as a closet with sliding doors. There must also be drawer space, either built-in or separate. The latter requires an adequate amount of uninterrupted wall space to accommodate the chests. On either side of the bed there should be room for a night table and lamp. What about a dressing room? You may want to use part of the bedroom as a place for a dressing table with a mirror and space for cosmetics and such. Or you may want to plan a separate small room for this purpose (Fig. 10-15). Either way, it will help to reduce congestion in the bathroom (Fig. 10-16).

Fig. 10-15. A separate dressing area is a desirable feature. Here light is provided by a skylight, since there are no other windows.

Fig. 10-16. Your bathroom will remain less congested if you have a separate dressing room.

A certain amount of care should be exercised in planning the location of windows and glass doors. Do you like to sleep with curtains drawn or open? If you prefer opaque curtains which keep the room dark no matter what is going on outside, then the placement of the windows and doors is not too critical. On the other hand, it you like to keep your curtains and windows open at night, you don't want windows located in such a way that the early morning sun shines right into your face while you're trying to snatch another 30 minutes of sleep. It's a nice feeling to have the sun shine into the room as long as it doesn't act as an alarm clock which can't be turned off.

Fig. 10-17. Ceramic walls accent this stall shower.

Second Bedroom

If the second bedroom is planned as nothing more than a second bedroom, then it will probably see little use except when you have overnight guests, one of you is sick or you have reached the stage in your life where you and your wife decide that sleeping in separate rooms is, after all, more restful. The rest of the time it is likely to develop into a place where things that have more or less outlived their usefulness will be stashed, especially if there is no practical storage space elsewhere. If that is the kind of room it is, all it needs is a closet of a reasonable size, a space for a chest of drawers, a chair or two, a night table, lamp and of course a bed.

Assuming that the available square footage is limited, it would seem more intelligent to plan this room as a combination second bedroom and study, library or hobby room. While even then it can still be fairly small, there should be room for comfortable chairs, a coffee table and possibly a desk of some kind. If it is to be used as a study or reading room, a small corner fireplace might be a desirable feature.

While a room like this would not necessarily require a direct access to its own bath, it should be located reasonably close to one because if and when it doubles as a guest room, it would be unpleasant for the guests to have to wander all over the house on their way to and from the bathroom.

Children's Rooms

Children's requirements tend to vary considerably from individual to individual. They also change as they grow older. As a general rule it is best to plan these rooms to be of a fairly good size, with as many built-in closets and storage spaces as possible. They should be uncluttered in design with plenty of window area for ample light. There has to be room for a single bed (or several, if the room is to be shared), several chairs, a table and possibly a desk and either built-in or separate shelves for books. Since children in their early years tend to be messy, a linoleum or other easy-to-maintain floor is usually the most practical choice. Walls should be finished in some sort of washable surface such as latex paint or washable wallpaper.

In addition children are often quite noisy. It is therefore a good idea to plan the location of their rooms as far away from the rest of the house as possible. Since there should be a separate bathroom for them, this may require some extra expense in terms of plumbing. However, the resulting peace and quiet for the grown-up faction is certainly worth the additional cost.

Guest Houses

The idea of a separate guest house, though certainly a luxury, is becoming increasingly popular. The advantages are numerous. First of all, if used for guests, it provides them with privacy and keeps them from being constantly underfoot. This makes the idea of a prolonged stay less painful for all concerned. Secondly, if by some happenstance a time should come when money is tight, guest houses can often be rented for sufficient amounts of money that may cover part or all of the mortgage payments. In future years when the children are gone and you may feel uncomfortable rambling around all alone in a huge house, you may want to move into the guest house yourself and rent the main house. That rental could provide you with a nice little extra income.

Ideally a guest house should contain a small bedroom, a living room with a small eating area, either a kitchenette or a small kitchen and a bathroom. In some areas zoning restrictions make it illegal to include a full kitchen in guest houses on the assumption that this would constitute a multiple dwelling. However, there are usually ways to circumvent such a regulation by adding some kind of kitchen facility after the guest house has been built.

When space permits it is a nice idea to design the outdoor space and plantings in such a way that the guest house ends up with its own

Fig. 10-18. A ceramic-tiled stall shower adds to the uniqueness of this bathroom.

reasonably private patio. That way, if you do ever find that you want to rent it, or live there and rent the main house, a degree of privacy is maintained for both. In this context there should also be a driveway leading directly to the guest house. Possibly it could even include some sort of covered car port.

Don't forget some means of heating the place. A fireplace might suffice in areas with mild winters, but elsewhere some type of gas, oil or electric heating unit is essential.

BATHROOMS

Most bathrooms are strictly utilitarian, containing a tub and, or shower, sink, toilet and just enough space for one person to do the various things which are supposed to be done in a bathroom. For most bathrooms that is just fine, but when it comes to the master bath, how about letting your fantasies run rampant?

Stall Shower. How about a stall shower with walls of ceramic tile (Figs. 10-17 and 10-18) and two showerheads? One could be high enough to stand under it upright and the other could be at a level which permits taking a shower while keeping your hair dry. A stall shower like that should be roughly 3 by 3 feet, although a few inches less would be acceptable. Making it much larger makes little sense, unless you like to shower with a friend.

Bathtub. Maybe you find a standard tub boring. If so, a sunken tub, designed to dimensions of your own preference and possibly lined with ceramic tile, might add a touch of elegance to the room. It can be rectangular, round or any shape that turns you on (Fig. 10-19). It can be large enough to let you lie in it full length, in which case the width should be just right to permit sitting up with the feet propped against the other side.

The Sink. Do you like an individual sink, free standing on a pedestal, or do you prefer pullman-type sinks set into a large surface area with a row of cabinets underneath (Figs. 10-20 and 10-21)? The latter is usually more practical, although some people like the former from a point of view of esthetics. Regardless of which you prefer, there should be provisions for a medicine cabinet, preferably built into the wall and a large mirror. Another mirror on the opposite wall would permit seeing oneself from both front and back. To accomplish this the two mirrors can't be exactly parallel. They have to be at a slight angle to one another. Walls in adobe houses tend to be slightly crooked anyway so this should present no major problem. Alternately, one might be hinged.

The Toilet. Regardless of whether you choose the cheaper small type or the more expensive larger version, the overall space

Fig. 10-19. If you find a standard tub boring, be creative with yours.

into which a toilet is placed should be not less than 3 by 4 feet. And while you're at it, put the toilet paper someplace where it can be reached without the need for major contortions.

Colors. Bathroom fixtures come in a wide variety of colors, but it should be remembered that those colors cannot be changed. If sink, toilet and tub are blue, you'll be stuck with that color and everything else in the room will always have to complement it. Unless you're absolutely certain that a certain basic color is what you'll be happy with for years to come, white fixtures might be a better idea. Then whatever color is used will be in terms of wall and ceiling paint, wallpaper and decorative details, all of which can be changed.

Fig. 10-20. Sinks are often set into a large surface area with a row of cabinets underneath.

Windows. Most builders seem to take it for granted that a bathroom window should be one of those tiny things. This is probably a hangover from building in cities where you wouldn't want your neighbor to look in from next door while you're doing your thing. But if there is no next door neighbor, a large window with a view of the outside would seem to be preferred.

One of the most sensational bathrooms I have ever seen had one entire glass wall with a sliding glass door looking out onto a small, fully enclosed patio. Since that patio was inaccessible from any direction other than the bathroom, complete privacy was preserved,

Fig. 10-21. When it comes to designing a bathroom, why not let your imagination run wild?

while at the same time, the feeling was created that one was taking a bath out in the garden.

On the practical side, don't forget that a bathroom needs a vent with an exhaust fan. It is also a good idea to arrange for some sort of special heating system because usually a great deal of time is spent in the bathroom in the early morning hours before the house has had a chance to get warm.

Chapter 11
Hobby Rooms

Anyone who would even consider the do-it-yourself aspect of building an adobe home is likely to be the kind of person who needs a place in which to work with his hands. Once the house itself is nearing completion, he may want to build bookshelves, make his own furniture or indulge in such hobbies as painting, sculpting or even building a model railroad layout. Regardless of what leisure time activity appeals to him, it is likely to involve the use of tools. This will result in noise and a certain amount of mess.

WORKSHOPS

Neither the living room nor the den are suitable for this sort of activity. Thus, a workshop or hobby room is probably of greater importance than one might initially think. If it is to be part of the house itself, try to place it as far away from the primary living portion of the house as possible. This will minimize the annoyance created when noisy power tools are being used. A simple cement slab floor is damage resistant and easy to clean. It is therefore preferred to wood, vinyl tile, brick or linoleum. Walls of raw wood, possibly with the studs exposed, simplify the task of storing tools within easy reach and of constructing utility shelves.

If an enclosed garage is part of the plan, it might be sensible to consider to enlarge it sufficiently to incorporate such a hobby room and workshop. This automatically helps to remove the noise and mess from the main house. But remember to include a means of heating the room if you want it to be usable throughout the winter months. The need for access to electricity goes without saying. You may also want to consider installing a sink and water faucet if the kind of work which you anticipate doing involves the use of water, even if only for the purpose of cleaning.

What size should such a room be? That depends entirely on what the planned activities involve. If you are hankering to construct massive pieces of furniture, you'll obviously need ample space. The final decision will probably be a compromise between what you'd like to have and what can be accommodated within the available space. Remember that such a workshop does not necessarily have to adhere to conventional room proportions. For example, if it is located in the back of a two-car garage, you may end up with a 20-foot long and 6- or 7-foot wide sausage of a room which may seem strange at first, but will actually prove to be very workable.

Don't forget to include windows. Not only are they needed to provide ample light, but even more important is the ventilation. No matter what you'll be doing in there, sooner or later you'll be using paints, or lacquer or some other material producing noxious odors. This will require easy access to a lot of fresh air. If a regular window is impossible for some reason, you may want to consider an openable skylight. Such skylights are equipped with a heavy-duty steel spring. They can be opened and closed easily from the inside and are commercially available. When properly installed they don't present any leakage problems. If none of this is possible, a vent with a reasonably powerful exhaust fan may suffice, but then all work will have to be done by artificial light.

STUDIOS AS WORKSHOPS

The workshop of an artist is a studio and since artists seem to be particularly drawn to the peculiar charm of adobe buildings, a brief section on the requirements for a studio seems indicated.

We might first analyze the different kinds of studios appropriate to various types of art forms. A sculptor's requirements tend to differ somewhat from those of a painter or a photographer. A musician will have still other needs.

A PAINTER'S STUDIO

Most painters like to work in a studio with a northern exposure, with large window areas giving ample indirect light, but no direct sunlight (Fig. 11-1). The size of such a studio room will depend largely on the type of painting being done. If the artist frequently works on huge canvasses or on full-size designs for murals, he will need ample space. He will need this space not only to accommodate

Fig. 11-1. Most painters like a studio with large windows facing north.

the painting itself, but also so that he can step back and examine his work from an appropriate distance and perspective. On the other hand, if he prefers working on a small scale, less room may be needed.

In either case, if live models are frequently used, the studio should include a small dressing room and adequate space for the model to pose. In that case it is preferred to have the studio located in a way which permits direct access from the outside. Then models won't have to go through the family living area in order to get to it.

Most such studios with their large windows and often high ceilings will be harder to heat than the average room. Provisions should be made to direct ample heat into the studio to keep it a comfortable place in which to work during the cold season. An additional convenience would be a half bath which includes a sink and toilet. The sink comes in handy to wash brushes and the like and the toilet keeps both the artists and the model within the confines of the studio.

The floor is a problem. A concrete slab would seem easiest to clean, but it tends to be hard on the feet for the artist who is likely to spend hours standing in front of his easel. A wood or other more resilient floor is more comfortable and gives a feeling of warmth. A good solution might be a wood or adobe-mud floor with some type of washable linoleum covering in the portion of the room where paints are likely to drip on the floor.

A PHOTOGRAPHER'S STUDIO

A photographer has different requirements. Most prefer to work with artificial light, so windows are unimportant. If they are included, the should be equipped with shutters to cut out all daylight when necessary. In most instances such a studio will have to be quite large and include ample storage spaces for props, backdrops and the like. The walls should be of smooth plaster or a similar surface, painted white to reflect light. The floor should be smooth to simplify the task of moving lights and camera tripods.

If models are used, the studio should be located to permit direct access from the outside. There will also have to be a dressing room with space for a makeup table and a rod to hang clothes.

In addition there has to be provisions for a darkroom. This includes plumbing, large sinks for the developing trays and place for an enlarger. Since this room has no window and is otherwise light tight, it will need some means of ventilation. It may also require an air conditioning unit in order to be usable during the hot summer months.

With the plumbing already in place, a half bath or possibly a three-quarter bath should certainly be part of the plan.

A SCULPTOR'S STUDIO

A sculptor's requirements tend to parallel those of a painter as far as light, northern exposure and overall size are concerned. He, too, will need access to water, a place for models to dress or undress and the necessary means of heating or cooling the place.

There are certain aspects in which the sculptor's requirements differ. Many of a sculptor's raw materials, such as marble, rock and metal are heavy and cumbersome to transport. While there seems to be no reason why a painter's or photographer's studio could not be on an upstairs level, a sculptor must not only consider that the floor of his studio will have to be firm enough to carry considerable weights, he will also need a means of backing a truck or van right up to the studio door in order to bring his materials into the studio. The finished work will be loaded onto a truck or trailer for transportation to the gallery or exhibition.

A MUSICIAN'S STUDIO

Here we are dealing with acoustics rather than light and the question of what to do with live models. The size of the room, its shape and wall surfaces determine the character of the sound produced by instruments or song. Smooth hard surfaces on walls and ceilings will tend to produce an echoing tunnel effect which will be annoying to the artist and make recording any kind of sound virtually impossible. A certain amount of curtains and hangings will help to minimize that effect, but too much could result in dead sound which is equally undesirable.

A room with a multitude of corners, angles and parallel walls where sound can bounce back and forth frequently results in a very respectable sound quality.

In order to protect family and neighbors from being exposed to hours of practicing music, the studio should most probably be soundproofed. If all walls are of adobe and of adequate thickness, that should take care of it. On the other hand, stud walls may need special soundproofing. The same will hold true for doors which lead directly from the studio to the living quarters. This soundproofing works in two ways. It not only keeps the music inside the studio, but it also prevents traffic and other disturbing noises from bothering the musicians.

The ideal size for such a studio depends on the use to which it will be put. There may have to be space and access for a grand piano.

If several musicians will frequently gather for group practice, the space must be sufficient for all of them. If test recordings are to be made, the quality of the sound is of greater importance than it would be otherwise.

With efficient soundproofing resulting in a room which is hermetically sealed, silent ventilation, heating and air conditioning become an important and necessary feature.

Obviously a great deal of thought should go into the planning of a studio. Many hours will be spent there so it is well worth the time and expense to do it right from the outset.

Chapter 12
Areas of Moderate Dimensions

These are the spaces which are necessary, yet are frequently overlooked by the do-it-yourself home designer.

UTILITY SPACES

What we're talking about here is room for the washer and dryer, the water heater, the central heating unit and a service sink. Let's take one at a time.

Washer and Dryer

Washers and dryers are relatively standard in size, measuring around 30 by 30 inches each. The washer requires attachments to the hot and cold water line, a drain leading to the sewer or septic tank and preferably a floor drain to minimze the danger of flooding the place if it ever overflows. Keep in mind that most washers will do that at one time or another.

The dryer may either be gas or electric. If it is a gas dryer, it needs access to the gas line. Furthermore it needs to be vented to the outside.

Most professional builders will habitually place the washer and dryer in a place which backs up to either the kitchen or a bathroom, thus reducing the need for additional plumbing. But a few dozen feet of additional plumbing are a relatively small item if you feel that a different location would be preferable. By all means think in terms of convenience rather than the saving of a few dollars.

A good proportion for a room for a side-by-side washer and dryer would be about 3½ by 5½ feet. Westinghouse produces a front-loading washer with the dryer mounted on top, designed primarily for apartments and mobile homes. (The identical unit is sold by Montgomery Ward under its own label.) By using one of these units the space requirement can be cut in half.

Water Heater

Water heaters come in varying capacities. Since the cost for a larger one is not a great deal higher than that for one with less capacity, it is certainly advisable to opt for one of sufficient size that will permit several members of the family to take showers without having to wait until sufficient hot water is again available.

When at all possible it is to be preferred to locate the heater reasonably close to where the hot water is being used. That way the time it takes until hot water is available at the tap is reduced to a minimum. Be sure that the hot and cold water pipes are not placed so close to one another that the temperature of one affects that of the other. Otherwise you're likely to end up with warm water coming out of the cold faucet. This can be annoying every time you turn on the tap to get a glass of cold water to drink.

Keep in mind that water heaters have been known to spring a leak or even to burst. This could result in expensive damage to floors, carpets, and furniture. For this reason it might be worth considering locating it in a space which is outside the main house. If that doesn't work, drop the level of the floor in its space a foot or so below the adjoining floor levels and incorporate a floor drain.

If the heater uses gas, a gas line will also have to be provided.

Central Heating

If it is at all possible to include a partial basement or even an adequate crawl space under the house, then that is the ideal place for the heating unit. If that is not feasible, a space must be found somewhere in the house. Provisions must then be made for the air ducts through which the air circulates to and from each room in the house.

The type of construction generally associated with adobe building often makes it difficult to find a logical place for all of these ducts. Where that is the case, a different type of central heating may have to be considered. The easiest to install are electric heating units which are placed along the floorboards. They take up virtually no room, require no structural consideration and are totally silent. Their drawback is that it takes a long time to heat a cold room and the cost of operation is fairly high. An alternate system involves circulating hot water through radiators or a network of thin copper pipes embedded in the floor. With this system the cost of the initial installation is quite high and it also takes longer to obtain adequate heat than with forced air. On the other hand, it is silent and the overall effect is most pleasant. It does require a second and separate water heater which might best be placed alongside the other water heater where provision for drainage and protection from water damage has already been made.

Service Sink

The service sink has already been mentioned in the chapter about kitchens. It is best located in a small, separate space adjoining the kitchen or pantry. It should include a door to the outside. Such a space can also be used for the storage of brooms, mops, cleaning rags and the like. If large enough it might also serve to contain a small supply of fireplace logs and protect them from rain and snow. A bare cement floor is to be preferred here because it will be unaffected by unavoidable water spillage.

Fig. 12-1. When the garage becomes a storage space, the cars are left out in the weather.

CLOSETS

In the long run there are few greater annoyances associated with living in any given house than a lack of closet and storage space. Living invariably involves the gradual accumulation of all sorts of things which even if not in daily use, one will want to keep. No matter what the number and size of closets and storage spaces, they always end up being filled to the brim. As soon as that happens most of us start taking things out to the garage and before we know it the car is left out in the rain and snow (Fig. 12-1).

The trouble is that such spaces take up a fair amount of square footage. Each square foot costs as much to build as any other, regardless of its eventual use. As a result we tend to shy away from alotting too much square footage to dead space (Fig. 12-2). Unless you are one of those rare birds who throws everything away the moment it has outlived its immediate usefulness, this is false economy.

There are different types of basic closets which are an absolute necessity. Each bedroom must have sufficient closet space for the clothes of the occupants of that room. Such closets must be 2 feet deep in order to accommodate suits and dresses on hangers without crushing them. If the closet is of the walk-in type, 6 feet is an ideal width. It provides for 2 feet of hanging space on each side and 2 feet of walking space. If only 4 feet are available, only one rod can be installed on one side of the closet (Fig. 12-3).

Shelves should be installed above the rod to hold suitcases, handbags, hats and whatever. A low shelf might be useful for shoes. One might also consider two rods, one below the other, to hang blouses, sweaters and jackets which do not require the full length from the upper rod to the floor.

The most practical type of closet door is a sliding door. They come in a variety of sizes, are relatively cheap and fairly easy to install. In addition, they don't use up space in the bedroom when left open.

Other necessary closets are a 2-foot deep coat closet in the entry hall and a linen closet. The latter should contain shelves and be large enough to hold linens, sheets and towels in such a way that permits taking them out without having to lift up a dozen sheets in order to get at a dish towel or face cloth. The contents of linen closets tend to be used in various parts of the house including bathrooms, bedrooms, the kitchen area and the dining area. They are often located somewhere in a hall, more or less equidistant from all parts of the house.

Fig. 12-2. The thickness of double-brick adobe walls permits the building-in of shelves and alcoves to display whatever we like to keep in full view.

Fig. 12-3. A large walk-in closet with a skylight is likely to be the delight of the lady of the house.

So much for the absolute necessities. But what do we do with old records, toys no longer in use, tools, skis, roller or ice-skates, and all the 101 diverse belongings which we rarely use but don't want to get rid of? If a regular garage is part of the plan, storage cabinets can be built-in. There will be more about that in a later chapter. If all you're planning on is an open carport, that will be a less than satisfactory location in which to store anyting worth storing at all.

The basements and attics of conventional houses traditionally served as ideal depositories for things one wanted to keep. After generations of use many attics have proven to be a veritable treasury of family history. But adobe houses are usually built directly on firm ground with no basement or even a crawl space and the flat roof makes an attic impossible. For this reason some type of large storage space must be planned for as part of the house itself. If there are stairs, the space underneath them might suffice. If not and if no other suitable area can be set aside, you might just consider a lean-to against one of the outer walls. If constructed of adobe and properly porportioned, it can be made to look quite attractive by giving the impression that it is an integral part of the house itself.

Children's rooms need more than the average amount of closet and storage space. While the clothes closet may not need to be as large as that for adults, they do need space for toys, school books, tools, baseball gloves, football helmets and the million and a half other things that they will accumulate and cherish.

Chapter 13
Fireplaces

An adobe home without fireplaces is like life without love. Something vital is missing. You will notice that I said fireplaces, plural. Much of the charm of older adobes results from the fact that there are fireplaces in practically every room. A fireplace is the focal point of any room (Fig. 13-1). It is its heart and soul, radiating a feeling of warmth and welcome to all who enter (Fig. 13-2).

Include as many fireplaces as you can afford in your original plan. If for some reason or other you can't or don't want to build all of them right away, be sure to pour adequate foundations wherever a fireplace might be built sometime in the future. It is necessary that fireplaces be planned for and preferably built during the early stages of construction because they require special consideration with reference to the strength and thickness of the foundation. The one in Fig. 13-3 is apparently ready to be tested. The adobe bricks in the foreground will be used in the construction of interior walls. Note the nailing blocks embedded in the wall at the left. They will eventually be used to hold a door frame.

Where should your fireplaces be? The living room and den are obvious candidates. A fireplace in the master bedroom is also a desirable feature. You may even consider putting one in the kitchen (Fig. 13-4) where it can be used in the winter to broil steaks on a hibachi.

There are two basic types of fireplaces. One is the conventional type. It is placed flat against or into a wall. The other, traditional in adobe homes, is the corner fireplace (Fig. 13-5). This latter type is

Fig. 13-1. An adobe fireplace built flush into a wall in an adobe home.

simpler to construct because two of its walls are already in existence. When no corner is available a *padercita,* a short piece of wall, can be built into the room. This creates a corner for a fireplace while at the same time serves to divide the room into several areas of activity (Figs. 13-6 and 13-7). A third possibility, although relatively rarely found, is a free-standing fireplace in the middle of the room (Fig. 13-8). There are conmercially available ready-made Swedish fireplaces or one can be sculpted out of adobe (Figs. 13-9 and 13-10).

The size of a fireplace should be in a sensible relation to the size of the room. A huge fireplace in a small room will tend to look as much out of place as would a small one in a large living room. From a practical point of view with an eye toward the amount of heat it will generate, the size is of less importance than one might think. I have seen quite small ones put out a great deal of warmth and huge ones which didn't seem to do much at all.

The fact remains that a fireplace is more important from the point of view of the esthetic pleasure it provides than as means of heating the house. Fireplaces, no matter how well constructed, are always inefficient sources of heat because an excessive percentage of the warmth they produce goes right up the chimney. With this in mind, design your fireplaces for the pleasure they will give and depend on an efficient heating system for warmth.

The traditional Indian fireplace was simply a firebox in the corner of the room with a straight chimney above it to draw out the

Fig. 13.2. In its stark simplicity a beautifully designed and executed corner fireplace in a remodeled old adobe.

Fig. 13-3. Fireplaces must be planned for and built during the early stages of construction.

Fig. 13-4. A corner fireplace in the part of the kitchen used as a dining area.

Fig. 13-5. A beautifully designed and executed traditional corner fireplace. It can be left with the brick design exposed or it can eventually be plastered over along with the rest of the walls.

smoke. While simple to construct, it is extremely inefficient as far as heat generation is concerned. It is also subject to sudden downdrafts which tend to blow ashes and glowing cinders all over the room.

An efficient modern fireplace (Fig. 13-11) consists of the following:

- foundation
- stem
- throat
- smoke shelf
- flue
- shell
- face
- hearth

Let's take them one at a time.

FOUNDATION

A fireplace is a great amount of weight concentrated in a small area. For this reason it will require a foundation of greater strength than is needed for other portions of the house. The average founda-

Fig. 13-6. A traditional corner fireplace built against a corner formed by one wall and one padercita.

Fig. 13-8. A free-standing fireplace partially completed in an adobe home under construction.

tion for a fireplace is a concrete slab. It is at least 1 foot thick and 4 to 6 inches larger than the actual fireplace. It must be reinforced with rebars and should rest on undisturbed ground. When in doubt, more foundation is always better than less. It would be rather disconcerting to discover after several years that the whole structure is beginning to lean and in danger of tipping over. As already mentioned, while you're in the process of pouring foundations for the whole house, include fireplace foundations in any place in which you can possibly envision that you might eventually want to add a fireplace. At that point the added cost is minimal, whereas if you have to start from scratch and pour an additional foundation later on, it might prove to be a complicated and expensive undertaking.

STEM

This is a masonry structure. It usually consists of concrete blocks which rise from the foundation to the base of the firebox. If the firebox is to be level with the foundation, no stem is needed. If it is to be raised above the level of the foundation, that is where the stem comes in. It is generally a solid construction with all crevices filled with mortar. An opening can be provided for an ash dump with a

Fig. 13-7. An unusual fireplace built against a shallow recess in the adobe wall.

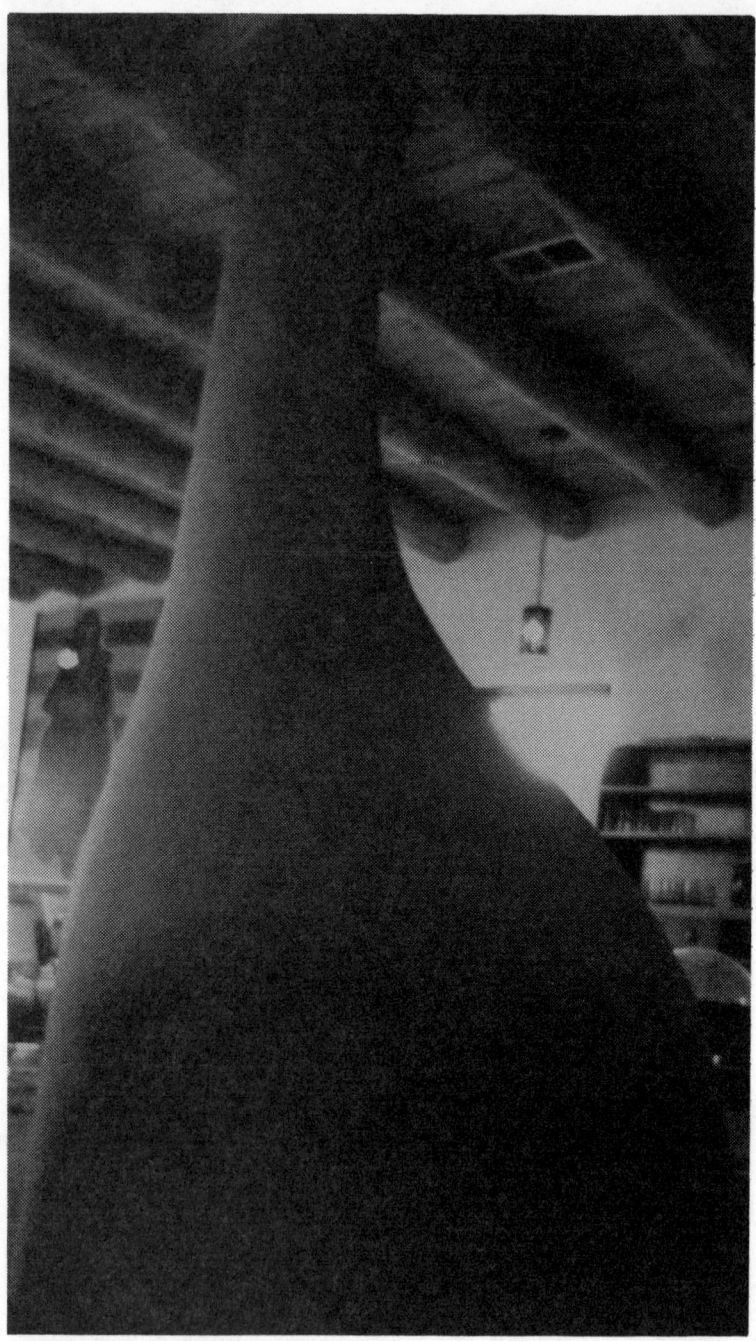
Fig. 13-9. An elegant free-form fireplace in a Santa Fe restaurant.

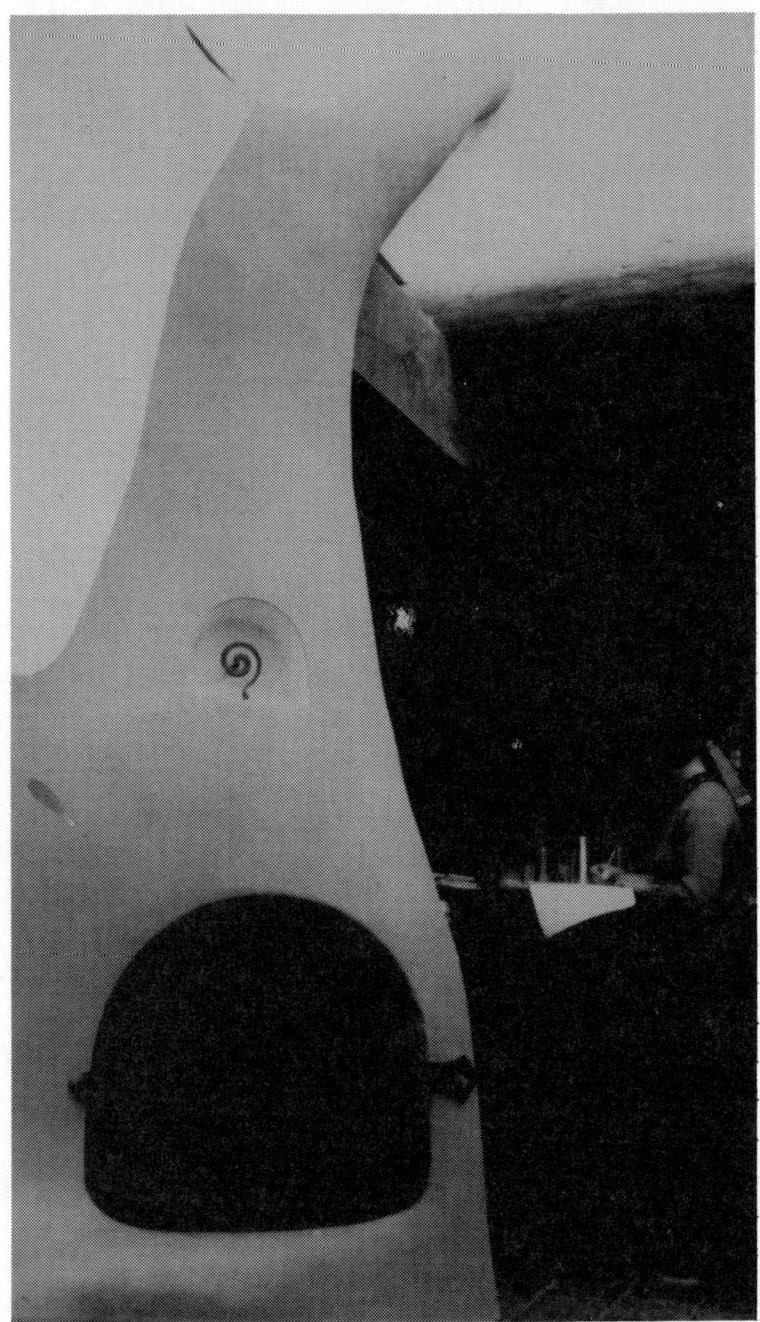

Fig. 13-10. A second view of a unique free-form fireplace in a restaurant in Santa Fe.

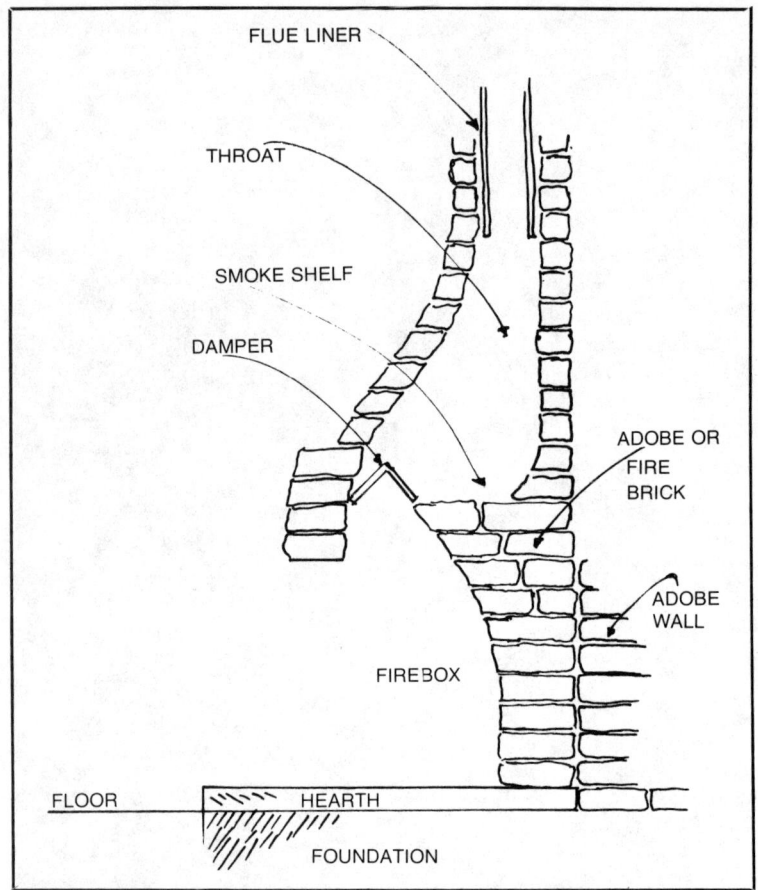

Fig. 13-11. Components of a fireplace.

means of removing the ashes from the outside. This is assuming that the fireplace is built against an outside wall. The height of the stem is not limited and if a fireplace is to be built into an upstairs room, the stem will obviously have to reach all the way up to the second floor.

FIREBOX

This is where your fires are going to be burning. It can be constructed of adobe brick or firebrick. Firebrick is mortared with fireclay or refractory cement. In some areas building codes required firebrick rather than adobe.

The trouble with adobe is that the mud plaster has a tendency to eventually crack away in chunks, requiring a replastering job from time to time.

The back wall of the firebox may be a continuous curve or it may be simply vertical for about a foot or so and then slant toward the room. This provides an angled surface which helps to deflect heat into the room. The side walls should be similarly angled to reflect warmth.

Since the opening of the firebox is what you'll be looking at, its shape should be pleasing. It may be a half oval, as is often the case with corner fireplaces, or a part of an oval with the top cut straight across or it can be rectangular, as is usually the case with conventional fireplaces built into the middle of a wall. In order to efficiently build symmetrical curved openings, you may find that it is useful to cut a template from a piece of plywood and then build the opening around that template.

THROAT

This is the upper portion of the firebox. It tapers to support the damper. You can buy prefabricated throats which simplify construction or it can be made of firebrick or adobe that is laid in such a fashion that each layer of brick extends beyond the edge of the one below it. This is called *corbelling*.

If a prefabricated metal throat is used it is important that there be a space between the metal surfaces and the brick. It should be insulated with fiberglass or rockwool. Any brick which actually touches the metal is in danger of being pushed out of place or cracked as the metal expands in the heat.

SMOKE SHELF

This is a necessary feature in the construction of any fireplace. It prevents downdrafts from reaching the firebox and blowing ashes or cinders into the room. In older fireplaces that were built without this feature, a stove-pipe damper often had to be inserted in the flue. When closed, this would prevent wind from blowing down the chimney. However, since it had to be open when the fireplace was in use, its usefulness was limited not to mention that fact that practically all the heat simply went up and out of the chimney.

FLUE

The simplest means of building the flue is to use clay-tile flue liners of the appropriate size. This results in a minimum number of joints and is cheaper than building the whole thing out of brick. It should be encased in brick and must be built up to extend at least 2 feet or more above the roof. Once the flue has been installed, it is a good idea to make a fire in the firebox and test the entire system to make sure that it works and draws all right.

SHELL

The shell is the main structure which surrounds the basic firebox and which can be built to any size and shape that seems appealing. Most building codes require a minimum thickness for the shell. It is usually 1 foot if the fireplace is built into a stud wall or if there is any wood adjacent to it. If it is built into an adobe wall, the masonry abode will serve as part of the shell.

The shell can be built of adobe, solid bricks, rocks laid in concrete or any other solid masonry material or combination of materials. This choice will depend on the requirements of the prevailing local building codes.

FACE

The face is strictly decorative and has nothing to do with the basic fireplace structure. It can be adobe plaster that is smoothed by hand to give it that slightly undulating effect—part of the charm of working with adobe. It can be brick, rough-hewn rocks, marble or any other non-flammable material. Whatever material is decided upon, take your time. This final result is supposed to be a thing of beauty, so don't mess it up by doing sloppy work in a hurry.

Virtually every fireplace face will include some kind of mantel. The sculpted adobe corner fireplaces usually simply have a narrow shelf built-in roughly at the level of the damper installation. Others may have wooden shelves projecting from the face. In this latter case, be sure to remember to build adequate supports deep enough into the face and possibly shell to support not only the shelf itself, but also anything that may eventually be placed on it.

HEARTH

A hearth is simply a projection of non-flammable material at the level of the base of the firebox. Its purpose is to catch sparks and prevent them from falling on flammable surfaces such as wooden floors or carpets. It normally extends in front of the firebox for about 1½ feet. If your floors are brick or a concrete slab, no hearth is needed. On the other hand, a raised hearth in front of a fireplace which is built up to the appropriate height may be extended on either side of the firebox, thus providing a pleasant place to sit.

There are prefabricated circulating fireplace structures available on the market such as heatilators. Some include fans which blow the warmed air into the room. In one unit they usually consist of a double-walled metal firebox, damper and throat. Using one of these units makes the job easier for the do-it-yourself builder, but he will be stuck with whatever sizes and dimensions are available. The installation involves building a floor for the firebox on which the unit rests. It will then have to be enclosed in a shell. This shell may have to be larger in order to accommodate the air ducts. As far as cost is concerned, it may come out about even because what is being paid for the prefabricated unit will be saved in other materials and time.

Chapter 14
Outdoor Projects

For some people a home is not complete without the added attractions of a garage, at least one patio, an outdoor barbecue and a swimming pool.

There is no doubt that these luxuries add to the charm and value of your home and some of them may be within closer reach than you think.

THE GARAGE

Considering what automobiles cost these days, it is amazing to realize how many large and expensive houses exist without a garage or even a carport. Leaving the cars outside in all kinds of weather is bound to be detrimental in the long run. In addition, there is the annoyance of getting soaked whenever it's raining or the annoyance of having to scrape ice and snow off of the windshields on cold winter mornings.

A two-car garage should be considered as a necessary minimum these days, not only for your own convenience, but also because it will seriously affect the resale value. Although the idea of selling right now may be the farthest thing from your mind, virtually every house is going to be sold eventually. If space and budget permit, a three-car garage may be even better.

Whichever you decide, make it big. Twenty by 20 feet is considered the standard size for a conventional two-car garage but unless both cars are VWs or other small compacts, that is really too small. First of all, once the car is inside and the doors are closed, you will want to be able to get from one side of the garage to the other without having to climb over the bumpers. You will also want to be able to open the car doors without smashing them into the side of the other car. Secondly, the garage will also be used to keep bicycles, scooters, lawn mowers and the like. With no basement or attic available for this purpose, it will end up being the primary storage space for all kinds of items. It makes little sense to one day find that your driveway looks like a used car lot because there is no room left in the garage.

The floor of a garage should be a concrete slab, a few inches higher than the ground outside so that rainwater won't run into it. Ideally it should be slightly slanted toward the front so that it can be hosed off and the water will run off to the outside. The walls need not be finished unless you plan to include a means of heating it during the winter. As a matter of fact, unfinished stud walls simplify the task of installing hooks or nails from which to hang things.

Since the average hood of a car is only about 40 or so inches from the ground, it might be a good idea to consider building storage cabinets out from the back wall, some 4 feet off of the ground. Though this would necessitate always walking around the back of the cars when trying to get from one side of the garage to the other, it

Fig. 14-1. There should be direct access from the garage to the house.

Fig. 14-2. Assuming the cost of building a garage is beyond the budget, how about a carport?

can provide a huge amount of storage space out of harm's way.

Standard garage doors are either 8 or 16 feet. There is no particular reason why you could not construct your own in any size that turns you on, however. Most drivers prefer one big door to two small ones because it seems to make getting in and out easier. Also, if you should ever decide to install an automatic door-opener, you'll only have to pay for one of them.

The location of the garage with reference to the main house will necessarily depend on the proportion and topography of the lot. Ideally there should be a door leading directly from the garage to the kitchen or some place near it (Fig. 14-1). This will reduce the chore of lugging groceries from the car to where they are needed. If this is not possible and the garage has to be built as a separate unit some distance from the house, then by all means, plan for a covered walk between the two. It simply doesn't make sense to be unable to get from one to the other in a downpour without getting soaked to the skin.

Assuming that the cost of building a real garage is beyond your budget, how about a carport (Fig. 14-2)? All we are talking about here is a few rough-hewn posts and a roof made of plywood and tarpaper or whatever other material seems practical. It should be slanted just enough to assure water run-off. Sides can be covered with bamboo screens or lattice work with creeping plants. Either of these will provide shade and reduce the direct impact of driving rain.

Direct access from the carport to the house is also a desirable feature. Attaching the carport directly to one side of the house reduces structural problems. It has to be a part of the house where there is no window, though because you wouldn't want to look out onto the carport and give the carbon monoxide, generated when starting a car, the opportunity to seep into the inside.

This floor should also be a concrete slab. It should be a few inches higher than the surrounding ground so that it won't be covered with water and mud from rain or melting snow. Don't forget to make provisions for electricity. You wouldn't want to have to stumble around in the dark.

The major drawback of a carport is the fact that it is no good for storage. Even though it is theoretically possible to hang storage cabinets from the roof to a level above the hood of the cars, the fact that they are exposed to all manner of atmospheric conditions, moisture and changes in temperature makes their usefulness rather limited.

PATIOS

One of the primary pleasures of living in the southwestern United States, where most of the building of new adobes takes place these days, is the fact that the climate is inducive to spending much of one's time outdoors. It is therefore of some importance to carefully plan the patio areas at the very beginning when deciding on the orientation of the structure on the lot. Consideration must be given to the prevailing winds, the heat generated by the sun on summer afternoons, the relation of the road and driveway to the patios and, in turn, to a means of providing privacy (Figs. 14-3 and 14-4) and access to and from the different parts of the house.

If at all possible it is often preferred to think in terms of several smaller patio areas rather than one huge one. A patio with a western exposure, expecially if there is a view of the mountains beyond which the sun will set each evening, can be beautiful. But the afternoon sun may heat such a patio to an uncomfortable degree. Therefore, it would require some shade trees to make it livable.

Another one, oriented toward the south and protected against northerly and northwesterly winds by the house itself, will be usable throughout the winter when the air itself may be quite cold, but the rays of the sun are warm enough to sit out and get a tan.

To the east a small patio could be walled in for total privacy. It might connect with the bedroom or bathroom or both, offering a

Fig. 14-3. On the Camino del Monte Sol in Santa Fe a beautifully maintained adobe wall with heavy abutments surrounds an old adobe home and its patio.

Fig. 14-4. An outside entrance to the patio is provided by the surrounding adobe walls.

view of the morning light through the window and glass door areas of those two rooms.

The north of the house is often the least ideal for usable outdoor space. It's not bad in the summer but in the winter, with a fair portion of the patio constantly shaded by the house, snow will tend to accumulate and refuse to melt. In addition, one side of the house must be the one where the water drains through the canales from the roof and the northern side of the house is often the one selected for this. It might also serve as the place in which to bury the septic tank and the associated leach field which tends to be responsible for excessively dense and rapid growth of grasses, bushes, shrubs and weeds. If this growth occurs in one of the to-be-lived-in patios, it could result in constant gardening work to keep it from becoming unmanageable.

Depending on the location of your lot with reference to neighbors, roads and the like, you may wish to enclose the entire lot, including all patios, with an adobe wall (Figs. 14-5 and 14-6). If equipped with a gate which can be closed, this not only assures total privacy, but is also useful in keeping small children from straying into the street. In addition it prevents the dog from running around loose and getting into all kinds of mischief.

Fig. 14-5. An adobe-brick wall provides privacy for a home in the downtown area of Santa Fe.

Fig. 14-6. Privacy is offered to the home by adobe walls surrounding the patio.

Fig. 14-7. Patios come in all shapes and sizes. This one is covered with flagstones.

Fig. 14-8. This patio area is distinguished by imaginative wall sections.

Fig. 14-9. This small patio is enclosed near the entrance door.

Always consider the view if there is any. A 6-foot or higher wall will tend to effectively cut off whatever view there might be. It is therefore up to you to decide in which direction you will want to compromise.

Patios may include lawns, areas covered with flagstone (Fig. 14-7), gravel walks, flower beds, fruit trees, an outdoor barbeque and even a swimming pool. They come in all shapes and sizes (Figs. 14-8 through 14-11).

Lawns are beautiful when well cared for, but the secret words are *cared for*. They usually need to be treated with fertilizer in the

Fig. 14-10. This adobe home includes a small patio.

Fig. 14-11. This small enclosed area serves as the patio for this adobe home.

spring and then have to be mowed throughout the summer in order to look nice. If you don't mind the job of repeated mowing, fine. Just be sure that the lawn mower can be stored nearby and doesn't have to be dragged across half of the house.

Flagstones make attractive sitting areas (Fig. 14-12). Place them loosely on the ground without the use of cement. Granted, weeds will spring up between them and will have to be pulled or cut. But when embedded in concrete, moisture has a way of seeping into the various cracks and during the next truly cold winter night it will freeze, expand and result in unsightly fissures.

Gravel walks tend to be more ornamental than practical. Gravel is commercially available in all colors, sizes and shapes. It looks nice but unless of a very small size, is not particularly pleasant to walk on (Fig. 14-13). Here too, weeds will have a tendency to grow through the gravel from the earth beneath. To avoid this you might want to consider covering the ground under the gravel with dark brown or black plastic sheets to effectively keep the weeds away. They should be carefully covered to the very edges because pieces of plastic may stick out here and there. They are quite ugly and will ruin the effect you've been after in the first place.

Shade trees provide shade in the summer but they shed their leaves in the fall, requiring constant raking of the ground for several

Fig. 14-12. This large walled patio is also covered with flagstone.

weeks. Fruit trees do the same and in addition they drop their fruit which, unless picked up, ends up rotting on the ground. All types of trees usually require dormant spraying in the early spring before the leaves start to bud in earnest. Otherwise they are likely to develop some kind of blight. In the higher elevations where below-freezing night temperatures are not at all unusual as late as early May, certain types of early blooming fruit trees, such as apricots, rarely bear fruit because their blossoms have been exposed to frost. Great apples are being grown in these same higher elevations in the Rocky Mountain states, but unless appropriately treated and sprayed, there is likely to be a worm in every apple. Also, birds just love to feast on the fruit just before it is ripe enough to be picked. Peaches also do fine in this climate, but again the birds may be the major beneficiaries unless you can figure out a way to keep them away.

When selecting patio furniture try to select the kind which is least affected by weather. Certain of the more expensive plastic and metal lounges, chairs and tables can be safely left outdoors in rain and snow. This is great because it becomes a bothersome chore to have to remove the outdoor furniture every time there is a change in the weather. Redwood is also weather resistant, but requires pillows and pads in order to be comfortable. Of course they will have to be protected from repeated exposure to moisture.

Fig. 14-13. A concrete covered walk leads to a patio area on the north side of the house and is easier to walk on than a gravel walkway.

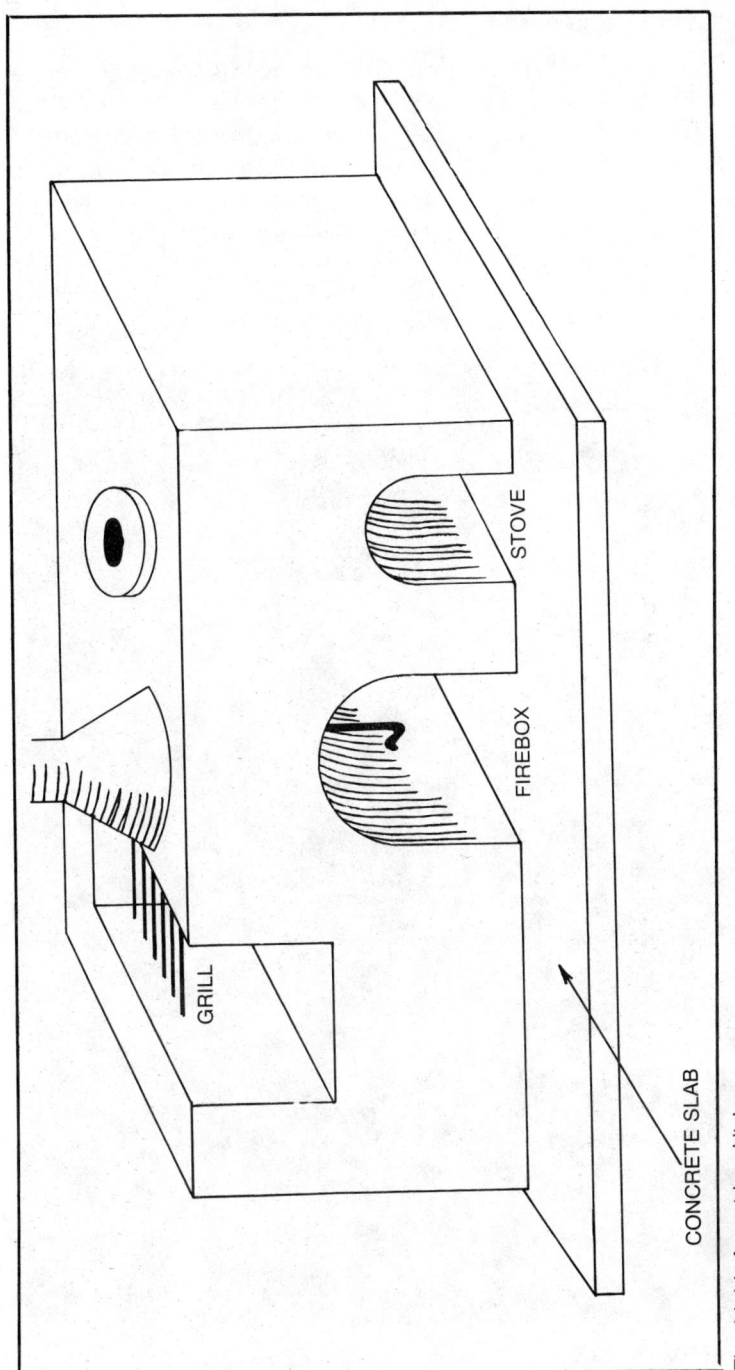

Fig. 14-14. An outdoor kitchen.

OUTDOOR BARBEQUES

Serving meals on the patio in the summer is a pleasant change from the usual routine. It is a nice idea to be able to do the cooking outside too. This can be accomplished with varying degrees of efficiency with anything from a simple portable barbeque or hibachi bought at the nearest discount store, to an elaborate outdoor kitchen built of adobe and including an oven, fireplace and stove.

To build such an outdoor kitchen, first decide on a practical location. It should form an integral part of the area of the patio where the appropriate tables and chairs are located. It is also helpful if it is

Fig. 14-15. A unique outdoor oven.

not so far from the house that all eating and cooking implements have to be carried long distances. Also consider the prevailing wind direction. An outdoor kitchen produces smoke and you wouldn't want to have to close every window on one side of the house to make sure that the house itself doesn't end up full of smoke.

Once the location has been decided upon, a concrete slab of about 5 or 6 by 15 or so feet should be poured. If the ground is firm and undisturbed it probably won't need any reinforcement or excessive thickness. It should be thick enough to minimize the chance of cracking and to safely carry the weight of the adobe structure which will be built on top of it.

While it is possible to use the top of the concrete slab as the base for the oven and fireplace, it is probably a better suggestion to place one or even two courses of adobe brick atop the slab. Recess it from the edge of the slab by about 1 to 1½ feet on one long side and less on the other three sides. This recess is needed to act as a hearth for the fireplace and oven (Fig. 14-14). The adobe courses make access to the fireplace and oven easier without having to always stoop all the way to the ground.

Then, on the left or right side of this base, adobe bricks are built up to a height of about 2½ feet into a solid structure which constitutes the base of the grill. It is then built up further on three sides, leaving sufficient space in the center for the grill. In the process of doing this, the iron grill rods are inserted at a sufficient height above the base to permit building a charcoal or wood fire underneath.

Adjoining this structure we build a beehive-type fireplace. This will not have to have the angled walls inside the firebox that are needed in interior fireplaces since we are not concerned with heating the patio. It also can probably safely eliminate the smoke baffle and damper. When building this structure entirely of adobe brick, hooks should be inserted which will permit hanging pots over the fire. The entire fireplace structure will take up little more than one-third of the overall outdoor kitchen unit.

Next to it an oven is built. Similar in construction to the fireplace, it will have a smaller opening in front. There is no chimney or flue (Fig. 14-15). We simply leave an opening at the top for which an appropriately sized metal cover must be obtained. A grill may be placed over that opening at the top which will permit hanging a chicken, or turkey or some such animal on a hook above the fire.

HORNOS

An alternate suggestion might be to forget about the oven and to build an authentic Indian *horno* on the third portion of the outdoor

Fig. 14-17. An Indian horno is used to bake bread.

kitchen (Figs. 14-16 through 14-20). A horno is a beehive-shaped enclosure used by the Indians to bake bread or to roast turkeys (Fig. 14-21). When baking bread a fire is built inside and left to burn until it is reduced to ashes, heating the horno itself to a high temperature. The ashes are then brushed out and the shaped bread dough is put inside. All openings, the larger front opening and the smoke hole are tightly closed and the bread bakes in the heat radiated inside by the hot adobe brick. If a turkey is to be baked, the coals are left in the

Fig. 14-18. An Indian horno can also be used to cook turkeys.

Fig. 14-16. Hornos are Indian ovens.

Fig. 14-19. Indian hornos can be found at the Taos and Santa Clara Pueblos in New Mexico.

oven and the turkey, on a metal pan, is placed on top of them. All openings are again tightly closed and the turkey is left to its own devices for several hours, cooking in its own juices.

To build a horno, adobe bricks have to be cut to the appropriate size. Or you might want to construct a special form and pour adobes of the size and shape needed. Once all of the bricks are in place, the inside can be left bare. The outside should be carefully plastered with

Fig. 14-20. Replicas of Indian hornos can be built in your own back yard.

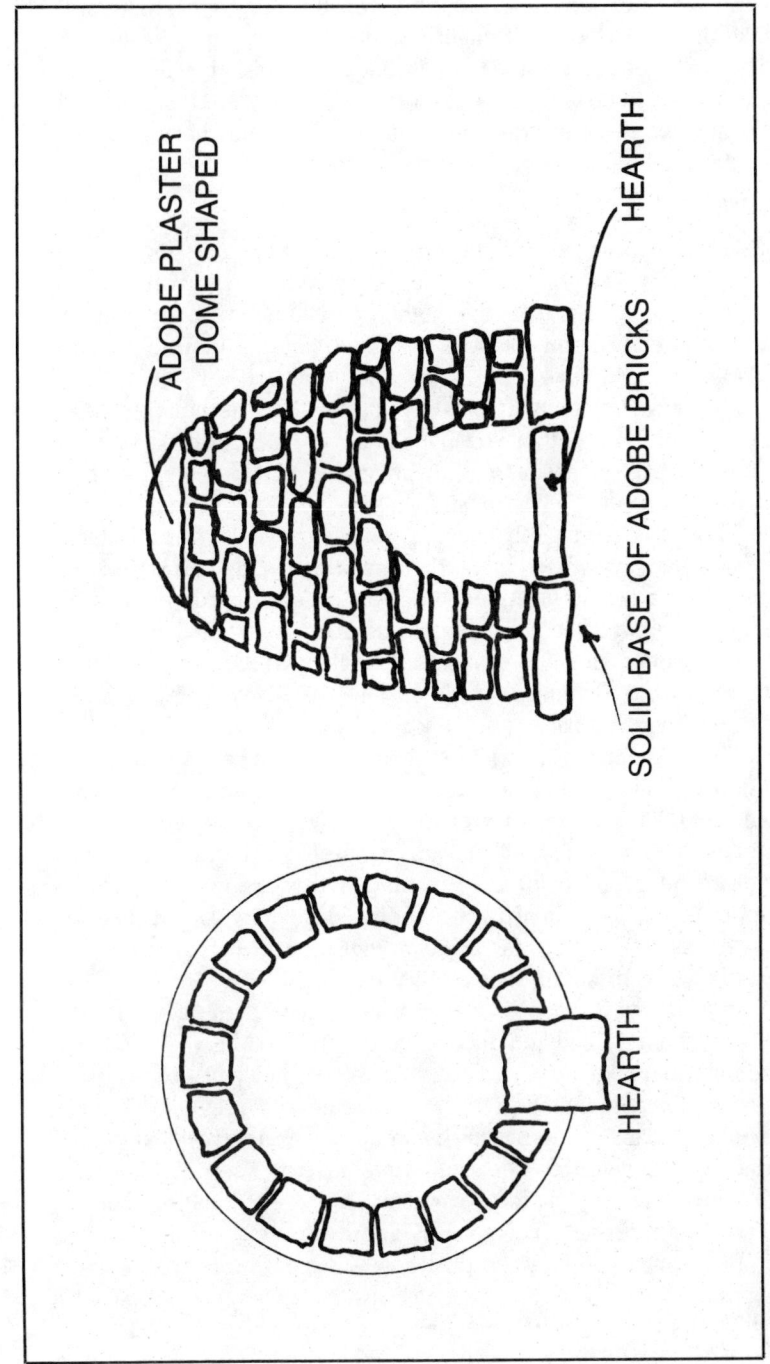

Fig. 14-21. Basic construction of a horno.

several layers of the usual adobe plaster in order to eliminate any cracks through which heat might escape. The ideal inside diameter of a horno for average home use is about 2 feet, with the width of the front opening measuring about 1 foot or a little more. Depending on the exact size of the finished horno, it will take somewhere between 100 and 200 adobe bricks to build.

SWIMMING POOLS

Once a status symbol of the super rich, swimming pools today are virtually taken for granted in regions where the winters are acceptably mild. Even in the higher elevations with their fairly severe winter weather for periods of five months, more and more pools are built each year.

A pool is a lovely thing to have regardless of whether you are an avid swimmer or whether you just like to take an occasional plunge. It is decorative, pleasant to sit by and gives an added dimension of elegance to outdoor entertaining.

Though never exactly cheap, it usually proves to be considerably less expensive when built at the same time as the house because excavating and the other needed equipment are already on the site and are being used to construct foundations and retaining walls.

Don't build an Olympic-size pool unless you are in training to compete in the Olympics. A dimension of 20 by 30 feet is about average. A much smaller pool tends to make it look like a displaced bathtub and much bigger will greatly increase the cost and problem of keeping it clean and heated. Though it requires in the neighborhood of 20,000 gallons of water to initially fill a pool, once filled the water is simply circulated through a system of filters and all that needs to be added from time to time is the amount lost through evaporation. A diving board is nice for the kids or anyone who likes to show off his or her expertise at executing fancy dives, but otherwise it would seem to be an unnecessary expense.

In areas where winter weather is of no consequence outdoor pools can be left filled and uncovered throughout the year. In such locations I have known of homes where the builder has extended a portion of the pool right into the house living room or even bedroom, providing a glass partition which can be lowered to just below the surface of the water to keep out wind or cold. This sounds like a lovely idea, but in practice I wouldn't be too surprised if it didn't prove to be more of a nuisance than it's worth.

Pools in parts of the country where severe winters are common do present some additional problems. In most cases they will have to be drained of all water with the onset of the cold season. What then remains is a relatively ugly hole in the ground into which small

Fig. 14-22. Equipped with a bubble enclosure, this pool can be used year around.

children or dogs may fall if no adequate protection is provided. The winds will blow large amounts of dust and dirt into it, resulting in a fairly unpleasant cleaning chore before it can be refilled in the spring.

One alternative is to install one of those plastic bubble-type pool enclosures which are kept inflated by a fan which blows heated air into the inside (Fig. 14-22). Thus equipped, the pool can be used year-round, no matter what the outside temperature is. The only real drawback is looks. Those pool enclosures tend to look like an incapacitated Goodyear blimp. The question which must be decided is whether your ability to use the pool for 12 months of the year is worth an oversized eyesore in your patio.

One word of warning. If you have small children, either teach them to swim as soon as they are old enough to crawl, or arrange for some sort of protection to keep them from falling into the pool. Each year we read about children who have drowned in pools. Make sure that it doesn't ever happen to yours.

Chapter 15
Utilities And Plumbing

The subjects briefly touched upon in this chapter are unglamorous and complicated, but necessary. Since all except the most experienced home builders will certainly want to have this work done by professionals, it seems unnecessary to go into great detail. For this reason we will simply provide what might best be described as a checklist.

HEATING

There are various ways in which you can heat your home. A few of the choices will be explained here.

Forced Air

Forced-air heating systems consist of a heater, ducts which carry the heated air to the various rooms in the house, additional ducts which draw air from the rooms back to the heater to be reheated, a fan to keep the air moving and two thermostats. The most efficient duct system brings the heated air into the rooms at the floor or baseboard level, while the return air is sucked out through openings near the ceiling. Since warm air rises to the ceiling, this results in less operation of the heater than would be required if the return air was pulled from the room at floor level.

One of the thermostats is located somewhere where the average room temperature can be expected, usually in a hallway. When the temperature at that location drops below that for which the thermostat is set, it activates the heater. The heater starts to heat the air and as soon as the air has reached a given temperature, a second thermostat, located in the duct system near the heater, causes the fan to start operating.

Ducts may be of a variety of material. Some can be embedded in earth without extra protection while others may have to be encased in concrete to avoid corrosion. In structures with basements or crawl spaces, the ducts can simply run beneath the house. Where there are no such spaces, they may have to be embedded in the earth or in the walls. Provisions must be made during the early process of constructing if this will be necessary.

Electric Heat

Electric heaters are usually laid along the floorboards. They look much like a floorboard with a narrow opening along the top. They require no special consideration in the construction of the house and they are clean, simple and quiet. However, it takes a little while to get a room heated to a comfortable temperature. They are also rather expensive in day-to-day operation, although in some areas utility companies offer reduced rates to homes heated with electricity. One of the advantages is the fact that each room can have its own thermostat, thus only the rooms actually in use need to be heated.

Hot-water Heaters

Hot-water heaters operate in two modes. One is referred to as radiant heat. It forces heated water through a system of thin, soft copper pipes which are set directly into the concrete slab or mud floor. This constitutes the base for the brick or tile used as the floor surface. This results in a very delightful even heating, but like electric heat, it also takes quite a while to heat a room to a comfortable temperature. On the other hand, once the floor surface has been adequately heated, it will retain that warmth for considerable periods of time. During cold winter months it might be desirable to include some type of time device which turns the heat on an hour or so before it's time to get up.

The other mode uses the heated water to operate radiators in the various rooms. Such radiator units are not particularly attractive, but can be dressed up to be less objectionable.

In either case, the various rooms can be equipped with individual thermostats which activate or deactivate separate water lines.

Fuel

The fuel used to operate the forced-air or water heaters can be natural gas, fuel oil, coal, LPG or electricity. Despite the huge increases in prices in recent years, natural gas is still the most convenient and probably least expensive in the long run if it is available in your area.

COOLING

Particularly in certain regions of the United States, cooling your house is vital to comfortable living. Some of the available options will be discussed now.

Cooling Through Evaporation

In areas with a low prevailing humidity level, evaporative cooling is practical, efficient and cheap. It consists of a unit usually mounted on the roof which contains sheets of some sort of absorbing material and a fan. Water is dripped slowly onto the absorbing sheets and the fan blows air across those sheets and into the house. As the water evaporates it cools the air and at the same time increases its moisture content.

Ideally the cooled air should enter the different rooms at some point near the ceiling, allowing it to descend within the room by its own weight. Each room so cooled must have some kind of ventilation. A slightly open door or window or the flue of a fireplace will permit air to escape and cooled air to continue to enter.

Air Conditioning

Standard air conditioning works on the same principle as the refrigerator, whether it uses gas or electricity. Circulating air is forced over a heat exchanger and then blown through a system of ducts into the various rooms. This type of air conditioning is usually unnecessary in the higher elevations where the air, even in the midst of summer, remains at a reasonable temperature regardless of the heat produced by the sun. In these regions the insulating quality of adobe will usually be sufficient to keep the house comfortably cool with the kind of ventilation afforded by opening windows.

On the other hand, in the low deserts such a cooling system becomes a virtual necessity if the house is to be livable during the summer heat.

Whether air conditioning or evaporative cooling is installed, it is usually possible to use the same system of ducts that serves the heating units during the winter.

ELECTRICITY

In order for the utility company to even consider hooking your house up to electrical service, the wiring, fuse boxes, switches, plugs and the like will have been inspected and approved. There are certain variations in the building codes with reference to electricity. Therefore, it is advisable to consult a licensed electrician before embarking on a do-it-yourself electrical installation.

In any case, be sure to include an ample number of outlets all over the house. There is nothing more obnoxious and potentially dangerous than to have a profusion of extension cords hanging around all over the place. Also remember that hallways and rooms which are habitually entered into at one end and left at the other require two-way switches in order to make it possible to turn the light on or off at either end. In rooms in which no ceiling light is provided, at least one of the wall plugs should be on a switch so that floor or table lamps can be turned on or off when entering or leaving the room.

GAS

Most gas companies will connect or disconnect gas appliances at no cost in order to make sure that such installations are performed by professionals and that there are no leaks.

PLUMBING

Like electrical conduit and gas lines, all plumbing must be planned in advance and incorporated into the basic structure of the house. The main water supply line leading into the average house should be at least ¾ inch in order to provide adequate water quantity and pressure. Pipes may be of copper, galvanized iron or, where building codes permit, plastic. Copper is more expensive than galvanized pipe, but it lasts longer. All metal-pipe installations require all manner of specialized tools, not to mention a fair degree of the knowledge of working with the tools and material. Hire a plumbing contractor. It's likely to be cheaper in the long run.

If your home is located within access to a city water system, you will most likely have no choice but to tie into that system and pay for the water being used. If your building project is way out in the boondocks, you may have to drill a well. Check around for a professional well driller who is familiar with the area because he will have a fair idea as to the best location in which to drill your well as well as the depth to which he may have to drill. He will not guarantee water at any given depth, but will charge you by the foot. This includes the cost of casings and such. The bid should also include a pressure tank of adequate size and the necessary pump. The size and power of the pump may depend on the depth from which the water must be pumped. Wells are not cheap, but once drilled the water is free forever except for the small amount of power used to operate the pump. With the prevailing cost of water in some areas these days, many homeowners are drilling their own wells despite the fact that access to a city water system is available.

Where there is water there has to be a sewer. Again, if a city sewer system is available, the logical thing is to hook into it. Where that is not possible a septic tank must be placed below ground at the appropriate level and hooked up to a seepage pit or leach field. Get professional advice to make sure that the septic tank does not contaminate the drinking water and that the seepage pit or leach field is located in an area where an excessive amount of plant growth does not interfere with the use of patio or garden areas.

Chapter 16
Remodeling An Old Adobe

So far we have talked and thought in terms of putting a brand-new structure onto an empty piece of ground. Now let's examine what is involved if you happen to find an old adobe with lots of charm that is located on a beautiful lot and you decide to buy and restore it (Fig. 16-1). At first glance this may seem to be quite a bit simpler than it will eventually turn out to be.

First of all you have to examine the old structure in order to determine whether or not it is worth remodeling. Many really old adobes were built on inadequate foundations such as rock without cement mortar. The simple fact that the walls are still standing is not necessarily proof that they will continue to do so.

If what you have found is the nearest thing to a ruin, no matter how charming it may look from the outside, it may prove to be the better part of valor to tear the whole thing down and start from scratch. You can save the still usable adobe bricks and wooden beams, latillas and vigas though. This decision should be based primarily on the soundness of the foundations and on the condition of the walls. If the foundation is of concrete and without noticeable cracks or of rocks embedded in concrete, again without any major cracks which would indicate that it has shifted in some distant past, then it is reasonably safe to assume that it will be capable of continuing to support the structure. This should include whatever is involved in the remodeling process.

Such an examination will probably necessitate a certain amount of digging around the foundation and the removal of large amounts of

Fig. 16-1. An old adobe is in the process of being remodeled. New lintels have been placed above window openings and new plaster applied overall. Note the huge abutment against the left wall. This may or may not contain a fireplace even though no chimney is evident.

dirt in order to get a good look at the foundation itself. Don't assume that just because one little corner looks fine, the rest will also be in satisfactory condition. Look at all of it. If there are only one or two cracks somewhere, it may be possible to dig a hole underneath and pour a new foundation under that portion of the old one which seems to be in doubt.

What is the condition of the walls? Has the plaster washed away and has run-off water started to affect the bricks and mortar? If so, it may still be salvageable if the wall is thick enough. A 10- or 14-inch wall which is starting to show serious signs of decay may not be worth salvaging. At best, it may require replacement in parts. Unless in really terrible shape a thicker wall using two adobes side-by-side of 20-, 24- or 28-inch thickness can probably be repaired.

The roof is likely to be in worse shape than anything else. Adobe roofs, particularly the kind traditionally used in building old adobes are certain to start to leak and gradually decay when left unattended for any length of time. In all probability the roof will have to be removed down to the vigas, decking or latillas and be com-

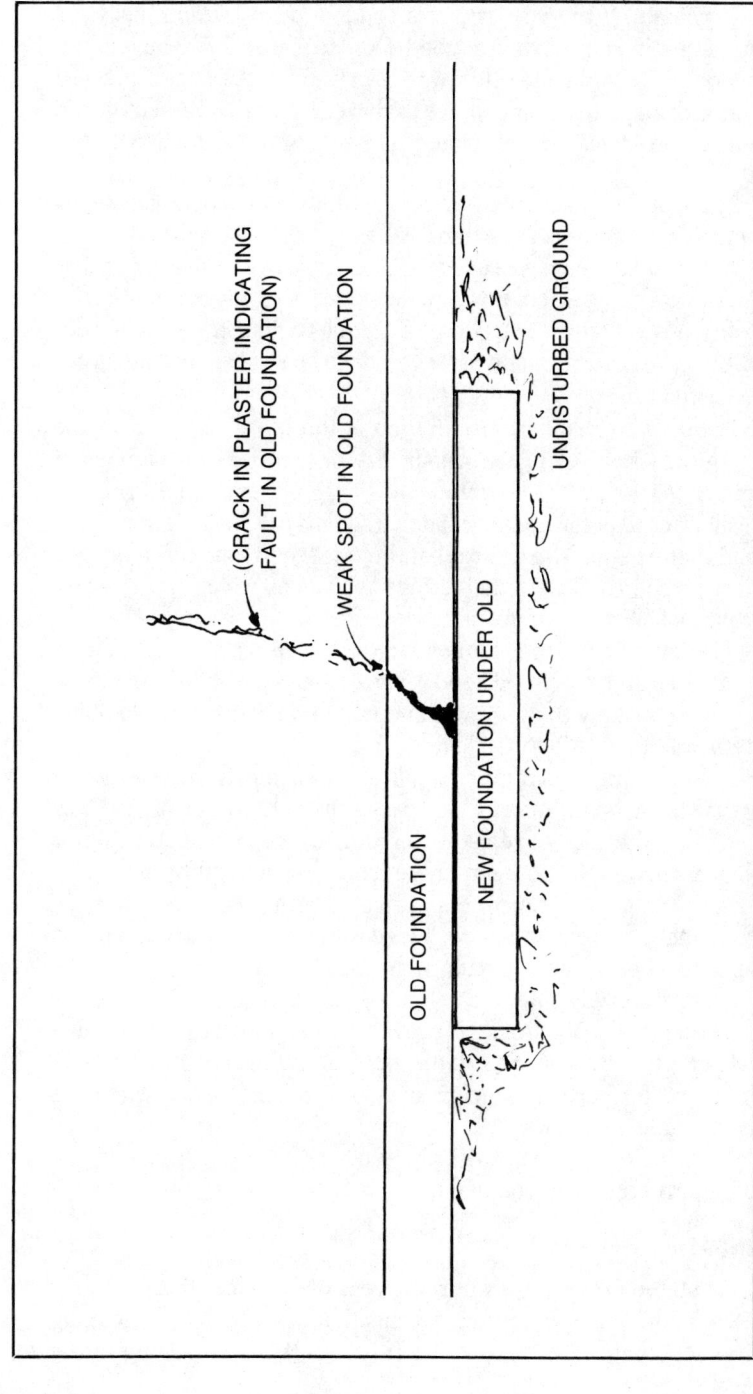

Fig. 16-2. A new foundation supports the old one.

pletely rebuilt. If the roof appears to have been leaking badly for some time, it is probably a good idea to carefully examine the condition of the vigas and other woodwork. Have they been affected by water damage to a point where partial or total replacement would appear to be indicated? A related question is the condition of the bond beam.

Many of the old adobes were built with wooden bond beams or without bond beams altogether. Unless you can be certain that a satisfactory bond beam was used in the original construction and that it is still in good condition, it will be necessary to remove not only the roof but also the ceiling structure in order to pour a new concrete bond beam that will then be strong enough to support the new roof and ceiling.

Another important consideration is the physical layout of the existing structure. Are you satisfied with the size and number of rooms or will you want to tear out walls and build additions? Probably you will want to put in bigger windows and maybe sliding glass doors to lead to the patio. Make sure that there is space to accommodate a modern kitchen and all of the various appliances which are a necessary part of today's comfortable living.

The condition of the plumbing must also be carefully examined. Rusted or leaking pipes will need replacement. As a matter of fact, it is not at all unlikely that you will find that an entirely new plumbing system will have to be installed.

Another and often rather complicated problem is the question of how to provide heat. In many old adobes the only source of heat was provided by the many fireplaces throughout the house. Cutting or buying enough wood to keep an entire house heated by means of fireplaces can be a nuisance, expensive or both. Some kind of more convenient means of heating the house will have to be added, but this can prove to be rather difficult in an old structure.

It is reasonably safe to say that remodeling an old adobe, even one in acceptable condition, will prove to be not much less expensive than building a new one. Still, if the location and the usable portion of the old structure are of sufficient appeal, it can be a worthwhile and satisfying undertaking.

Let's look at some of the basic specifics involved in adapting an existing structure to your needs.

FOUNDATIONS

As stated previously, where there is doubt about the solidity of an existing foundation, excavate beneath it and pour a new foundation to add support to the old one (Fig. 16-2). When adding to the

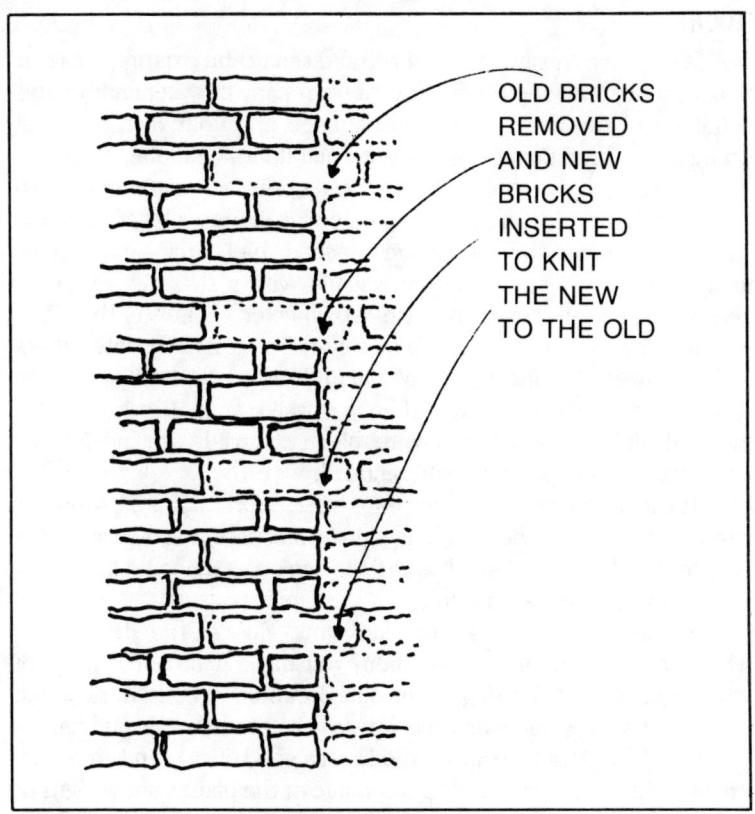

Fig. 16-3. Integrating a new wall into the old one.

house, pour the foundation for the addition down to a low enough level so that it extends under the old foundation for at least a foot or so. It can then be built up with a higher stem to the future level of the flooring. While you're at it, decide if you want any additional fireplaces. If so, pour those foundations to the appropriate size and thickness and include reinforcement with rebars at the same time.

WALLS

Where a portion of a wall will have to be rebuilt or where a new wall is to abut against an old one, the replacement will have to be integrated into the old structure (Fig. 16-3). To do this, remove some of the old bricks in alternating courses, scraping away the old mortar and loose dirt and then fit new bricks into those spaces with new mortar. This combines the new and the old into an integral whole.

FLOORS

Whether to maintain, preserve and repair the existing floors in an old adobe, or to replace them with something new depends on the condition of the floors, the material used and your own personal preference. Traditionally, old adobes had floors of adobe. Here the ground was simply leveled, tamped and sprinkled with moisture to cause it to harden. It may have been covered with a layer of adobe plaster containing some straw and a second level of the same plaster minus the straw, subsequently washed with a thin mix of adobe selected especially for its reddish-brown color. This was then hardened in the old days by pouring ox blood all over it and in later years with mixtures of boiled linseed oil and turpentine. Such a floor seems to have a carpet-like texture when one walks on it. It can be damp mopped, dusted and even waxed. When covered with Indian rugs here and there it is very lovely indeed.

It can also serve as the base for brick floors, but if flagstone or ceramic tile are to be used, it will necessitate the pouring of a concrete slab. In very small areas tile can sometimes be laid on an adequately tamped mud floor.

If the original old adobe had wood floors, the decision of whether to repair or replace them will depend on the quality of workmanship and the degree of deterioration. Wood floors which have been walked upon for generations will have a certain unevenness which is quite attractive if the wood is of a good quality and color. On the other hand, if a sufficient percentage of the planks show signs of rot, it may be better to tear up the whole thing and start from scratch.

DOORS AND WINDOWS

Assuming the lintel above a window opening is in good condition, the size of the window can be increased downward or it can be turned into a door without any structural problems. All that needs to be done is to remove the old window frame, cut out the adobes below, remove some adobe mortar where new nailing blocks are needed and then install the frame for the new window or door.

To install a new window where none existed previously or to widen a window or door will involve a degree of structural precaution. With no existing lintel to carry the weight of the roof, or in the case of widening an existing opening, the fact that the old lintel has to be removed and replaced means that supports have to be provided to carry that weight until a new lintel has been put in place. The simplest way of doing this is to cut wooden beams to the length which

Fig. 16-4. Small, permanently closed windows set directly into the thick adobe wall can add charm to your home.

equals the distance from the floor to the bottom of the vigas. These beams are then wedged vertically between the floor and each of the vigas which lie atop the part of the wall where the opening is to be cut or enlarged.

With these supports in place, the hole can then be cut into the wall or the old lintel removed and the opening enlarged as desired. At the top of the opening a recess of at least 1 foot on each side must be provided to receive the new or larger lintel. Once that new lintel is firmly in place and secured, it will carry the weight of the roof. The temporary supports can then be removed.

Sometimes it is desirable to have some small, permanently closed windows to bring light into a dark hall or corner of a room. If they are small enough and are not located directly under a viga, an opening for them can be cut safely without installing any temporary supports. Such a window will require only a minimum lintel and no other framing at all. Simply place the glass into the opening and plaster around it with adobe plaster. By shaping the plaster accordingly, you can produce any shape window that might seem attractive in that particular place. It can be round, oval, rectangular with rounded corners, L-shaped, T-shaped, triangular or whatever turns you on (Figs. 16-4 and 16-5).

CEILINGS

Unless the roof is a total disaster, the ceiling in an old adobe is likely to be in pretty good shape and one of its most beautiful features. It is therefore important that if additions are built, the new ceilings blend in with the old. It is somehow disconcerting to have one part of the house with ceilings of vigas and latillas and the new part with plain plaster ceilings. By matching the style to the greatest degree possible, the house will present a feeling of unity rather than one consisting of two portions: one old and the other new.

ROOFS

Assuming that the roof of the old adobe is in good enough shape to be retained and repaired where needed, certain considerations must be kept in mind when planning additions. Which way does the water run off? If the addition is on the side of the run-off, the new roof must be at the right level and correctly slanted to permit the water to run off across it. In that case the old coping may have to be removed. Otherwise the water will run in narrow streams across the new roof, increasing the likelihood of eventual damage.

Fig. 16-5. Permanently closed windows can be any shape you like.

Fig. 16-6. Where a bearing wall is to be removed, some alternate means of support may have to be installed.

Fig. 16-7. A decorative vertical beam may be used to support part of the ceiling and roof.

If the addition is not on the run-off side, the old coping can be left in place. But then the new roof must be slanted in a different direction to assure run-off away from the coping.

REMOVING WALLS

Many of the older adobes consist of many small rooms, several of which may be profitably combined into fewer but larger ones. This would involve the removal of interior walls. The first determination which has to be made is to make sure that the wall in question is not a bearing wall. Check the vigas. If it is obvious that the vigas on both sides of the wall are one and the same and that they extend from one bearing wall to another bearing wall through the top of the non-bearing wall that is to be removed, then it is safe to assume that the wall can be knocked away without impairing the structural solidity of the house as a whole.

That having been determined, decide whether you want to knock out all of the wall or whether it might be attractive to maintain a short section of it as a partial partition and a decorative corner on either side. If there is a fireplace in one of those corners or if you have decided that you would like to install a fireplace there, then it goes without saying that a short section of the wall will have to be maintained. Such a short partition or *padercita* (little wall) need not rise straight up to the ceiling. It is more attractive to recess it in regular or irregular steps, thus reducing its length as it rises up.

In removing all or part of a wall, it will pay to do the work slowly, removing one brick at a time. Some will certainly break or crumble, but a large number can be salvaged and stored for later use elsewhere. Doing it that way also helps to not accidentally damage electrical conduit or gas lines which might have been built into the wall. Where such lines are discovered they will, of course, have to be removed and their ends secured to be certain that there is no danger of electrical short circuits or gas leakage.

If the interior wall that is to be removed runs parallel to the direction of the vigas, it is safe to assume that it is not supporting any weight. But if there is any doubt, it might be a good idea to ask a professional, either a builder or an architect, to take a look at it. After all, you don't want to take a chance of having the whole place collapse around your ears.

If all or part of a bearing wall is to be removed, precautions will have to be taken to install some other means of supporting the weight of the ceiling and the roof (Fig. 16-6). In that case vertical beams will have to be inserted under each of the vigas on each side of the wall for the entire distance to which the wall is to be knocked out. With these supports in place, the obsolete portion of the wall can

Fig. 16-8. Attractive and decorative buttresses built against an old patio wall provide strength.

then be removed. Recesses will have to be cut into the tops of the parts of the wall to be retained and a lintel of the appropriate size and strength must be inserted. It must be large enough to safely support the ends of the vigas on both sides of the former wall. If the opening is really wide, say 15 or more feet, it might be advisable to place an attractive vertical beam under the center of the crossbeam as a permanent additional support (Fig. 16-7).

If such a wall is equipped with a sturdy bond beam, it might be advisable and attractive to retain that bond beam and possibly one or several courses of adobe brick beneath it and insert the crossbeam below. There should still be adequate height to permit people to walk without hitting their heads. It will also help to screen the fact that the vigas on either side of the wall are not in the identical position.

REPAIRING EXTERIOR WALLS

Frequently exterior walls show cracks in places where the foundation has weakened. Aside from strengthening the foundation by pouring a new section of foundation under the weakened portion of the old one, the wall itself will need repair and possibly some strengthening. If the crack is simply in the plaster and does not extend to the brick portion of the wall itself, it can simply be replastered because the new foundation should inhibit any further movement of the wall. On the other hand, if the wall itself is cracked, it will require more extensive reworking.

If the crack happens to be in a place where you would like to install a window or door, a new lintel can serve to hold the wall together. If the wall is to remain solid or if a major portion of the crack remains above or below the new window or above the new door, then a sufficient number of the old bricks may have to be removed to permit inserting new bricks with new mortar. This may be done safely by removing only a small section at a time, repairing it and then removing the next section.

In cases where the wall has been seriously weakened, a buttress can be erected against the wall on the outside. This is a frequently used means of supporting the walls of old adobes. It can be rather attractive when it becomes an integral feature of the overall adobe structure (Fig. 16-8).

REINFORCING OLD FOUNDATIONS

Aside from adding new sections of foundation under weak spots of the old one, it is frequently necessary to protect the base of the wall where it meets the foundation from continued water damage. To do this a narrow concrete foundation reinforcement should be run along the outside of the old foundation and the base of the wall. To accomplish this a trench must be dug around the entire outside of the house down to below the frost line. This trench will serve as a form for the newly poured cement, but a wooden form will have to be built to a height of about 1 foot so that the newly poured foundation reinforcement will rise to about that distance above ground level. Once the cement is poured but is still workable, it should be finished on top as a beveled ledge, slanting outward to permit rainwater and melting snow to run off away from the wall. Be sure that there are no cracks between this new foundation and the wall itself where water might collect and seep into the wall or freeze and cause damage.

Chapter 17
Solar Adobe

By far the largest number of adobe structures, both old and new, can be found in areas with a relatively arid climate. In other words, they are found in areas with an above-average amount of sunshine. It is therefore not surprising that in recent years much has been done to combine adobe building and solar heating.

Architects and builders involved in solar construction are constantly experimenting with new ideas, but basically there are two methods of using the energy of the sun: active and passive.

SOLAR COLLECTORS

An active system uses *solar collectors* (Figs. 17-1 and 17-2). They are flat boxes covered with a sheet of glass and black painted metal sheets above about 4 or 5 inches of air space. Inside these panels the air heats quickly to about 170 degrees Fahrenheit. It is then forced by a system of ducts and fans toward a material which will absorb and maintain this heat. This can be a space under the house filled with large-size gravel contained in some sort of chicken-wire enclosure or it can be a fairly large body of water, such as a storage tank or even a swimming pool.

When gravel is used for heat storage, the room where it is stored (usually a cellar below the floor level of the house) will become quite hot and the hot air can be circulated throughout the house in the same manner used in standard forced-air heating systems. Experience seems to indicate that a solar-collector surface of approximately one-third of the square footage of the dwelling is

Fig. 17-1. Solar collector panels apparently added after the house was built.

required in order to produce sufficient warmth to keep it at a comfortable level for several sunless days during even the coldest winter.

Figure 17-3 is an active solar dwelling, built of adobe, but with little regard to what is generally referred to as adobe style. It uses 28 solar collector panels on the south slope of the roof, pumping the hot air into a heat storage area underneath the house and then distributing that heat to the various rooms in the house in the usual forced-air heating manner. This house is located in the Arroyo Hondo area near Santa Fe. Its owner says that the heating remains effective for three to four sunless days, even during the coldest winter months.

The picture in Fig. 17-4 was taken in the basement where a large area, encircled by steel posts and wire mesh, contains large gravel piled about 4 feet high. On sunny days the hot air from the solar collector panels is forced into the gravel, raising the temperature to 150 or more degrees.

If the heat generated by the solar collectors is used to heat water in a storage tank, this heated water must then be circulated to water radiators throughout the house (Fig. 17-5). By far the most comfortable, but also expensive, means of using water to heat the house is to embed water lines in the floor base beneath brick, tile or flagstone floors. It results in a slow warming which rises evenly from all portions of the floor. The floor itself will retain a degree of warmth for some time even when the water begins to cool. In houses with

Fig. 17-2 Solar collector panels have been installed on the roof of a conventional adobe home.

Fig. 17-3. An active solar dwelling.

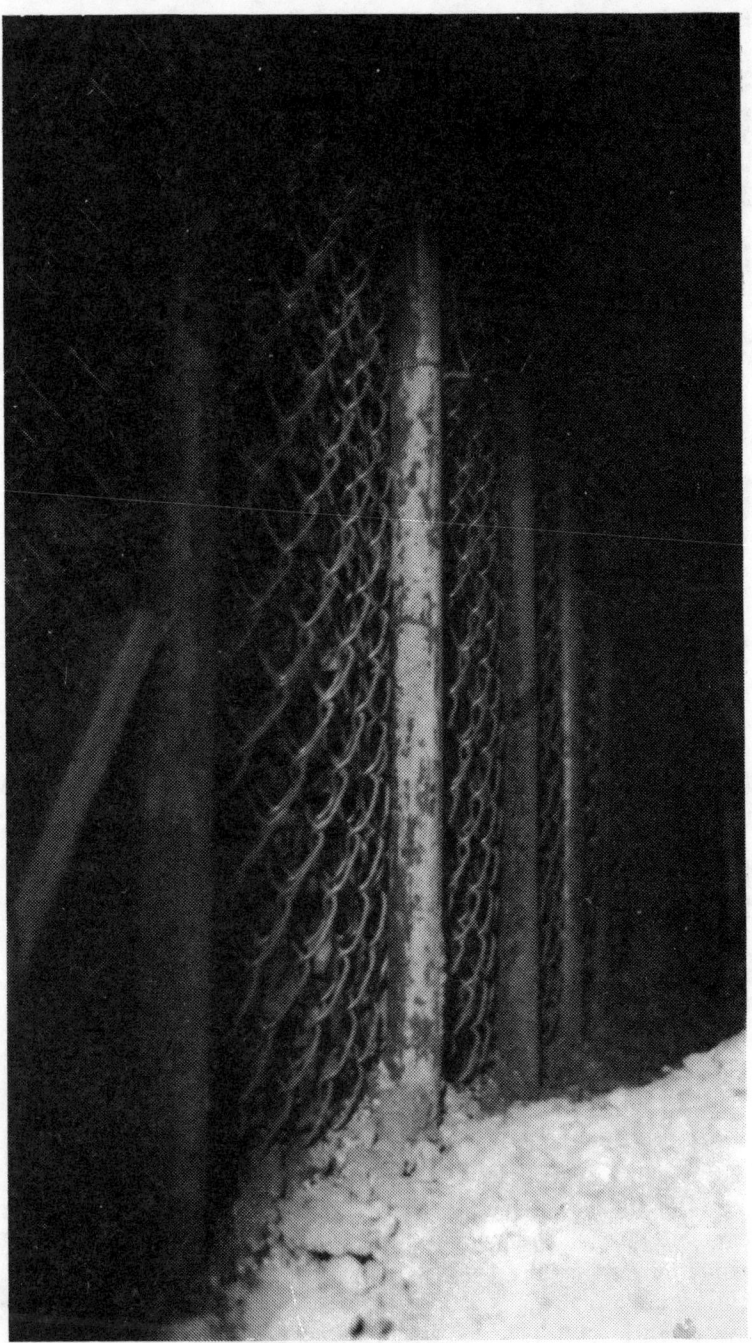
Fig. 17-4. Gravel is piled high in this basement.

Fig. 17-5. A solar collector panel, placed against a workshop building in the back yard, is being tested to see if it will suffice to produce the needed amount of hot water. The hot air which collects in the panel is being sucked through the circular duct by the fan which can be seen in the extreme foreground. It is then forced on to its destination.

wood floors or where for some other reason this type of heating is not practical, regular water radiators can be installed.

Heating a swimming pool in this manner and using its water to circulate through the heating system in the house would not seem practical. A swimming pool has a huge surface exposed to the cold air outside and would tend to cool too fast to be effective. If covered by a heated enclosure, its water would probably become too warm to be used for a refreshing swim.

Fig. 17-6. A passive solar home.

Fig. 17-7. A passive solar-heated home in the final stages of construction.

PASSIVE SOLAR HOMES

Passing solar homes operate on a different principle (Fig. 17-6). In such houses large window areas are installed to catch the rays of the sun, usually faced inside by massive walls of adobe or some other heat-absorbent material. The walls should be painted a dark color to maximize absorption and minimize reflection. The sun hits these walls and warms them sufficiently to give off heat for considerable periods of time after the sun has set. This type of heating is not sufficient to spread throughout an entire house, however. Therefore each room not facing the sun must be equipped with appropriately placed skylights through which the rays of the sun can shine and warm a given portion of the opposite wall.

When using this passive system, care must be taken to provide for ventilation and a means of reducing the effect of the sun's heat. Otherwise they will become virtual hot boxes during the summer.

In Fig. 17-7 a passive solar-heated home is in the final stages of construction atop one of the higher hills around Santa Fe. Built into the side of the natural rock in a manner similar to that used by the cliff-dwelling Indians long ago, it will use the heat-absorbing capability of the natural rock to store solar warmth for cold nights and sunless days.

The southside of the house, constructed of concrete blocks with adobe supports (far right of Fig. 17-8) includes a greenhouse covered by glass panes. The rays of the sun heat the concrete-block wall beyond it, transferring the warmth to the interior. Louvres at top and bottom can be opened during the summer to avoid excessive heat.

The flat roof of Fig. 17-9 is speckled with skylights, one for practically every room. These skylights are placed in such a manner that the sun will hit an interior wall which is designed to absorb the warmth and retain it throughout the night and to some extent a sunless day. The rays of the sun shining in through a sky light, light and warm a thick interior wall constructed of natural rock (Fig. 17-10). This will retain the warmth for a considerable length of time. Also built into the wall is a fireplace which will be used to heat the room if the sun should fail to shine for several days in a row.

GREENHOUSE SYSTEM

A variation on this system is the so-called *greenhouse*. Patios, balconies, verandahs or other areas on the south side of the house may be enclosed with glass or clear plastic. This will form a kind of storage space for the sun-heated air which can then be funneled into

Fig. 17-8. A greenhouse covered by glass panes is being included in the construction of this solar adobe home.

Fig. 17-9. This flat roof is speckled with skylights.

the house. If glass is used in a permanent installation, means must be included to either remove the panes of glass or to open sections of it during the summer. Otherwise the heat would become unbearable. On the other hand, plastic can simply be used during the winter and then removed and thrown away. Plastic to enclose even a fairly large area would cost no more than maybe $20 or $30. Though cheap and efficient, it is not particularly attractive and may be impractical in a location where frequent strong winds may cause it to tear.

In Fig. 17-11 a framework has been constructed for a greenhouse. It will face south-westerly. When finished it can be covered with glass or clear plastic, thus serving during the winter as an additional source of solar warmth. At the same time it will provide a windbreak for the door leading to the patio.

As just mentioned, plastic is cheap and can be thrown away in the spring. Glass, on the other hand, is permanent. But it does require ample means of ventilation, either through the use of louvres or removable panels, This will avoid excessive heat during the summer months.

In Figs. 17-12 and 17-13 a glass-enclosed area on the south side of the house serves as the casual dining area and plant room. The

Fig. 17-10. The rays of the sun light warm a thick interior wall constructed of natural rock.

Fig. 17-11. A framework has been constructed for a greenhouse.

thick adobe walls are painted dark brown and absorb the warmth of the sun, keeping the house comfortable long after the sun has set.

SOLAR HOME COSTS

While the idea of solar heating sounds awfully nice, it does have its drawbacks. Solar collector panels and greenhouses, both of which can usually be installed on existing structures not originally designed for solar heating, tend to be unsightly. There is really no good way to hide them from view because they need to have an unobstructed exposure to the sun. Passive solar homes, on the other hand, must be designed and built as such from the start. The huge expanses of glass often result in a less than harmonious appearance however, especially when used in adobe structures which according to tradition call for smaller window areas.

The cost of building a solar home is still relatively high, usually some 10 per cent more than a conventional home. On the other hand, the cost of heating fuel has risen to such an extent during recent years that the average monthly heating bill for an average-sized house tends to exceed $100. This makes the potential savings offered by solar energy meaningful. In addition some states, includ-

Fig. 17-12. This glass-enclosed area serves as the casual dining area and plant room.

Fig. 17-13. By enclosing a glass balcony with a southern exposure, a greenhouse effect is being created. It then produces heat for the home.

ing New Mexico, offer tax rebates or deductions to people building solar homes or solar commercial structures.

It should be emphasized here that designing and building an efficient solar home, whether adobe or some other type, is a job for experienced experts. No one who has not studied its characteristics, advantages and limitations should undertake such a task without the help and advice from an architect or builder who has been involved with the subject for some time.

Glossary

adobe: A term said to have been derived from either the Spanish (*adobar* = plaster) or the Arabic (*at - tub* = brick) or the Coptic (*tobe* = brick). In modern usage is stands for the mud mixture used in adobe building, for the bricks made of adobe mud and for the structures built of adobe.
adobe brick: Bricks made of adobe mud, sand and straw that are dried in the sun.
adobe plaster: Mortar made of the same material and used for exterior and interior plaster of adobe-brick walls.
arroyo: A creek bed, usually dry most of the year except during the spring runoff.
asphalt roofing felt: A felt-like material impregnated with asphalt and used in the form of shingles or sheets in the construction of roofs.

bath, full: A bathroom consisting of a tub with or without shower, sink and toilet.
bath, half: A bathroom featuring only a sink and toilet.
bath, three-quarters: A bathroom with a stall shower, sink and toilet.
bearing wall: A wall which supports a portion of the ceiling and roof.
bond beam: A beam of concrete or wood, laid across the top of bearing walls to support the vigas or roof beams.
buttress: A solid adobe protrusion built onto the outside of adobe walls to improve their strength.

canale: An open drain, U-shaped in cross section. Its purpose is to drain the water off of the flat roofs of adobe structures.

cliff dwelling: Adobe-brick structures built against and into the vertical sides of cliffs by the Pueblo Indians in order to be more easily defended against hostile nomadic Indian tribes and the invading white man.

coping: An extension of the bearing walls above the upper surface of the roof, usually approximately 1 foot high. Canales are placed through holes in the coping to allow water run-off.

corbelled: An expression used for the type of brick construction, usually employed in the building of fireplaces where each brick sticks out a certain distance beyond the one below it.

course: A row of adobe bricks.

covenant: A contract between two or more persons. In real estate, a covenant usually implies some type of legal restriction or entanglement.

curtain walls: Thin nonbearing interior walls constructed of wooden studs and plasterboard.

damper: A means of shutting off the flue of a fireplace. It is located in the fireplace throat.

decking: The ceiling material placed atop the vigas or ceiling beams.

dormant spraying: The spraying of trees and shrubs with insecticide in the early spring before they start to bud.

easement: The right of utility companies and others to encroach upon a lot for the purpose of constructing power lines or to provide access to an otherwise inaccessible area.

face: The decorative outer surface of a fireplace.

fill: Earth piled into a hole or depression. Foundations may not be built on top of fill, but must sit on undisturbed ground.

firebox: The portion of a fireplace in which the fire is set.

fire brick: A special type of brick appropriate for use in the construction of fireplaces.

fire clay: A clay mortar used in fireplace construction.

flue: The inside of the chimney.

footing: Foundation.

gringo block: A wooden block approximately equal to the dimension of an adobe brick. It is inserted into the wall to permit nailing.

guy wires: Wires attached at an angle to a vertical post or beam to keep it in position.

hearth: A platform in front of a firebox, made of masonry or other nonflammable material and designed to catch ashes and cinders.
hibachi: A small portable grill in which charcoal is burned.
horno: A beehive-shaped Indian oven, used for baking bread or cooking turkeys.

joist: A wooden support for floor coverings.

kiva: A circular ceremonial chamber, built by the Peublo Indians either above or below ground. It is used primarily for religious ceremonies.

latilla: Thin wooden stakes, usually aspen or cedar, which are placed across the vigas to provide the ceiling and the base for the roof.
leach field: A system of perforated pipes layed below ground. The sewage flows from the septic tank into the leach field which permits it to soak into the ground.
lintel: A beam above a door or window opening, designed to support the weight of the wall and roof above that opening. It is usually wood.
LPG: Liquefied petroleum gas, stored in tanks and used in areas where access to natural gas is unavailable.

masonry: Construction of brick, stone, concrete, or a combination thereof. Adobe walls are considered masonry.
mezzanine: An indoor balcony or platform located above the main floor but below the second story.
mortar: In adobe building the adobe mud which is spread between the courses of adobe brick to hold them firmly together.
mud: A term frequently used with reference to adobe.
multiple dwelling: A dwelling designed to house more than one family.

nailing block: A piece of wood of any dimension inserted into an adobe wall to permit nailing.

padercita: Literally meaning little wall. The term applies to partial walls, usually constructed in order to permit locating a corner fireplace in a room where the use of an actual corner is impractical.

parapet: Coping.

partition walls: Curtain walls.

patio-type brick: Nonporous brick used in the construction of brick floors and brick walks. Also known as *solids*.

plumb line: A line with a lead weight at one end, used to make sure that a wall or post is perfectly vertical.

pueblo: Communal building or group of buildings used by the Indians in the southwestern United States.

Pueblo Indian: The term applied by the Spaniards to the Anasazi Indians who lived (and still live) in permanent communities.

rebar: A steel reinforcing bar embedded in concrete construction to add strength.

refractory cement: Cement which is resistant to great heat.

retaining wall: A wall built to prevent the soil at an embankment or cut from sliding.

seepage pit: An underground pit designed to perform the same function as a leach field.

septic tank: A tank in which sewage decomposes before it is permitted to seep into the ground.

shell: The masonry enclosure of a fireplace which must be of adequate thickness to protect wood or other flammable materials located nearby.

shim: A block of wood or other material designed to keep vigas in place.

smoke shelf: A recessed portion in a fireplace designed to prevent downdrafts from blowing ashes and cinders into the room.

solids: See patio-type bricks.

spanish tile: Curved clay tile used in the construction of gabled roofs.

stem: A portion of the wall between the foundation and the actual adobe wall. Constructed of concrete blocks, it prevents water from damaging the adobe. Also the concrete-block base of a fireplace.

subfloor: A floor, usually of plywood, placed below the actual hardwood floor.

template: A pattern of wood or other material used as a guide in building given shapes.

territorial style: An adobe building style recognizable by the intricate brick design around the coping.

throat: The part of a fireplace between the smoke shelf and the flue.

toenailing: Nailing at an angle through two pieces of wood.

tongue-in-groove: Boards with a protrusion along one side and a matching indentation on the other. When placed together they result in a tight fit.

undisturbed ground: Firm ground with no fill. All foundation trenches must be excavated down to undisturbed ground.

vigas: Straight round tree trunks with all bark and branches removed and used as ceiling beams.

winch: A system of pulleys which permits hoisting heavy weights with a minimum of power.

Additional Reading

ABCs of Making Adobe Bricks. New Mexico State University, Las Cruces; Cooperative Extension Circular 429.

Adobe and Rammed Earth. United Nations, Housing and Town and Country Planning Bulletin #4.

Adobe Architecture. Myrtle Stedman; Sunstone Press.

Adobe Book. John F. O'Connor; Ancient City Press.

Adobe—Build it Youself. Paul Graham McHenry; University of Arizona Press.

Adobe Construction Methods. L. W. Neubauer; University of California, Agricultural Experiment Station, Extension Service.

Adobe Fireplaces. Myrtle Stedman; Sunstone Press.

Adobe News. Bi-monthly publication; P. O. Box 702, Las Lunas, New Mexico 87031.

Adobe or Sundried Brick for Farm Buildings. U.S. Department of Agriculture, Farmer's Bulletin #1720.

Adobe—Past and Present. William Lumpkins; Museum of New Mexico; Case-Thompson Printing Company.

Adobe Remodeling. Myrtle Stedman; Sunstone Press.

A Qualitative Comparison of Rammed Earth and Sundried Adobe Brick. University of New Mexico Press.

Build with Adobe. Marcia Southwick; Sage Books.

Build Your Own Adobe. Paul and Doris Aller; Stanford University.

Earthen Home Construction. A & M College of Texas, Texas Transportation Institute, Bulletin #18.

Handbook for Building Homes of Earth. U. S. Department of Housing and Urban Development, Division of International Affairs.

Making the Adobe Brick. Eugene H. Boudreau; Fifth Street Press.

Mud, Space and Spirit, Virginia Gray, Alan Macrae and Wayne McCall; Capra Press.

New Mexico Home Plan Book. George Fitzpatrick; Rydal Press.

Taos Adobes. Bainbridge Bunting; Museum of New Mexico Press.

The Manufacture of Asphalt Emulsion Stabilized Soil Bricks. International Institute of Housing Technology.

Index

A

Acoma Pueblo	36
Abodar	11
Adobe	18
buildings, monumental	26
dwellings, modern	40
history	18
insulating quality	82
relics	20
uses	69
Adobe bricks	70
hardware	73
labor	74
Air conditioning	213
Albuquerque	22
Anasazi Indians	21
Apaches	20
Apartment houses	52
Arabs	25
Architect's scale	54
Arizona	22
Ash dump	179
Asphalt, hot	120

B

Balconies	239
Bandelier National Monument	22
Basements	64, 103
Bathrooms	152
bathtub	152
colors	153
exhaust fan	155
sink	152
stall shower	152
toilet	152
windows	154
Beam ceilings	116
Bedroom	144
second	149
master	145
Beds, flower	196
Blocks, gringo	89
Brick floors	101
Buildings, commercial	52
site	61
Buttresses	18

C

California ranch-style	12
Car port	152
Ceilings	114, 224
beam	116
interior finish	116
options	123
Central heating, location	164
Ceramic tile	106
Chaco Canyon	20
Children's rooms	150
Chimayo	32
Chimneys	123
China	25
Clear title	64
Cliff dwellings	22
Closets	166
Colorado	22
Commercial buildings	52

253

Concrete floors	105	depth	79
Condominiums	52	purpose	79
Considerations, practical	62	reinforcing old	230
Convertible sofas	144	rock	80
Cooling	213	trench	80
Cooling through evaporation	213	Four Corners area	22
Corbelling	183	Foyer	125
Covenants	67	Fruit trees	196
Cristo Rey church	36		
Curtain walls	98		

D

		Gabled roofs	120
		Garage	158
Damper	183	Gas	214
Darkroom	160	Gravel roof	119
Den	132	Gravel walks	196
Designs, unconventional	58	Greenhouse system	239
Dining area	140	Gringo blocks	89
Dining room lighting	143	Glass	240
Dogon people	25	Governor's Palace	26, 56
Doodles, perfecting your	54	Guest houses	150
Doodling in future terms	53		
Doors	89, 222	**H**	
Dressing room	146, 160	Hallways, other	126
Driveway	152	Hearth	184
Dryer, location	163	Heatilators	184
		Heating	211
E		electric heat	212
Electricity	214	hot-water	212
Entry hall	125	forced air	211
Exterior walls, repairing	229	fuel	213
		History of adobe	18
F		Hobby room	157
Face	184	Horno	44, 203
Fiberglass insulation	183	Hotels	52
Fire clay	182	Houses	52
Firebox	182	apartment	52
Fireplaces	171	guest	150
conventional	171		
corner	171	**I**	
foundation	176	India	18
types	171	Indians	21
Flagstone	196	Anasazi	21
Flat roofs	96	Pueblo	18, 21
Floors	101, 222	Insulation, fiberglass	183
brick	101	rockwool	183
concrete	105	Island kitchen	136
patio type	103		
pattern	104	**K**	
plan	55	Kitchen	130
solids	103	Kitchen, island	136
vapor barrier	103	Kitchenette	151
wood	108	Kiva	20
Flower beds	196		
Flue	183	**L**	
Forklifts	110	Lamaseries	25
Foundation	79, 220	Las Trampas	35
concrete	80	Lawns	196

254

Lear, William P.	53
Legal restrictions	64
Lighting	130
dining room	143
living room	130
Lintels	90
Living room	129
Living room lighting	130
Lot	65
access	65
legalities	67
location	65
size	65
topography	65
LPG	65

M

Mali	25
Mantel	184
Master bedroom	145
Materials, vinyl	107
Mesa Verde	22
Missionaries, Spanish	26
Modern adobe dwellings	40
Monumental adobe buildings	26
Musician's studio	161

N

Nambe	26
Navajos	21
Neighborhood	63
New England saltbox	12
New Mexico	20, 22

O

Old foundations, reinforcing	230
Oldest House	26
Options, ceiling	123
roof	123
Outdoor barbeque	196, 202

P

Padercita	172, 228
Painter's studio	158
Parapet	122
Passive solar homes	238
Patios	190, 239
furniture	199
type floors	104
People, dogon	25
Photographer's studio	160
Plumbing	214
Pool, swimming	196, 208, 236
Power tools	157
Practical considerations	62
Professional advice	57
Pueblo	20, 21
Pueblo Bonito	20
Pueblo Indians	18, 21
Puye Cliffs	22

Q

Queen Isabella	18

R

Rancho de Taos	26
Reading room	144
Rebars	83
Reinforcing old foundations	230
Removing walls	228
Repairing exterior walls	229
Resale value	67
Restrictions, legal	64
Rockwool insulation	183
Room	129
children's	150
dining	140
dressing	146, 160
hobby	157
living	129
reading	144
sewing	144
study	144
Roofing felt	120
Roofs	96, 224
flat	96
gabled	120
keeping dry	118
options	123

S

Saltbox	12
Santa Fe	26
Second bedroom	149
Second story	81
Sena Plaza	56
Septic tank	65
Service sink, location	165
Sewers, access	65
Sewing room	144
Sculptor's studio	161
Shade trees	198
Shell	184
Shrubs	66
Sky City	22
Skylights	239, 123
Smoke shelf	183
Solar	231
collectors	231
home costs	242
homes, passive	238
Spanish missionaries	26
Stem	179
Studio	158

as workshops	158
musician's	161
painter's	158
photographer's	160
sculptor's	161
Study room	144
Surroundings	65
Swimming pool	196, 208, 236

T

Taos Pueblo	12, 43, 46
Territorial style	41
Tibet	25
Tile, ceramic	106
Throat	183
Tools, power	157
Trees	66
fruit	196
shade	198

U

Unconventional designs	58
Utah	22
Utilities, access	65
Utility spaces	163

V

Vent pipes	123
Ventilation	158
Verandahs	239
Vigas	109
Vinyl materials	107

W

Walks, gravel	196
Walls	81, 87, 221
curtain	98
really necessary	98
removing	228
repairing exterior	229
thickness	81
Washer, location	163
Water heater, location	164
Where to build	61
Windows	89, 222
Wood floors	108
Workshops	157
Workshops, studios as	158